Dress, Body, Culture

Series Editor **Joanne B. Eicher,** *Regents' Professor, University of Minnesota*

Books in this provocative series seek to articulate the connections between culture and dress, which is defined here in its broadest possible sense as any modification or supplement to the body. Interdisciplinary in approach, the series highlights the dialogue between identity and dress, cosmetics, coiffure, and body alterations as manifested in practices as varied as plastic surgery, tattooing, and ritual scarification. The series aims, in particular, to analyse the meaning of dress in relation to popular culture and gender issues and will include works grounded in anthropology, sociology, history, art history, literature and folklore.

ISSN: 1360-466X

Recently published titles in the series

DRESS, BODY, CULTURE

Old Clothes, New Looks

Second Hand Fashion

Edited by
Alexandra Palmer and Hazel Clark

Oxford • New York

First published in 2005 by
Berg
Editorial offices:
1st Floor, Angel Court, 81 St Clements Street, Oxford OX4 1AW, UK
175 Fifth Avenue, New York, NY 10010, USA

Berg is the imprint of Oxford International Publishers Ltd.

Library of Congress Cataloging-in-Publication Data
A catalog record for this book is available from the Library of Congress.

British Library Cataloguing-in-Publication Data
A catalogue record for this book is available from the British Library.

ISBN 1 85973 852 4 (Cloth)
     1 85973 857 5 (Paper)

Typeset by JS Typesetting Ltd, Wellingborough, Northants.
Printed in the United Kingdom by Biddles Ltd, King's Lynn.

www.bergpublishers.com

To our boys, Wyndham and Hugo, and Jacob, with thanks.

Contents

Part 1: Historical Perspectives

Part 2: Trading Cultures

Part 3: Contemporary Refashioning

Figures

Notes on Contributors

Hazel Clark (PhD) is Chair of Critical Studies at Parsons School of Design (New School University) New York. She has published and taught internationally on the history and theory of design. During the 1990s she lived and worked in Hong Kong, where she was Head of the Swire School of Design, Hong Kong Polytechnic. Her research and teaching from that period encompassed Hong Kong fashion, design and cultural identity, and publications included: *The Cheongsam* (Oxford University Press (Images of Asia), 2000); 'Fashion, Identity and the City: Hong Kong', *Form/Work: an interdisciplinary journal of design and the built environment* (Sydney: University of Technology, 2000); 'The Cheung Sam: Issues of Fashion and Cultural Identity', in *China Chic: East Meets West* (Yale University Press, 1999).

Carole Collier Frick (PhD) is Associate Professor in the Department of Historical Studies at Southern Illinois University, Edwardsville. Recent publications include a monograph entitled *Dressing Renaissance Florence* (The Johns Hopkins University Press, 2002), and a chapter entitled 'Francesco Barbaro's *De re uxoria*: a silent dialogue for a young Medici bride' in *Printed Voices* (Toronto, 2004). She is currently working on another monograph, *Performing the Feminine,* on the roles of Renaissance women.

Karen Tranberg Hansen (PhD) is Professor in the Department of Anthropology, Northwestern University, USA. Her research in Zambia is concerned with work and housing in the urban informal sector, household dynamics, and consumption. She is the author of *Distant Companions: Servants and Employers in Zambia, 1900–1985* (Cornell University Press 1989), *Keeping House in Lusaka* (Columbia University Press 1997) and *Salaula: The World of Secondhand Clothing and Zambia* (University of Chicago Press, 2000).

Heike Jenß is a PhD candidate and temporary lecturer at the Institute of Cultural History of Textiles, Dortmund University, Germany. She works in the research project 'Uniforms in Motion: The Process of Uniformity in Body and Dress' and investigates practices of consumption and performance in contemporary youth-culture. Her publications include articles for webzines, international magazines and scholarly articles such as 'Identity Wear: Über Authentizität in Kleidern' in *Jugend, Mode and Geschlecht*, Elke Gaugele and Christina Reiss (eds.), (Campus Verlag, Frankfurt, 2003).

Beverly Lemire (PhD) is Henry Marshall Tory Chair in the Department of History & Classics and the Department of Human Ecology, University of Alberta, Canada. Currently the co-editor of *Textile History*, her books include *Fashion's Favourite: the Cotton Trade and the Consumer in Britain, 1660–1800* (Oxford, 1991) and *Dress, Culture and Commerce: the English Clothing Trade before the Factory* (Basingstoke, 1997). With Ruth Pearson and Gail Campbell she co-edited *Women & Credit: Researching the Past, Refashioning the Future* (Oxford, 2001). Her forthcoming book is titled *The Business of Everyday Life: Gender, Practice and Social Politics in England, c.1600–1900*.

B. Lynne Milgram (PhD) is Associate Professor in the Faculty of Liberal Studies at the Ontario College of Art and Design, Toronto, Canada. Her research on gender and development in the Philippines analyzes the cultural politics of social change with regard to fair trade, women's production and trade of crafts, and microfinance. This research has been published in edited volumes and in *Atlantis: A Women's Studies Journal* (2002), *Human Organization* (2001), *Research in Economic Anthropology* (1999) and *Museum Anthropology* (1998). She has also co-edited, with Kimberly M. Grimes, *Artisans and Cooperatives: Developing Alternative Trade for the Global Economy* (University of Arizona Press, 2000). Her current research explores Philippine women's engagement in the global trade of secondhand clothing.

Terry Satsuki Milhaupt (PhD) is currently an independent researcher based in New York City. She received her MA in East Asian Studies from Columbia University and her PhD in art history from Washington University and was awarded research grants from the Agency for Cultural Affairs in Japan (1996) and the Metropolitan Museum of Art (1992, 2002). Her publications include 'The Chinese Textile and Costume Collection at the Metropolitan Museum of Art' in *Orientations*, April 1992, 'Tsujigahana Textiles and their Fabrication' in *Turning Point: Oribe and the Arts of Sixteenth Century Japan*, 2003 and 'The Museum Artifact' in *Moving Objects: Time, Space and Context – International Symposium on the Preservation of Cultural Property*, March 2004.

Lucy Norris (PhD) is a postdoctoral fellow in the Department of Anthropology, University College London. Her research investigates the life-cycle of clothing in contemporary urban India, focusing on practices of disposal, recycling and the transformation of clothing into hybrid products in the global market. To date, this research has been published in *The Journal of Material Culture* (2004) and in the edited volume, *Clothing and Materiality* (2004). Previously the Collections Manager at the Horniman Museum, London, she is also the co-author (with M. Hitchcock) of *Bali: The Imaginary Museum. The photographs of Walter Spies and Beryl de Zoete.* (Kuala Lumpur: Oxford University Press, 1995).

Hilary O'Kelly (MA) is Lecturer in Design History at the National College of Art and Design, Dublin, Ireland. She received her MA in the History of Dress from the Courtauld Institute, London. She has lectured in Dress and Design History in the National College of Art and Design in Dublin and the Crawford College of Art and Design in Cork. She also worked as Visual Arts Co-ordinator at University College Cork. She has contributed to several books on fashion including *Chic Thrills* (1992), *Fashion in Photograph 1900–1920* (1992) and written reviews for *The Irish Times*, *Circa Magazine* and *The Irish Craft Review*.

Alexandra Palmer (PhD) is the Nora E. Vaughan Fashion Costume Curator, Textile and Costume Section at the Royal Ontario Museum, Toronto, Canada. She is also adjunct faculty in the Graduate Programme in Art History, York University and in Fine Art History, University of Toronto. Her book *Couture & Commerce: The Transatlantic Fashion Trade in the 1950s* (2001) won a Clio award for Ontario history. She is editor of *Fashion: A Canadian Perspective*, (University of Toronto Press, 2004), and is currrently exhibition editor for *Fashion Theory*. She has authored chapters in *Framing Our Past. Constructing Canadian Women's History in the Twentieth Century*, (McGill-Queens University Press, 2001); and *The Culture of Sewing: Gender, Consumption and Homedressmaking*, (Berg 1999). She is now working on a book, *20th Century Culture and Couture in Toronto*, which has been supported by a grant from the Social Sciences and Humanities Research Council of Canada.

Margot Riley (MA) is an independent scholar living in Sydney, Australia. She is a cultural historian with special interest in textiles and dress and her professional experience includes curatorial positions with the Powerhouse Museum (Sydney) and the Historic House Trust of New South Wales. She currently works as a Picture Researcher at the Mitchell Library, State Library of New South Wales.

Victoria Rovine (PhD) has mounted more than thirty exhibitions at the University of Iowa Museum of Art. Her research is focused on West Africa, with extensive fieldwork in Mali and has published *Bogolan: Shaping Culture through Cloth in Contemporary Mali,* (Smithsonian Institution Press, 2001). Her current research concerns African fashion designers in global markets for which she received a Getty Foundation Curatorial Research Grant as well as grants from the Rockefeller Foundation and the National Endowment for the Arts.

Acknowledgments

The co-editors Alexandra Palmer and Hazel Clark are indebted to Jean Duce Palmer who took time away from her own lecture preparations for the careful copyediting, and to Daniel Faria for his patience, assistance and care with the bibliography and to Andrea Retfalvi for the index. We would also like to thank Kathryn Earle, Ian Critchley and their colleagues at Berg, and reviewers Joanne Eicher and Nicky Gregson for their thoughtful comments. We are grateful to the Nora E. Vaughan Curatorship Fund, Royal Ontario Museum for supporting this project. Finally, we wish to thank all of our authors, without whom this book would not have been possible.

In alphabetical order, our authors acknowledge the assistance they received:

Hazel Clark thanks Margery Au and Teresa Ho for their insights, and Piera Chen and Cecilia Chu for additional research assistance;

Karen Tranberg Hansen wishes to acknowledge the generous support of her research on the second hand clothing trade from the Social Science Research Council (USA), the Wenner-Gren Foundation for Anthropological Research and Northwestern University.

Heike Jenß thanks all her interviewees for their kindness and interest in her project. She also thanks Volkswagen-Stiftung for funding and her colleagues in the 'Uniform in Motion' project in Dortmund and Frankfurt for discussions on the subject and in particular Gabriele Mentges for her guidance and support.

Beverly Lemire thanks the Social Sciences and Humanities Research Council of Canada and by a Killam Research Fellowship for their support towards the research for her chapter. Versions of this chapter were presented at the conference 'The Circulation of Secondhand Goods', European University Institute, Florence, and at the Pre-Industrial England Seminar, the Institute of Historical Research, London. Dr Lemire also thanks Laurence Fontaine, Maxine Berg, Negley Harte, Giorgio Riello, Bruno Blondé, Lynne Milgram and Ruth Pearson for their comments and conversation on this subject.

Lynne Milgram conducted the field research for this paper over several periods in 1995, 1998, 2000, 2001 and 2003. Financial support for this research was provided by the Social Sciences and Humanities Research Council of Canada (SSHRC) through a Doctoral Fellowship, Postdoctoral Fellowship and a Standard Research Grant and by the Ontario College of Art and Design, Faculty Research Grants. In the Philippines, she was affiliated with the Cordillera Studies Center, University of the Philippines Baguio, Baguio City, where she thanks colleagues for their generous support. Dr Milgram also thanks the co-editors, and offers a depth of gratitude to the residents of Banaue, Ifugao.

Terry Satsuki Milhaupt thanks Claire Cuccio, Brad Fratello, Dorothy Ko, Soyoung Lee and Leila Wice for their careful reading of the manuscript and insightful comments, and the Department of Asian Art, Metropolitan Museum of Art for their support. She dedicates her chapter to her mother, Grace Unemori, and maternal grandmother, Chie Kumashiro, who taught her to cherish old pieces of cloth.

Lucy Norris wishes to thank all those dealers in Delhi who generously provided of their time in conducting this research, and Sunita Bhaduria and George Samtabhai for invaluable field assistance. She also thanks the UK Economic and Social Research Council, which funded her doctoral research and postdoctoral fellowship from which her chapter is drawn. She also thanks colleagues in the Department of Anthropology, University College London for their helpful comments on drafts of her chapter.

Hilary O'Kelly would like to thank those who shared their memories of childhood with her; Catherine McNulty and family, Mary Murray, J J Bunyan, Bea Thunder and The Irish Countrywomens Association, Barna, Co. Galway. She would also like to thank colleagues, friends and family for discussions and suggestions on the subject; Dr Paul Caffrey, Nuala Fenton, Orla Fitzpatrick, Lisa Godson, Brendan, Colette and Breffnie O'Kelly, Vera Ryan and especially Prof W. J. Smyth, Department of Geography, University College, Cork. For permission to use sources from their archives she gratefully acknowledges the Head of The Department of Irish Folklore, University College Dublin, and their librarian Emer Ni Cheallaigh.

Alexandra Palmer would like to thank vintage professionals Lynda Latner and Cameron Silver for their time and insights, and Eileen at Norma Kamali for her assistance. She is grateful for the support and interest of colleagues and friends David Howard, Peter McNeil and Catherine Tait, and to students Laura Parsons and Christina Remenyi. Additionally she owes a debt to colleagues Anu Liivandi and Karla Livingstone, as well as Jean Charing at the Royal Ontario Museum, Toronto, Canada, for their patience with her projects.

Margot Riley thanks colleagues in the Original Materials Branch, Mitchell Library, State Library of New South Wales, for their support and interest in her research, and in particular, Alan Davies, Richard Neville and Shirley Walker for generously sharing their enthusiasm for, and superior knowledge of, the Library's collections.

Victoria Rovine thanks her colleague Kristyne Loughran Bini for many conversations and emails on the subject of African fashion. She also thanks Aurore Durry of XULY-Bët for her time and the introduction to Lamine Kouyaté. Thanks are due to Ly Dumas, Hélène Joubert, Pamela Golbin, and others in Paris. Dr Rovine is also grateful to the Getty Foundation for a Curatorial Research Grant that enabled her to conduct research in Paris, and to Florence Babb for her advice and support.

Introduction

The idea for this book originated in a chance conversation over ten years ago when we, the editors, discovered a shared scholarly interest in second hand clothing. As a museum curator and a design historian, specializing in dress and textiles, we were both professionally engaged with the 'old' and its reinvention and reinterpretation as the 'new', and also interested in understanding the ways that second hand clothes have been transformed and reused in a variety of social, economic and cultural contexts in the past and today. We wanted to develop our understanding of second hand clothing from a multidisciplinary and cross-cultural perspective, and this enabled us to draw upon a diverse range of scholarship. So we embarked on this collaborative project inviting contributors whose specializations include anthropology, sociology, economics, art history, fashion and design history and theory. These multiple views have enabled us to provide insights from historical and global perspectives into how, where and why clothes have been and continue to be reconsumed, transformed and given 'second lives'. By focusing on the global trade and consumption of used clothing this book aims to expand the understanding of the fashion system as well as question assumptions about the origins of fashionable dress, and indeed how one considers what is fashionable. The histories given here reveal varied contexts of used clothes, urban and rural, and clearly demonstrate that consumer agency and taste are the final determinations of sales, costs and, ultimately, the fashionability of dress – even, and perhaps especially, in second hand.

At the time of our initial conversation, existing research on second hand dress and fashion was scarce and disparate, yet always insightful and intriguing. One of the seminal articles was by Madeleine Ginsburg (1980) who was the first to articulate the historical significance of the trade in used clothing. Her interest was undoubtedly influenced by her profession as a curator of historical dress at the Victoria and Albert Museum in London, a well-known repository for used and discarded fashionable clothing. Her hands-on experience with historical garments clearly revealed that continual wear, alterations and long-term use were as common in luxury goods as for garments worn everyday. Museum collections of historic costume clearly document the material culture that testifies to the constant updating of former fashions, as well as to the reuse of textiles and dress that are cut down and altered for later use, economically salvaged into children's wear or put into domestic utility as pieced quilts. From a critical perspective this opens up the important question of how and why cultures value previously worn garments and confirms that the study of used clothing demands engagement with a diversity of academic approaches and time frames.

During the decade that intervened before the publication of this book, second hand dress has become the focus of greater attention within the global fashion system and in academe. The important work of Appadurai (1986) and Kopytoff (1986) has developed our understanding of the value and valuing of commodities from a cultural perspective. Kopytoff's 'cultural biography of the object' has become a standard academic text in material culture studies that serves to inform our understanding of, and relationship to, used clothes from historical, cross-cultural as well as social and economic dimensions. Allerston has noted how, 'in the early modern period the second-hand trade performed key social and economic functions' (1999: 46), and Lemire (1988 *passim*) has added extensively to our understanding of the social and economic role of clothes in exchange since the seventeenth century. Commodity value is established within and between cultures and affects the material and aesthetic value of used clothing. This becomes of particular interest in relation to the role of fashion as an expression of identity. Angela McRobbie (1989) was the first to identify the subcultural consumption, use, commodification and creative transformation of second hand clothes into fashion by young female consumers. McRobbie's essay clearly indicates how issues and practices of consumption are key to our subject, while more recent research has added to our understanding of the contemporary consumption of second hand goods (Gregson & Crewe, 2003).

The trade in second hand dress has a history as long as the manufacture of cloth and garments. Its rationale during the Middle Ages and Renaissance was as a means for poorer people to acquire better quality and also fashionable clothes. The expansion of the trade then was not only due to need, but also to the exotic appeal of items from other parts of the world. The uniqueness of the garments in their new settings signified the wealth and social status of their owners. Ginsburg (1980); Lemire (1988, 1990a, 1990b, 1991, 1997); Roche (1994); Allerston (1999); Hansen (1997, 1999, 2000a, 2000b); Palmer (2001: 194–206) have all added to our knowledge of the trade in Western fashionable dress from the sixteenth to the late twentieth century. A conference, *The Circulation of Secondhand Goods*, held at the European University Institute in Florence, Italy, in October 2002 also provided an exchange of the latest scholarly interest in garments presented in the wider context of the second hand trade in general.

Reusing previously worn fashion is predicated on excess production of cloth and garments in societies that manufacture more than they need. Clothes are cast-off before they are worn out. Thus the defining principal for a second hand market is both economic and cultural. One group or class's discards, or rags, are taken up by another group or class and regarded as riches because this is their best access to quality, style and change. The class connotations of wearing something otherwise out of reach of one's socio-economic range, be it from master to servant, or purchased or traded on the open market, has even been legislated through sumptuary laws in Europe (Baumgarten, 2002: 182–207; Ribeiro, 2002: 20, 80). Each class and culture has established its own fine line between what is considered appropriate for re-commodification and what is not. Appadurai has highlighted a distinction in what he refers to as 'the dilemma of distinguishing wear from tear. That is while in many cases wear is a sign of the right sort of duration in the social life of things, sheer disrepair or decrepitude is not' (1996: 75).

Used clothes also serve as clear markers of the baggage and detritus of a culture. For some they carry negative and unsettling associations of poverty, immigration and displacement. Old clothes are also firmly associated with disease and death. From the Middle Ages to the twenty-first century's concern with AIDS, the West Nile virus and SARS, used clothing continues to be suspect. Recently the Panafrican News Agency warned that millions of people might be exposing themselves to serious health problems including scabies, radioactivity, ringworm, skin infections and tuberculosis by wearing second hand clothes without washing them (Lee, 2003: xxiii). Scholars of consumption have begun to address these more unsavory aspects of second hand clothing that includes the residues of bodily secretions and smells that make 'charity shop spaces problematic, no-go areas' (Gregson, Brooks & Crewe, 2000: 110, 104).

The tactile nature of cloth and the fact that clothes are worn on the body means that they can represent, and indeed often stand in for, human beings more forcefully than any other objects. Taboos against wearing used clothes are culturally determined and can have both positive and negative associations that trigger strong emotional responses. East Asian cultures have beliefs that clothing carries the presence of the deceased who are very much 'honored' and thus kept 'alive' in the present, by means of a tactile *memento mori*. Perhaps this is also one reason why costume and fashion exhibits in museums are so popular, because of the associated presence or aura of a former wearer. The popularity of the numerous displays from the wardrobe of the late Princess Diana serves as a clear exemplar. But by the end of the twentieth century many cultural taboos had been eradicated as the exchange of used clothes develops on a global scale spurred on by fashion as much as by genuine need. The trend for wearing 'vintage' second hand clothes that emerged in western urban dress serves as illustration.

In the late 1980s and in the 1990s fashion designers also began to show interest in used items. High fashion reconstructions based upon second hand dress, best exemplified in the practice of the Belgian designers, brought used clothing literally into contemporary and avant garde fashionable circles, as well as into theoretical discourse. Caroline Evans (1998) and Alison Gill (1998) have discussed deconstruction and reuse of garments in the work of designer Martin Margiela. The inclusion of second hand items as new fashion posed challenges to the fashion system itself. If old clothes became the raw material of 'new' fashion, what constituted the new? While past styles have always been subject to fashionable reinterpretation by those who may not have seen and certainly have not worn them before (Baines, 1981; Davis, 1979) we have entered a new and different phase where actual items of clothing are not simply being transformed for their use value but become fashionable commodities that contribute to a complex global trade. It has been remarked that, 'A long chain of charity and commerce binds the world's richest and poorest people in accidental intimacy. It's a curious feature of the global age that hardly anyone on either end knows it' (Packer, 2002: 54).

As fashion and as anti-fashion statement, second hand clothes have been absorbed into the fashion system in different ways in different parts of the world. They have also developed their own forms of communication, through informal channels such as conversation and at a more organized level via publications outside of the mainstream. 'Thrifters' journals have contributed to consumer consciousness of second hand fashion especially amongst younger people in western countries. The more alternative, 'fan-zine' types of publications are typified by *Cheap Date*, launched in June 1997 in Britain and subsequently in the USA, that positions itself as an alternative style magazine. According to its founding UK editor, Kira Jo-liffe, 'What originally inspired us is the freedom that second-hand buying, or at least getting things cheap, can provide. It's a cliche, but you don't need a lot of money to look sexy, glamorous and cool. We all make some duff decisions, but at least they were cheap. And then there are the tri-umphs...' (Frost, 1997). The magazine has continued its alternative feel, in its design and its contents. It condones creativity by the young and not so well off, such as students, and even promotes alternative and ironic con-sumer practices. 'Shop dropping' is a Situationist type of act promoted as the antithesis of shoplifting. In this rogue event, used items are 'dropped', as anonymously as possible, onto the racks of retail shops selling new and fashionable clothes, then photographed, to see how well they fit – or not – into their new setting. The caption to one photograph described a 'Crappy polyester shirt. We added pataphysical swirls for office fun. Dropped in *J. Crewe*. The shop was very busy, and the shoppers looked bemused' (*Cheap Date*, 2001).

Some contemporary consumers have also been attracted to second hand clothes for political and ethical reasons. Since the late 1960s hippie movement, young people who have espoused 'alternative' lifestyles have worn used garments. In Britain in the 1980s the 'New Age Travellers' who chose to live life on the road wore second hand clothes, often thickly layered for protection, warmth and for ease of transportation (de la Haye & Dingwall, 1996). The political and the functional melded in their dress which became a self-conscious marker of their lifestyle and identity. The deliberate adoption of used clothing as a mark of uniqueness is not only a contemporary or a western phenomena. In the late nineteenth century aesthetes and bohemians in Europe wore second hand dress as a mark of cultural status (E. Wilson, 1998; V. Wilson, 1999). As subcultural styles increasingly influenced mainstream fashion in the second half of the twentieth century, second hand clothes gained a place in western countries and in their turn, ironically, became acknowledged into the global fashion system as signs of a contemporary or postmodern identity. Used clothes continue to operate as global commodities, valuable for their economic, cultural and fashionable status, for which there are historical and cross-cultural precedents.

While the study of fashion must always be within its historical, social and cultural contexts, second hand fashion fascinates because it is not only styles that are being recycled, but the actual garments themselves. The rationale for its appearance as a global fashion phenomenon at the millennium is undoubtedly multifaceted and also predicated on a number of factors particular to our own times. However, as a phenomenon, this book demonstrates that it is neither regionally localized nor exclusive to the contemporary. As a practice it provides challenges to the international fashion system, which has always purported to be concerned with the strictly new. In contributing to the discourse of fashion second hand adds to the complexity of defining the term fashion itself. As Breward has remarked, fashion 'requires a method of analysis that takes account of multiple meanings and interpretations' (2000: 26). It is the conundrums and contradictions associated with the trade, consumption and wear of second hand clothing, past and present, across the globe that make it especially relevant to fashion research.

Part 1

Historical Perspectives

Introduction

Alexandra Palmer and Hazel Clark

The specific and detailed studies that comprise this section reveal how the second hand trade has historically played a highly significant cultural and economic role around the globe. While its principal rationale was as a means for poorer people to acquire fashionable clothes, the trade varied in detail according to temporal, social and cultural factors. Scholars are still in the process of uncovering the material culture that provides evidence of the roles of second hand clothes as valued commodities and as markers of social change. Museums are the best-known cultural repositories of the material remnants, though as dress curator, Anthea Jarvis, has remarked, 'I have gradually come to realize that at least half of the nineteenth-century children's clothes in my own collection, especially those made of silk, are made from recycled women's dresses' (2003: 140). What is especially interesting about her statement is not its veracity, but that it is only fairly recently that curators and academics have begun to acknowledge that many extant textile and dress artifacts, are in fact not iconic examples of a single period or style, but often complex composites with multiple histories that should in turn be examined from multiple perspectives.

This section demonstrates historically how used clothes have played key economic, social and cultural roles within different periods and societies. The chapters also indicate how primary source material can require reinvestigation and reinterpretation to provide insight into the previous use and value of a garment or piece of cloth. Clothes and textiles can be mundane as well as significant cultural markers of power and social and economic influence. This is clearly seen in ecclesiastical vestments, artifacts that museum collections often hold as archetypal examples of textiles that trace the development of silk weaving and design. Yet these highly symbolic forms of ceremonial clothing commonly utilize textiles that were donated to a church because of their high economic and cultural value. Once offered, they were usually reused by incorporating them into vestments or as precious

9

wrappings for sacred bones preserved in reliquaries. The Hispano-Moresque silk embroidered shroud of Saint Lazare of Autun survives because it serves as a trophy of war and religion. This fragment is considered important because it was originally part of a garment worn by Abd-al-Malik in 1007 until his death a year later. Its embroidered bands mark his victory against the Christians in 1007. In 1146 the historic, cultural and economic value of the expensive silk was reinforced and added to when it was given and used to wrap the relics of Saint Lazare, Bishop of Autun in Burgundy, France (Marcelli & Wallut, 2003). Today the fragment, which represents a small number of extant early silks, is significant for scholars because it serves as a marked document of textile technique and design that scholars can use when assessing and dating other related silk fragments. In this case, both the function and the sociocultural meaning of the garment and cloth have changed in its reuse, while the cultural value of the piece is still being reconfigured.

Eighteenth-century dresses of rich silks are another stock of museum dress collections that are only beginning to be re-evaluated in their complexity. They were often preserved and acquired because the rich textiles represent a high point in French silk production and design. However, most of these garments were remade and updated during the eighteenth century itself because the silk was so valuable, yet the dresses tend to be dated according to the style, not the original silk. Now museums are unraveling and more consistently cataloguing not only the dress style, but the date of the actual silk, and noting alterations that indicate other dates, styles and forms of wear that are no longer as evident in the dress (Baumgarten, 2002). Even in nineteenth- and twentieth-century dress it is not uncommon to find dresses made up from eighteenth-century silks as fashionable dress and fancy dress (Cooper, 1997). Today eighteenth-century silk dress fragments are used by interior decorators for cushions and trims on furnishings, giving these valued textiles another life as well as new cultural interpretations.

More recently on a more prosaic level, many women keep clothes that they believe they will never wear again but are too good or important to discard (Banim & Guy, 2001). Others donate such pieces to museum collections. For the benefactor, being able to have a suitable repository for their garments assuages complex sentiments that their clothes embody. A donation that is kept in perpetuity confirms the 'correctness' of their taste and validates the worth of the garment that also holds personal memories and other meanings that may or may not be recorded by the museum. Clearly clothes, as documents of our material culture, are loaded with individual and collective meanings. Regardless of rank and as far back as the Heian period (794–1185), it was expected that audience members would throw garments onto the stage for the Noh entertainers in lieu of admission fees. 'In this way a variety of clothing styles, from simple hemp garments worn by commoners to elegant silk robes of the nobility, fell into hands of performers' (Takeda, 2002: 71).

Each of these examples demonstrates the ongoing importance and effort required to recoup meaning and/or economic value from previously worn garments, either through donation, sale or barter. Though this exchange is not always straightforward it is repeatedly and consistently performed throughout time and cultures, because of the possible worth of clothes – however that worth might be interpreted at a given time. This key theme, the construction of and change in value, is documented in the following chapters, which move across time and geography.

To begin, Frick describes clothes as expensive commodities that were sold and resold in Renaissance Florence keeping their value for decades – an old understanding of 'investment dressing'. She shows that used clothes retained a high economic and social value not only for the original consumer, but that the status of the goods was also transposed to the high end second hand clothing vendors, the *rigattieri*, and even to the locations of their shops. As Frick reveals, though the aristocracy paid dearly for expensive clothing, even forty-three years later it retained its value so much so to be 'enough to feed, house and clothe a family of four for a year'. Clearly this important economy had a profound social and cultural impact. The ongoing importance of the second hand trade is further elucidated by Lemire who adds yet another aspect of it to her long term study (*passim*), and to its vibrant history, whereby the actual and assumed value inherent in garments was reflective of prevailing social and economic conditions. As Lemire writes 'second hand defied the proscribed models of market exchange'. It cannot be understood or examined only theoretically, but through a conglomeration of detailed historical records she reveals that used clothes made up an active trade, honest and dishonest, that played an enormous role in the ongoing transfer of goods. She also highlights the importance of taste, fashion and location, as in the case of outdated men's wigs, which had little or no value in major centers, such as London, but did so when despatched to rural Irish settings, or older leather breeches being sent to an interested market overseas.

Margot Riley's chapter maps the fascinating role of second hand dress in Australia from the eighteenth century to the early twentieth century and develops the global perspective by placing second hand dress firmly within the discourse of a nation that was founded on the discards of European society. As she notes, some of its first settlers were convicts 'transported for theft of wearing apparel, a potent reminder of the value of clothes as a commodity'. Riley's case history establishes the critical role that second hand clothes played for its settlers and aborigines, in the founding and making of a nation. The importance of context for understanding dress is well illustrated in the aboriginal 'clothing misuse' that she attributes to lack of interest and experience in Western dress forms, and that confirmed the 'primitiveness of the blacks' for the new colonial settlers. This chapter highlights the neglected role of second hand fashion in the construction of Australian societies.

The final two chapters in the section also emphasize the historical significance of used clothing in relation to social change. In Japan the context for second hand kimono is laid out in three different settings and times by Terry Milhaupt. She shows how this garment has been transformed socially and culturally in history. It has and continues to be revered but also to be adapted to new roles and social symbols, and even in its fragmentary state is still worthy of study. Hilary O'Kelly questions our understanding of the value as well as the meaning of second hand clothes, which she shows are transformative, in both positive and negative ways. She illustrates this in the clothing sent by Irish immigrants in America to loved ones still in Ireland. The second hand clothes are poignant symbols of the immigrants' success and independence, and she traces an aspect of the ephemeral power of clothing to transform and single out the individual within a community.

Together the authors in this section illuminate not only the vital economic and social roles that second hand clothes have historically performed, but they create a cumulative picture from many viewpoints of the deep cultural and symbolic significance of second hand dress for a wide variety of individuals from traders to consumers within a global setting. Clearly second hand clothes have powerful meanings within the history of dress and material culture that have only begun to be interpreted and understood.

1

The Florentine 'Rigattieri': Second Hand Clothing Dealers and the Circulation of Goods in the Renaissance

Carole Collier Frick

A 'Cloth' Town

In the economy of Renaissance Florence, the textile and garment industry dominated the urban marketplace for consumer goods. In addition to the 909 household heads Franceschi found who listed some aspect of the woolen cloth business as their occupation at the turn of the fifteenth century, Herlihy and Klapisch-Zuber counted 866 clothiers in 1427 that identified themselves by some aspect of the clothing trade within the city.[1] Clearly, the commerce in cloth, clothing and accessories provided a livelihood to many hundreds of households. The occupation of *rigattiere*, or used-clothing dealer, had an important role in this city industry. As newly finished cloth in general was an expensive commodity produced for the rich, and new luxury cloth was certainly out of the reach of most, the shops and inventories of the dealers in second hand clothing filled an essential function for the rest of the urban populace, that of providing them with garments and personal/household linens at a cost they could afford. They acted in effect as the first clothing retailers. This chapter will consider those Florentines who practiced this trade, to try to situate the used-clothing dealer within the guild community itself. The question of who the *rigattieri* were, whether primarily males or females practiced this trade, and what their socio economic role was in the complex economic life of the city will be explored. It appears that these tradespeople served an important function in the commerce of cloth and clothing in the early modern period. Some even got rich. But whether he or she was an official male guildsman regulated by communal statute, or one of the independent female vendors who traversed the crowded marketplace on a regular basis, the men and women who acted as *rigattieri* were crucial to the circulation of textile goods among the various social strata of the city. The entire populace, from the poor to the wealthiest, participated in this commerce as consumers of these locally produced textile products.

Scholars have attempted to understand the circulation of goods and services in the economies of the early modern time period. See, for example, the work of Elizabeth Sanderson (1996, 1997). These studies, for the most part, have focused on alternative currency models such as barter systems, and been centered on northern European cities such as London and Paris. Beverly Lemire's work has recently included the utility of used clothing as a means of exchange within these models (1998). Patricia Allerston's study on the place of second hand clothing in Venice, expanded our understanding of this currency southward, by examining this practice specifically within the Italian guild setting (1999).[2] While she has focused on sixteenth- and seventeenth-century Venetian practices, this essay will endeavor to extend the scope of scholarship to the city of Florence. Here, fourteenth- and fifteenth-century urban guild records and family log books among other Florentine archival sources, will be utilized to begin to examine the second hand clothing trade in the city.

The Guild Marketplaces

The Florentine chronicler Giovanni Villani, in his *Cronica* of 1336, re-ferred to the earliest guild of used-clothing dealers informally as the Arte di Baldrigari. It was first formed in 1266 as the retail guild of second hand clothing, cloth, household linens and related items of cloth (Davidsohn, 1956: IV: II: 328). Each city in Italy had its own name for this occupation. In Bologna, it was *regattieri*, while the completely different term *strazzaruoli* was used in Venice.[3] In the city of Florence by 1280, some fourteen years after the guild was first organized, the formal designation for the used-cloth-ing dealers' guild was the Arte de' Rigattieri e Linaiuoli. They were at the bottom of the list of the five so-called 'middling guilds' or Arte Mediante, that were brought down to the status of the lesser guilds in 1293 (Staley, 1906: 45–6).[4] This association grouped together used-clothing and linen retailers, linen-producers, and tailors – all livelihoods that dealt with supply-ing the basic clothing needs of the local population.

Goods had been sold in the various fixed marketplaces established from the earliest history of the Commune.[5] The *rigattieri* as a group dominated the ready to wear textile market (Davidsohn, 1956: IV: II: 328). By providing a commercial venue for used items of clothing brought to them for sale by private citizens or bought up at public auction, and by buying up traditionally home or convent-produced linens and goods willed to the Church, the *rigattieri* sold their acquired inventories within retail stalls in one of the town's many outdoor marketplaces (Frick, 2002: 21–2, 36, 38–9). The local resale of used clothing in Florence was here coupled with the marketing of a variety of household linens. Personal linens-making was one of the few areas of Renaissance clothing that remained for the most part unprofessionalized, and women on all levels of society sewed continually on an informal basis, often selling their output to these guild-run venues in the city. By dealing in a category of clothing for the most part outside guild incorporation, the *rigattieri* were undoubtedly able to keep their shelves cheaply stocked. Statistics compiled in 1442 show that the Arte dei Rigattieri e Linaiuoli handled imported and domestically made doublets (*farsetti d'ogni ragione*), bed linens (*choltre e chopertojo*), and towels and tablecloths (*sciugatoi e tovaglie da tavola*) as well as its basic staple of used clothes (Pagnini, 1765–66: IV:1–8).[6] Also included in this complex commercial center were those more elusive participants, independent female vendors (*venditrice*) selling veils, caps and headscarves, and roaming shop workers, seamsters, seamstresses, and shoe-makers.[7]

The rich and prestigious silk guild (Arte della Seta) on the opposite end of this spectrum oversaw the other textile marketplace in Florence, consisting of luxury goods such as jewelry, pearls and gemstones, as well as an extensive inventory of imported silk accessories – from doublets and hosiery to hats and silk embroidery. Silver and gold thread, purses, buttons, and veils, as well as embroidered fringes, ribbons, scarves and caps, all made of silk, also could be found in the shops policed by the city's silk dealers (*setaiuoli*) (Davidsohn, 1956: IV: II: 85–6.) Clothing, then, made using these expensive materials would subsequently have been privately commissioned from tailors, seamstresses, or specialty workers like belt-makers or headdressmakers, by individual families. New luxury clothing was not made up and offered as ready-to-wear. Prestigious though the silk dealers and their luxury merchandise may be, the *rigattieri* were more numerous – by 1427, being only second in numbers to the ubiquitous shoemakers (*calzolai*). In fact 159 people declared their occupation as *rigattiere* in Florence in 1427.[8]

Significance of the Trade

So, what did it mean that the used-clothing dealers were such a big part of the marketplace? How were the wares of the *rigattieri* different from those of today's second hand or Salvation Army shops? For one thing, in thinking about these professionals, we must be careful to discriminate between them and old clothes or rag dealers, who went by the different term of *rivenditori*. The second hand clothing dealers occupied a different role in the diffusion of still-wearable and therefore presentable material resources of this Renaissance city. Even within the upper reaches of society, the personal log books (*ricordanze*) of rich merchant families list the expenses of having 'new' garments made with 'used' cloth (*panno usato*), which people were always careful to distinguish from 'old' or 'worn-out' cloth (*panno vecchio* or *panno triste*).[9] Few people were above patronizing the shop of the local *rigattiere*, who performed the recognized and valuable economic service of providing affordable textiles to the public at large.

Secondly, we should remember that in the Renaissance, good cloth and the clothing made from it retained its value for years; even decades. In her work on used-clothing practices in Venice, Allerston has written that this is probably the reason we do not have clothing that has survived from early modern Italy (1999: 47). Because these durable textiles, such as silk brocade and finely finished wool, were such valuable commodities, clothes and cloth continued to work and be reworked, over and over, by their owners, like other major investments can be today. In order to understand the importance of used clothes in early modern societies, we have to rethink the place of clothing to these people. Clothes were their ultimate consumer goods, not only immediately useful in a variety of ways, but also representing a prudent investment of one's hard-earned florins.

Luxury clothing that may have been commissioned by a family for an important rite of passage such as a wedding, claimed a corporate ownership. Rather than 'belonging' to the individual for whom it had been made to wear in a family ritual, the gown, or cloak, or ensemble, acted as part of the larger family's goods. These material resources could be taken apart, stripped of their ornaments and sold as separate pieces. They were a resource to be deployed in a family economy when it was strategically necessary. In other words, good clothing was something a socially mobile family group could save and re-enter into the marketplace, confident that its value would have held over time. On March 2, 1451, four years after his marriage to Caterina Strozzi, prosperous silk merchant Marco Parenti sold some fourteen garments to the firm of Giovanni di Filippo e Chompagni rigattieri. This sale included four cloaks, six overgowns (some fur-lined), a worn-out (*triste*) fox lining, two women's gowns and three pairs of red stockings. For all these items, which had belonged to his parents, Parenti received 242 florins (*ASF, Carte Strozz*, Ser II, 17bis: 31V). In 1490, waiting many years after his wife Caterina's death, Parenti finally sold her sumptuous wedding gown of expensive *chermisi* (kermes) red and a pair of gold-embroidered sleeves, both of which he had had made for their marriage in 1447. For these two used garments, which he had assembled some forty-three years before, a *rigattiere* paid him 57 florins. To understand how much this amount represented in the fifteenth-century economy, 56 florins were enough to feed, house and clothe a family of four for a year at mid-century. What does this tell us? First of all, that Parenti was rich, and secondly, that clothing, even used clothing, could be expensive. The *rigattieri*, as brokers of these family investments, thus could play a significant role in the early modern economy, assuring the necessary movement of these luxury goods.

Social Status of the *Rigattieri*

However, the *rigattieri* were only one of the minor guilds in Florence. If their role was so significant to the economy and they seemed to be so prevalent in the city, why were they only afforded lesser guild status? This status had developed over time. The very early commercial marketplace of Florence in the thirteenth century had had a few dozen small associations (*societas*) of crafts and tradespeople, from purveyors of goat hair to dealers who rented horses and other 'beasts'. Beginning in 1293 the Commune consolidated the numbers of its guilds and reorganized workers into seven major and fourteen minor guilds, for only twenty-one in all. At this time, all crafts and tradespeople were incorporated into this formal guild network that established the infrastructure for the commerce of the city, and this would stand until the sixteenth century. Anyone left out of this incorporation process was effectively marginalized by his or her exclusion. Women especially would be forced out of the new guild structure, as we shall see below (Herlihy, 1990: 162).[10]

The new hierarchy of trades and crafts became well known and rigid, conveying social status or lack thereof on the basis of one's position in the guild ranking. At the top were the seven major guilds that supplied, organized and regulated international trade. The judges and notaries headed this, followed by the foreign cloth dealers, the wool guild, the bankers, the silk guild, which included the goldsmiths and jewelers, the doctors and apothecaries, and the furriers. All of these associations dealt directly in either the production or dissemination and policing of luxury goods, the commodities for which Florence would become famous. From four-pile, cut- and figured silk brocades and linings of ermine to the finest English wool finished in Florence and dyed scarlet with kermes, the sumptuous wares created by this guild production were in high demand during the Renaissance period.

The minor guilds, of which the *rigattieri* were the second most numerous, concentrated their energies on the local market. Here, the top of the hierarchy began with the butchers, and continued on down through the blacksmiths, shoemakers, stonemasons and woodcarvers, before we find the used clothes dealers, who would eventually be grouped into the same guild as the tailors and linen merchants (Staley, 1906: 61–2). These occupations, while they may have been essential for the urban population, were not major players in the lucrative long-distance commerce upon which the fortunes of the city were based. Therefore, their social ranking reflected this fact. However, even given this second-tier social ranking for second hand clothiers, some of these urban merchants did quite well. In 1457, *rigattiere* Niccolo di Benintendi, had a net worth of some 1515 florins, which included a farm out in the Tuscan countryside valued at 529 florins. He also owned his own home (over and above his net worth), which was situated in the quarter of Santa Maria Novella where he lived with his wife and family, near the same central city location of his shop (*ASF, CAT,* 822: 567R).[11] Fifteen years later, Florentine merchant Benedetto Dei, writing in his *Cronica* in 1472, ranked another used clothes dealer, the 'righatiere tTomaso,' among the richest men in the city, putting him about hundreth on a list which began with Lorenzo de' Medici himself (Dei, 1984: 85–6).

Location, Location, Location

By looking at the Catasto of 1427, we can also ascertain in general which quarters of the city had concentrations of specific artisans. The historic center of the commercial life of Renaissance Florence was encompassed by the quarter of San Giovanni, and this area seems to have housed the most used-clothing retail shops, with a total of seventy-six heads-of-households from this quarter declaring their primary occupations as dealers in second hand clothing and textiles. This represented almost 50 percent of the *rigattieri* of the city. To get some sense of proportion for these figures, in the same quarter there were some thirty-three tailors (*sarti*), twenty-five goldsmiths (*orafi*), and twenty-four furriers (*vaiai*), all doing business from their shops. With more than twice the number of *rigattieri* than any of these other occupations, used-clothing dealers would have been prominent among the cloth and clothing merchants (Herlihy & Klapisch-Zuber, 1981).[12]

They certainly dominated the textile shops in the local market venues, especially at the location of the Mercato Vecchio, which dated back to 1225. (This is now Piazza Repubblica, the large square in front of the modern post office.) Due to its central position in the economic world of the city, this market was referred to in thirteenth-century sources in Latin simply as the *foro* or the 'marketplace.'[13] Along the streets in the same quarter of San Giovanni associated with the international luxury trade, streets such as Via Pellicciai, Via Calimala, Via Vacchereccia, Por Santa Maria and Via Porta Rossa all near the modern-day Piazza della Signoria, the shops overflowed with exotic, newly-woven, gold and silk-embroidered items, not second hand clothes and basic linens (Carocci, 1884: 31, 49, 143–6, 151; Guccerelli, 1985: 49–50, 71–2, 78–9, 88–9, 350, 376). Used clothing shops that carried personal linens would not have signified the desired identity Florence as a city wished to project to its wealthy and often foreign clientele. Benedetto Dei, for example, characterized his hometown by foregrounding its most exotic offerings. His description of the economic life of the city begins 'Beautiful Florence has forty-four shops of goldsmiths and silversmiths and jewelers in the center of the city and thirty-two shops of establishments that finish and cut cloth of crimson and scarlet and purple...' and then goes on to enumerate the far-flung, cosmopolitan locations to the East, such as Turkey, Greece, Persia and Constantinople, to which city merchants exported the most luxurious of Florentine textiles (Dei, 1984: 83).[14] Given the city's reputation for luxury wares then, the locations of its second hand shops would have been relegated to the large and diverse, but locally patronized venues like the Mercato Vecchio, where used clothes would have blended in with a wider range of utilitarian wares. This was where the average citizen could have purchased an already-made-up garment.

In 1457, three tax declarations from men who made their livings as *rigattieri* do locate their shops (*botteghe*) in this main piazza. Domenico di Filippo Rinaldi, age 52, paid thirteen florins per year for the rent on his shop, while 50-year-old Niccolo di Benintendi shared a bottega with another second hand clothing dealer, one Bartolomeo di Michele (*ASF, CAT*, 815: 133R; 822: 567R).[15] Their shop must have been quite large, as Niccolo paid roughly 18 ½ florins for his half of the rent, and valued the merchandise inventory at a respectable 500 florins. Even the famed architect Filippo Brunelleschi only made 100 florins a *year* while building the Duomo for the Cathedral of Florence. A third, older, used-clothing dealer by the name of Giusto di Dolfo (age 74), reported on his tax statement that he too had had a bottega in the Mercato Vecchio in the mid 1430s, but had had to let it go for unknown reasons. He was able to sell his *entratura* or right to do business there, however, for 200 florins (*ASF, CAT*, 822: 730R). Clearly, this area was the center of the second hand 'rag trade' in the city of Florence, and a spot in this lucrative retail market was a prized commodity.

Other important markets for textiles by the fifteenth century included the so-called Mercato Nuovo, further south toward the Arno in the same quarter of San Giovanni, as well as the environs of the old grain market of Orsanmichele, on the main thoroughfare of Via Calzaioli (Guccerelli, 1985: 78–9). These stalls servicing the local trade were however, mixed some-what with more exclusive shops. There was no formal commercial zoning in place, and in Florence as elsewhere in early modern Europe, wholesale shops and retail outlets for cloth and cloth products could operate side-by-side with used clothing, bedroom linens, cloth ends and industry-doffings dealers, shops for notions (*merciai*), and sometimes even the old clothes dealers (*rivenditori*) (Carocci, 1884: 31–59).

In 1427, the *rigattieri* were also prominent among the trades doing busi-ness in the quarter of Santa Maria Novella, adjacent to San Giovanni and site of the modern train station. Here, forty-two second hand clothing deal-ers had established themselves, even outnumbering the ubiquitous shoe-makers (Herlihy & Klapisch-Zuber, 1981). What is interesting about the *rigattieri* as a group however is that, as major retailers, they were, by and large, absent from the more industrial sections of town, especially the quar-ter of Santa Croce. In this quarter, their numbers drop off precipitously, only 7 percent of the city total filing taxes from this area, where leather and wood workers were most numerous, employed as purse makers *(borsai)*, slipper and clog makers (*pianellai*), and were neighbors with some thirty-five shoe-makers (Herlihy & Klapisch-Zuber, 1981).

The Circulation of Clothes

Along the streets of these many commercial venues, *rigattieri* then plied their trade. By combining the sale of household and person linens with second hand clothes, their primary function was to supply the necessary basic linens for the people of the city. As Herlihy and Klapisch-Zuber have shown, after waves of plague which had begun in 1348, the typical household size of fifteenth-century Florence left the average home in 1427 with only 4.42 people (1985: 282). Many of these household units would not have had a woman's expertise in the home to sew, or have sewn, the traditional domes-tic everyday linens. These linens ranged from underwear, caps, scarves and veils, to towels, tablecloths, napkins, pillowslips, sheets, and other wash-able items. In fact, one out of six households in Florence was composed of widowers, bachelors, brothers, orphaned children, or 'seemingly unrelated' individuals. A significant number of these unusual demographic groupings would not have included any females at home, and would have had to rely on the shops of the *rigattieri* for all their household cloth and clothing needs (Herlihy & Klapisch-Zuber, 1985: 291).

The second function of this occupation was to provide a commercial outlet for the female home producers of personal and family linens (*panni lini* or *biancheria*), who were excluded from guild participation. Whereas communal records show clear evidence of a professional female presence in the late thirteenth-century economy, by the time of the consolidation of the guilds in 1293, women begin to drop out of sight on formal guild matriculation lists (Herlihy, 1990: 96, 102; Staley, 1906: 68).[16] In its exclusion of women, the guild system in the city of Florence was one of most restrictive in Europe. In the northern cities of Paris and Cologne for example, some textile crafts, such as silk-weaving, were seen as feminine occupations with their own guilds, but in Italy and especially in Tuscany, the guild system shut out women completely (Doren, 1940–48: I: 145, n. 3, 146, nn. 1–4). Historians have attributed this to the legacy of Lombard law in the region, which disallowed female self-representation in the court system, requiring a designated male representative (*mundualdus*) to serve as legal intermediary for a woman in any case brought before the court. Women were not able to be legally independent, therefore signing contracts or entering into any business agreements on their own was forbidden to them (Herlihy, 1990: 162, 167). As Alessandro Stella has shown from his study of the late fourteenth- and early fifteenth-century tax surveys (*Estimi*) between 1352 and 1404, the number of women designating themselves with an occupation drops significantly, and is replaced by 'helper of' or 'worker at' the place of the occupation, indicated by the word 'at,' '*ista*' in Italian (Stella, 1993: app. 2: 284–8, 293). Over time then, females were increasingly forced by necessity to work as simple outside suppliers of textile goods on an extra-guild, informal basis. If a male craftsperson held guild membership, he retained control over his product from its creation to sale. However, the vast majority of female craftspeople, being denied guild entrance, had to find other ways to support themselves in this urban economy. For women, hawking their needlework independently or selling it to a male *rigattieri* with a fixed shop location were their only options to participate in the potentially lucrative textile market, but on a subordinate and marginalized basis.

A third significant role that the *rigattieri* played was to provide the Commune with professional evaluations of clothing and accessories which had been brought to the merchants court (*Mercanzia*) for various legal purposes. Whether part of a trousseau, dowry, bequest, or sale for unknown personal reasons, the worth of the goods had to be legally set by this specialized court. The males who worked as *rigattieri*, based upon their experience in the textile marketplace buying and selling clothes, were well situated to do this work.[17] For example, on June 7, 1456, the *rigattiere* Caroli de Carradorili was summoned to the merchant's court along with three other men, to look at textile goods consisting of a woman's gown (*una ghamurra paonaza da donna*), a worn-out bedcover (*una coltrice trista*) and two quilts (*due primacci*). Their evaluation of these textiles brought their owners 15½ florins total. In August of the same year, one of the same *rigattiere* was back in court, evaluating another four items for one Simone Taddi, this time pricing them at 20 florins (*ASF, Mercanzia*, 288: 41V, 72V). That next March, one Francesco del Nero *rigattiere* was in court to give a valuation on a number of luxury items for the de Stufa family, which included a woman's crimson velvet gown with brocade sleeves, a blue-violet overgown embroidered in gold with twenty-seven pearls, and a white belt with silver decorations set in gold. The *rigattiere* valued these items at 55 florins (*ASF, Mercanzia*, 288: 196V). The repeated presence of the second hand clothing dealers at these court proceedings would certainly have provided the opportunity for continual professional contact with these valuable and costly textile goods and with their owners or owners' representatives.

And therefore a fourth role of this occupation is not surprising. By their intimate involvement in the assessing of goods, they linked themselves as minor guildsmen and their own shops, with the high-end expensive wares produced by the major guilds and marketed in their shops. In fact, mapping the circulation and consumption of material goods demonstrates that many of the luxury items originally purchased in the shops of the silk merchants would be recycled by their owners, either willingly or unwillingly, and begin a second life in the inventories of the shops of the *rigattieri*. For example, following an explosive political crisis in the month of April 1478, the Commune confiscated the possessions of an outlaw family (Martines, 2003). Pazzi family leaders and accomplices were put to death for their attack on the young male heirs of the Medici family and their personal effects were then publicly auctioned. Beginning on June 1, 1478, officials of the communal mint (or *Zecca*), began the procedure of selling these assets. Florentine apothecary Luca Landucci wrote in his diary that the clothes and household furnishing of the Pazzi and others filled the auction house from end to end, because of the great wealth of the family (Landucci, 1883: 22).[18] Another auction of the personal belongings of Piero de' Medici, held at Orsanmichele beginning on July 9, 1495, was even more spectacular, the dissemination process of his *cosi e panni* (literally 'things and yardage') lasting for months, until November 14, 1495 (Landucci, 1883: 111, 118). The opportunity for the *rigattieri* to bid on and acquire wares for their *botteghe* would have been seized in these historic opportunities to add to their inventories.

Venditrice or '*Rigattiera*'?

The physical setting for the ancient marketplaces of Florence as we have seen, was complex in its juxtaposition of layers of urban society. Full male guildsmen worked in close proximity to subordinated craftspeople and peripatetic female vendors who threaded their way through the stalls, carrying their goods on their backs. Known as *venditrici*, they were eyed with suspicion by the more established shopkeepers, who perceived them as a threat that endangered the regulated urban marketplace. From repeated attempts within the guild statutes of the *rigattieri* to police this potentially disruptive element, we can see that for the guild community, these females represented a constant source of anxiety.

Early in the fourteenth century (1318) a *venditrice* had had to post a surety of 20 lire per year to the second hand clothing guild to be able to sell her wares, but by 1371, the guild temporarily prohibited women from working the neighborhoods of the city at all, saying that these females manipulated unsuspecting wives into buying their merchandise by wheedling their way inside their homes, causing them to squander their husbands' money (Sartini, 1940–48: 170). These peripatetic female vendors were often given the informal title of '*rigattiera*', in addition to being referred to as *venditrice* (Doren, 1940–48: 1: 203, no. 3).[19] What this actually meant however is unclear. It seems from the sources as though the term '*rigattiera*' came to be used as a generic pejorative label for any independent female entrepreneur, whether or not she was a purveyor of used clothing.[20]

On the streets of Florence then, a certain number of the active participants in the cloth and clothing business lacked any guild supervision. Historians have noted the overt societal discrimination against these female needle-trade workers/vendors operating freely without obvious male control, a bias that was part of the larger patriarchal framework of fifteenth-century Italy (Brown, 1986: 216). In 1427, out of a small number of women (some forty-four) who declared an occupation in textiles or related crafts and trades when filing their taxes as heads-of-households, only seven listed themselves as a '*rigattiera*,' representing about 17 percent of this total (Herlihy & Klapisch-Zuber, 1981). We can surmise however, that this under-reporting of female occupations would have been due to the fact that only the head-of-household reported to the city officials, and females did not usually occupy this familial role. In addition, the perceived 'disruptive' nature of this work may have discouraged married women with family from actively engaging in it, relegating such work to single or unattached female workers.

It also seems as though female procurers of domestically produced linens who did business exclusively with other females on an informal, personal basis, avoided censure of their economic activities by communal authorities. Women's own letters to family members are full of references to items of clothing and household linens being commissioned, designed, paid for, repaired, washed, and re-sent through female networks of friendship and affiliation. The correspondence between one merchant husband and his much younger spouse provides a good source for these practical matters of cloth and clothing between women. As Francesco Datini and his wife Margherita were often separated due to his business responsibilities (and his desire to be personally independent), Margherita took care of the bulk of the domestic affairs, which included the making, laundry and repair of clothes and family linens. Her letters to Francesco contain repeated mention of the various females (by name) who worked in one or another aspect of fulfilling the sometimes minute textile needs of their households (Rosati, 1976: 25–152). For just one example among many, in a letter of June 5, 1395, Margherita discusses the personal linens made by a woman by the name of 'la Lapa,' as well as the twenty undershirts (*camice*) made for Francesco and herself by 'the wife of Fensi' (*la moglie di Fensi*), among other things (Rosati, 1976: 62–3). From thread and cloth, to orders for a new underblouse (*camicia*) or headcap (*cuffia*), every item of intimate clothing was made by some woman's hand.

Often, the females of a family dealt with women in a convent who were either nuns or young unmarried women temporarily residing there, or other females of unknown relationship to them. A large number of religious communities had been established around 1350 in Florence, and by 1540, there were over forty convents for women in the city. Every family of middling class and above would have had some female relative living in this relatively fluid ecclesiastical community. In fact, the higher on the social spectrum one's family was, the more likely it would be that one would have multiple female relatives living within convent walls with varying degrees of permanence. This was due in part to the difficulty of providing adequate marriage dowries for girls from wealthy families (Trexler, 1972: 1329–50). That these convent-bound women produced thread, cloth, and specialty clothing items (embroidery and other fine needlework) is well known, and the notion that their own female kin would have a utilitarian connection with this essential, but informal industry seems clear. Margherita Datini dealt with the women at the monastery of Santo Nicolaio, writing to her husband about some thirty handkerchiefs made by a Mona Vivola, and twenty-four large ones by Mona Chita, as well as a dozen 'fine' napkins (*sotile*) and as many tablecloths, as well as five pairs of large sheets made by the same Mona Chita. A portion of these linens she encloses for him. And again just four days later in another missive to her husband, Margherita sends along four new handkerchiefs, again made by Mona Chita (Rosati, 1976: 62–3, 67). From the frequency of this correspondence and the detailed nature of its domestic concerns, one can get a sense of the amount of energy demanded of women in providing household linens from within the intimate settings of home and convent.

Work though it may have been for Margherita, it was not paid labor. If a woman were to move outside these informal webs of contact between individuals known to each other personally, if she were to begin vending to strangers, thereby establishing commercial networks for purely remunerative motives, then she was open to being castigated by the larger guild community for behavior inappropriate to a proper female. She would be transgressing these gender-specific realms and be punished for it with the label of '*rigattiera.*' In other words, a female '*rigattiera*' was not the same thing as a male '*rigattiere*' in Renaissance Florence. Her only recourse for establishing a legal, if meager income, was to sell her domestically produced cloth goods to an established male guildsman with a shop, thereby relegating herself to supplying his customers with needed linens on a piecework basis (Greci, 1996: 88–91).[21]

Reinventing Fashion

As mentioned above, not only were entire clothing ensembles sold by their owners to the *rigattieri* or to a pawnbroker (*sensale*), but also bits and pieces of outfits that had been created for family celebrations such as baptisms, weddings and funerals. In this way, *rigattieri* provided the opportunity for buyers of luxury fabrics to continue to make their initial investment work for them, rather than freezing their capital in ritual objects no longer in use. For example, in January of 1496, the wealthy patrician Andrea Minerbetti availed himself of needed capital by selling not only garments of his own, but also eight gowns which had formed part of his wife's trousseau, and more humble clothing from his deceased father. From his sale to the *rigattiere*, Minerbetti received some 230 florins, which he then used to pay off a family creditor (*BL, acq&don*: 229: 2: 11R).[22]

Pieces of ensembles like sleeves were detachable from the bodice to which they would be laced, and were listed separately in family account books. They were also *sold* separately from the outfit of which they had once been a part. Red and green striped sleeves, fashioned especially to go with a crimson dress, could find themselves coupled with a gown of *pavonazza* (dark blue-violet), after a trip to the local *rigattiere*. The sleeves of a Renaissance garment often reflected the latest fashion statement, and in Florence there were over a dozen recognizable cuts of sleeves, as well as variations for men and women. Within the bounds of communal sumptuary law, the combination of a newly purchased sleeve with an existing gown would have multiplied the choices available for sartorial creativity (Rainey, 1985: 2: 648–56).[23] But that was not all. Bodices could be detached from skirts, or an overgown sold separately from the gown that it had originally been made to cover. With at least twenty different types of gowns to choose from in fifteenth-century Florence, fourteen or so styles of headwear, ten kinds of fitted garments that were usually quilted, five varieties of belts, and almost two dozen different kinds of ornaments for gowns, cloaks, and hats, any one of which could have ended up in the inventory of a *rigattiere*, the permutations of clothing elements would have stimulated fashion innovation (Frick, 1995: 437–8).

Gold cloth was lined with turquoise, white with watered blue (*sbiadato*), tan velvet with dark blue-violet silk (Frick, 2002: 172). Whether fur or silk satin, the Renaissance favored unusual combinations of colors for gowns and linings, some unusual and even jarring to the modern eye. As linings were also made, sold, and then *re*-sold independently, these original color pairings could and would have changed dramatically, according to the taste of the customer. Italian Renaissance clothing consisted of many layers of thin garments worn one over the other, thereby facilitating addition or subtraction depending upon the weather or the season, so there would have been an infinite number of choices available to the consumer with the cash, for creative combination and recombination of various pieces of second hand clothing in fifteenth-century Florence.

Conclusions

The used clothing sector of the Florentine garment business then was important to the overall economy of the city. Not only did these dealers supply affordable clothing and linens to the average citizen, they also acted as brokers for the handmade output of female pieceworkers operating from their homes. Further, these *rigattieri* were able to facilitate the movement of goods by offering previously owned but still usable items for sale in a public marketplace. This prevented the stagnation of the considerable outlay of funds rich Florentines spent on personal display, and instead, returned their purchases to the marketplace, where owners were able to recoup their liquid capital, and live to invest another day. The lower reaches of society were able to access bits and pieces of luxury goods, albeit used, while the upper reaches of society were able to recycle their extravagance. Clothing practices among the urban population were influenced by the adaptive reuse of hardy textiles, allowing individual recombination of various garment pieces to emerge. And in the meantime, hundreds of guildsmen and female textile-workers and vendors participated in this circular market, and a few managed to get rich. The *rigattieri* functioned to weave together gender, class and emerging personal identity in this early modern economy.

Notes

1. For the wool-workers see (Franceschi, 1993: tab. 20: 143). For other clothiers (Herlihy & Klapisch-Zuber, 1981). Many thanks to Rebecca Emigh for her assistance with this database.

2. See the work of Patricia Allerston, where she identifies the guild records of the *L'Arte degli Strazzaruoli* as one valuable source of information on the second hand clothing trade.

3. For Bologna, see *Le Arti di Bologna di Annibale Carracci.* (Marabottini, 1979: fig. 14). For Venice (Allerston, 1999: 48).

4. The lists are within *Le Consulte della Repubblica Fiorentina*, I: 75–97 (Staley, 1906).

5. These records are contained within the matriculation lists of the Guild of Silk Merchants in the State Archives in Florence. *Archivio di Stato Firenze* (hereinafter 'ASF'), *Matricole del' Arte di Por Santa Maria*.

6. See Giovanni di Antonio da Uzzano, *La pratica della mercatura*, 1442, under 'Gabelle di Firenze' (Pagnini, 1865–6).

7. For example, Davidsohn, in his *Storia di Firenze*, discusses the female vendors (*venditrice*) of herbal medicine, especially sought after to lessen the effects of the plague (1956: IV: II: 85–6).

8. The total number of people who declared *calzolaio* as their major occupation in 1427 was 264. However, see the caution about these figures above in note 1. (Herlihy & Klapisch-Zuber, 1981). Also see Davidsohn's earlier figures on shoemakers (1956: IV: II: 104).

9. *ASF, Carte Strozziane*, Ser. II, 17 bis, fol. 39R. Here in 1453, Marco Parenti, a rich merchant, is having a simple long dress made for his wife of used cloth ('una gamurra rosata per la donna di panno usato').

10. Guild membership in Florence after 1293 carried concomitant political power, thereby excluding female crafts and tradespeople.

11. Niccolo was 50 years old, had a 40-year-old wife and nine children, age 2–15. Their house was in the Via dell' Amore (now Via S. Antonio).

12. The only business which outnumbered the second hand clothing shops in San Giovanni was that of shoemaker, with 116 *calzolai* filing their tax forms from this quarter in 1427.

13. See *ASF, Matricole del' Arte di Por Santa Maria dal 1225 al 1532*.

14. 'Florentie bella à 44 botteghe d'orefici e d'argientieri e gioiellieri drento alla città, e à 32 botteghe di fondachi che schavezzano e tagliano panni di grana e scharllatti e paonazi…'

15. *ASF, Catasto* (Florentine Tax Survey) of 1457.

16. Herlihy cites the *Arte dei rigattieri* statutes of 1296 which regulate the work of female vendors ('venditrices pannorum') but do not allow them matriculation and therefore full guild membership.

17. And obviously, females could not have fulfilled this function, being legal minors not able to speak on their own behalf.

18. He writes, '… ch'enpievano da l'un lato a l'altro, ch'erano molte ricche.'

19. From the guild statutes of the Rigattieri e Linaiuoli (*Rig. & Lin.* V, f 51) (Sartini, 1940–8). The critical text reads: 'et seducunt mulieres … ad dampnum virorum'.

20. Klapisch-Zuber, for example, has found evidence of a husband bringing suit against his second wife for her disruptive entrepreneurial activities as a peripatetic *weaver*! He calls her a thieving '*rigattiera*' (1992: 42).

21. See Greci on the exclusion of women from the guilds in Italy.

22. Biblioteca laurenziana, acquisiti e doni (Laurentian Library, Acquisitions and Gifts).

23. The Florentine communal statutes regulating consumption, especially of female dress, were amended some 80 times between 1281 and 1531.

2

Shifting Currency: The Culture and Economy of the Second Hand Trade in England, c. 1600–1850

Beverly Lemire

Spending shapes our fiscal and social lives; the timing of purchases and selection of goods are, in turn, mediated by age and social standing, income and social networks and, above all, the historical context in which these exchanges take place. The possessions used, reused and amassed in greater or lesser quantities represent objective worth as well as more qualitative values within their social milieu (Douglas & Isherwood, 1979; Douglas, 1996). I began my study of the second hand trade some years ago, in order to understand the consumer process better in all its complexities. Since that time I have been drawn back to this phenomenon, finding in it a medium through which to appraise great societal transformations, seen from the perspective of the everyday practices of common people, where the nuances of gender and social rank found clear expression (Lemire, 1988, 1990a, 1990b, 1997). The intricate material lives of our ancestors are a source of fascination and a means of illumination, for, as Fernand Braudel observed, 'at the very deepest levels of material life, there is at work a complex order, in which the assumptions, tendencies and unconscious pressures of economies, societies and civilizations all contribute' (Braudel, 1981: 333). In that regard, the apparently trivial exchange of worn garments for new china or the pawning of a petticoat for short-term credit take on much larger significance (Lemire, 1991: 76–7; Mayhew, 1861–2: vol. 2, 27).

The second hand trade will be considered first as a socially defined tool enabling consumption, but without seeing the purchase itself as the end game. The mechanics of a trade that fulfilled a number of complex intersecting needs for generations of plebeian and more affluent men and women will be summarized. Financial, monetary and economic histories have charted the formalization and standardization of mediums of exchange, of financial institutions, of economic growth, creating clear chronologies measuring the advance of regional or imperial economies, the appearance and regulation of coherent systems of sanctioned coinage, currency and other fiscal instruments. This is a record of progress, framed by hierarchical concepts of the movement from primitive to more advanced economies (Ashton, 1924; Earle, 1989a; Wrigley, 1988; Daunton, 1995). Does this narrative accord with the full reality within Western societies? The formalization of currencies and banking systems over the early modern period also paralleled unprecedented developments in trade and industry. But what of the complex, often messy, fertile expressions of economic life which persisted for generations on street corners and by kitchen doors? The longevity of these alternate economic practices requires a cogent re-examination, where the stuff of culture and social interaction are recognized for their organic links to the economic.

Clothing and bodily accoutrements will be a particular point of focus, as they possessed multiple characteristics including utility and status marking. At the same time, second hand apparel and accessories functioned as a type of alternate currency, circulating during a time when there was a scarcity of coinage, during the gradual formalization of fiscal media. Fashion was also a significant factor in the determination of value of these goods and its role demands consideration. A full re-examination of these facets will shed new light on the significance of the trade itself.

Everyday, Second Hand

In the long period of human history in the West before the full force of industrialization changed the world, the scarcity of goods ensured their careful husbanding. Use and reuse defined the everyday for all but a tiny minority of the population. However, by at least the late sixteenth century, dramatic and progressive changes in trade and manufacturing were stimulating regional economies, changing social relations, as scarcity slowly and very gradually began to give way before a rising abundance (Thirsk, 1978; de Vries, 1984; Roche, 2000). The second hand trade fits into this process as a stimulus to exchange, as an essential prop in the structure of plebeian commerce that grew in scale and significance over the course of this era. The majority of women and men transformed their hard-won income into material goods that fit their immediate needs and expressed their relative position within the family and community hierarchy; this 'form of self-fashioning' as Keith Wrightson terms it was, 'not simply self-directed, for the adoption of a particular pattern of material life also invariably imparts messages to a larger social audience' (2000: 299). Utility combined with social, religious and gender expressions whether through the wearing of a white linen handkerchief or petticoat-breeches in the seventeenth century, or the adoption of corduroy breeches or muslin aprons in the eighteenth century. All these goods were defined by virtue of their consumption, consumption itself being 'the sole end and purpose of all production', according to Adam Smith (1776, reprinted 1976, II: 660). But this assertion presents only part of the complex potential inherent in goods after purchase. The commodities accumulated by non-elite women and men represented many things including savings, investments, if you will, which retained values that could be realized. Furthermore, the value of these commodities was enhanced by the extensive second hand markets through which the liquidity of these items was assured. As authors in this volume show, consumption was a multifarious process and was rarely the final act in this social and economic interplay. This fact was also well known to contemporaries. Goods were bought to enjoy and use, but also as a bulwark against future needs or hazards. Adam Smith was also well aware of the mutability of used goods, as indicated in his rumination on a poor man in receipt of old clothes; these, Smith theorized, 'he exchanges for other old cloaths which suit him better, or for lodging, or for food, or for money, with which he can buy either food, cloaths or lodging, as he has occasion.' Smith goes on to observe, 'it is by treaty, by barter, and by purchase, that we obtain from one another the greater part of those mutual good offices which we stand in need of.' What Smith terms the 'trucking disposition' stood at the root of the second hand trade, where material goods retained many of the functional elements of money, as mediums of exchange and repositories of practical value (1776, 1: 27).

From its inception, the second hand trade depended on the existence of a modest surplus of goods in the general population beyond bare necessity, the capacity of laboring and middle ranked people to buy items filtered through other hands, some from other social ranks. Certainly calamity could bring waves of items on to the market if, for example, soaring food prices squeezed the last ounce of resources from communities under stress. But for the second hand trade to flourish, common people had to have more than single garments to cover their nakedness; there had to be at least the small occasions of surplus, as well as the desire for extra, the means to bring comfort and reflect some material complexities in their lives and on their persons. Over the early modern era, the purchases of common folk were the subject of contemporary comment in England, especially where social hier-archies were challenged, as pins, buckles, laces, ribbons and hosiery trickled then poured through retail channels and into work-roughened hands (Bald-win, 1926: 157–9; Thirsk, 1973: 53–64).[1] England was not alone among her European neighbors in having laboring and middling ranks who could afford these niceties; but in north-western Europe it was among the earliest to express these trends in such a dynamic form. This capacity to consume showed itself in the market for clothing in the late seventeenth century, a fact that Margaret Spufford has shown incontrovertibly. Spufford confirmed a widespread capacity to purchase new garments and that 'people below the level of gentry were relatively well-clad; indeed, almost all of them had some new clothes' (2000). This is a critical discovery, confirming the centuries-old observation by Gregory King that in his country clothing purchases repre-sented a quarter of total national expenditures in 1688 (Harte, 1991: 278). These garments combined with the cast-offs flowing between mistresses and servants, to swell the tide of second hand wares. Gradually, but inexorably, this growing plenty permitted the intermingling of articles from different social stations, of varied quality, across the ever more permeable barriers of rank.

By the mid-sixteenth century, London's second hand trade was long estab-lished and growing in size. The convergence of these dealers was noted by John Stow later that century, about that time when new buildings were set up harboring 'brokers, sellers of old apparel, and such like' outside the City walls along Houndsditch. Thieving Lane, Westminster, almost in the shadow of Whitehall, also hosted a vibrant second hand trade by the later years of Elizabeth's reign (Stow, 1987: 117; Korda, 1996: 191). Each decade saw the progressive expansion of a trade which defied the prescribed models of market exchange, frustrating and dismaying some theorists who wished for a simple, regulated, one-way system from producer to seller, then buyer. The second hand trade ensured a more malleable and complex commerce in used items, parallel to an elaborate pawning network which secured loans or credit through the pledging of goods (Sanderson, 1997; Lemire, 1998). In both instances, the hat, ring, shift, waistcoat or cloak slipped from its status as a thing to wear and display and was transformed into a type of alternate currency, linking the seller or borrower to the market arena. This traffic fueled day-to-day transactions.

In recent years there has been growing interest in currency substitutes, what some have called 'non-money', alternative currencies which facilitate exchanges in local regions or among broad memberships. These mechanisms are presently employed in various developed nations, sometimes as a means of protest against existing economic and political forms, to enhance alternative community values; other examples can be found in developing regions, or in nations rocked by financial crises, as a way to get by (DeMeulenaere, 2000; Liesch & Birch, 2000; Schraven, 2000). Operating 'parallel to the national currency to perform as a medium of exchange' these possess many of the characteristics of money – 'unit of account, medium of exchange and store of value' (Schraven, 2000) – without being authorized by governments. The formalization and perseverance of these currency substitutes into the twenty-first century suggests the significant utility of these forms. It also compels historians to rethink the practices common within the early modern economy, the habitual commutations which persisted across centuries. In turn, these examples point to the importance of species of goods that are both generally available, had a value commonly agreed-upon within a wide market and whose mutability ensured a ready translation into cash or other goods. There were a number of such categories of goods in early modern England. Margaret Hunt (1999) has uncovered a complex trade in seaman's tickets, which moved freely within the seafaring neighborhoods of London as an accepted pecuniary token among the shopkeepers, pedlars and denizens of the East End, one of several specific commodities spawned in this neighborhood, whose value was accepted and whose exchange was assured within those precincts. In some respects, these circulated like bills of exchange whose ultimate worth was guaranteed by government payment. In similar dockside neighborhoods, Peter Linebaugh identified the circulation of chips, pieces of wood less than three feet in length, as one of the important traditional perquisites for shipyard workers. A 1767 letter describes the scene in which 'upwards of two thousand, mostly Women' assembled on Wednesdays and Saturdays, 'to take from thence the small Chips and Gleanings of the Yard'. Perquisites, like chips, were compensations provided in addition to monetary wages, a practice that continued until the enforcement of exclusively money payments in shipyards at the end of the eighteenth century. During the long reign of chips, shipwrights and carpenters were assured an income while they waited months for the eventual payment of their earnings, using the chips to settle debts or purchase goods in the interim, their value accepted by local residents and the chips themselves framing the windows, doors, stairways, shutters and cupboards in surrounding streets (Linebaugh, 1991: 378–9). Both these mediums of exchange were commonplace in their particular neighborhoods, with the value of the items and the ease of their circulation assured by the familiarity of local residents with these objects, ensuring their ready acceptance as specie. But the use of these goods in a wider community was problematic since knowledge of their value could not always be assumed or their acceptance guaranteed. Precious metals and jewels were uniquely placed as mediums of exchange, but were the purview of the elites. With those exceptions, at this time, the other most transmutable goods were clothing and textiles. They were the most important of the alternative currencies, the most ubiquitous, the most readily transformed into cash or credit, goods whose valuation was assured, a fact known to thieves, common folk and honest dealers. Clothing was transposed into cash at the shopkeeper's counter, at the tavern rail, at the kitchen door, or could also secure short term credit from official and unofficial pawnbrokers – functions essential for a significant portion of the population from at least the sixteenth through the nineteenth century (Hows, 1847; Hardaker, 1892; Tebbutt, 1983: 1–36; Lemire, 1997: 75–118).

What accounts for the unique position of apparel and fabrics among what I call alternative currencies? First, the investment made, whether in a shirt, head cloth or breeches could be readily evaluated. A basic knowledge of textiles and their qualities was commonplace within the wider public, especially among women who took care of these items in the home; more detailed insights were equally apparent among specialist traders. A vibrant cloth culture ensured the ready circulation of clothing in formal and informal second hand markets, through regional, national and international chains of exchange. With little effort, Philip Henslowe, the Elizabethan theatrical entrepreneur and pawnbroker, turned 'a payer of blacke sylke stockenes' into ten shilling for 'goody streates', lending six shillings to the owner of 'A dublet & A payer of breches for a chylld'. Henslowe's accounts capture the dynamism of the second hand market in Elizabethan London where, as elsewhere in Europe, hats and boots, stockings and coats fueled local economies and individual budgets. Ann Rosalind Jones and Peter Stallybrass describe Henslowe's late sixteenth-century venture 'a banking system in clothes', with Henslowe relying on teams of women to organize this trade (Jones & Stallybrass, 2000: 31; Korda, 1996: 191–3; Earle, 1989b; Wiesner, 1993: 92–106). This style of enterprise was replicated by thousands of similar pawnbrokers and by many more dealers in clothes, salesmen and saleswomen, all of whom relied on the habitual acceptance of used garments as payments by generations of pedlars and shopkeepers. The liquidity of these goods was attested to by Mary Browne, indicted in London in 1700 as a receiver of stolen goods. Her extensive testimony paints a vivid picture of the easy movement of clothing through many hands, through channels not easily stopped by authorities.

> Mary Browne further sayth that about three dayes before Christmas last she received from Samuel Barber and Luke Matthews Stollen Goods; vizt a white Antherine Gowne a flowered Satten mantle lined with white persian three scarfes

a hood one paire of sheets and one sheet unmade up ... this informant heard Elizabeth Browne and Elizabeth Hatfield stole from Mr Aston in Leadenhall Street 15 or 16 dozen flowered Muslin Neckcloths which was sold ... to Katherine Hurste... This Informant Bought of Edward ffloyd and toothless Tom a parcell of wet linen which was stollen from Joseph Wade in Shorts Gardens about the middle of last summer; Edward Holland and little Ned stole a Damask Gowne and petticoat a silk Gowne two white striped petticoats two lineings for a Gowne and some Childbed linen from a person unknown which Goods this Informant sold to Jane Davis she knowing the same to be stolen... (MJ/SP/MSP1701 AP/45/108, London Metropolitan Archives)

London, like other great cities of Europe, was especially rich in used garments of every quality – little wonder that this trade attracted the greatest comment from contemporaries. In the sixteenth and seventeenth centuries, country towns like Leicester also had their 'Brogers or pledge women' buying and selling clothing and housewares house to house, as did Shrewsbury, Chester, Oxford and countless other cities and towns (Lemire, 1997: 99–104, 110–12). This was the easiest trade for poor women to gain a foothold, where the needs of neighbors and the ease of resale was guaranteed, where training in household textiles and clothing enabled a ready entry to both legitimate and illicit commerce. The female networks of legal and illegal trade reflect as well the responsibilities assumed by plebeian women to organize and secure credit for their household ventures, whether these were domestic or commercial in orientation. For several centuries, the vast majority of pawns brought to pawnbrokers were garments or domestic textiles, directed by women to meet individual and household needs, as part of the alternative currency system.

An early example of this trade is illustrated in the small remaining section of a pawnbroker's ledger, kept by a pawnbroker in Pistoia, Tuscany, in 1417 (Fig. 1). I include this example, though from a region remote from England, to underline the ubiquity of this practice and the general importance of apparel in second hand trade. Eighty loans were granted in the five-day period for which records survive, small loans guaranteed with humble pledges, most characterized as of poor quality and little value. The garments that could be spared in the spring of that year were the principal pledged goods (de Roover, 1948: 113–21). Investment in apparel became the sum and substance of plebeian budgeting, the source of liquidity for affluent and plebeian patrons of second hand dealers and pawnbrokers throughout Europe; England was no different in this respect.[2]

The statistics gleaned from surviving English pawnbrokers' ledgers over several centuries illustrate their role in this essential commerce. Figures 2

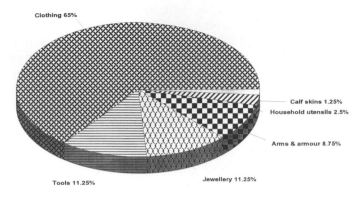

Source: de Roover, Table 6, p. 121.

Figure 1. Categories of Goods Pawned, Pistoia, Tuscany, 1417.

to 6 summarize the trade goods circulating through five English businesses, between the late sixteenth to the mid-nineteenth centuries. The pattern of Philip Henslowe's South London trade matched that of a less famous successor, John Pope, a haberdasher, pawnbroker and money-lender also based in South London, but later in the seventeenth century – for both men, sixty to 70 percent of their pledged goods were comprised of wearing apparel. Similarly, where probate inventories survive for ordinary pawnbrokers from the late seventeenth and early eighteenth centuries, these too confirm the primary importance of apparel as pledges.[3] A shop front illustrated on one of the several surviving trade cards produced by the late eighteenth-century

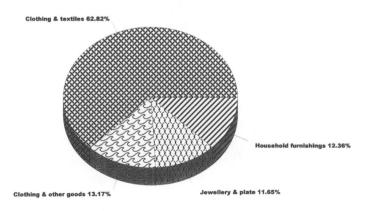

Source: Jones & Stallybrass, 30.

Figure 2 Categories of Goods Pawned, London, 1593–6.

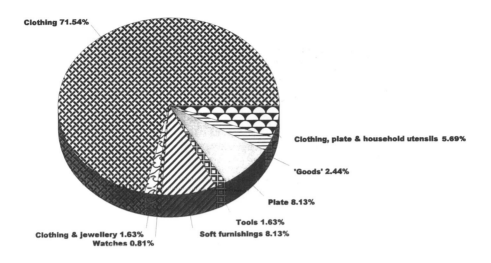

Source: C108/34, Public Record Office, London.
Note: Number of transactions: 123.

Figure 3. Categories of Goods Pawned, South London, 1667–71.

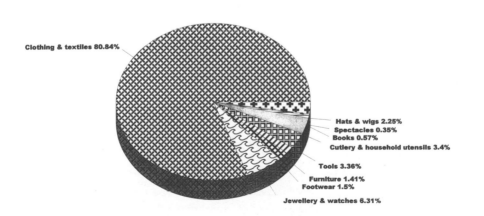

Source: Acc 38, York City Archives.
Note: Sample size: 2208 transactions.

Figure 4. Categories of Goods Pawned, York, 1777–8.

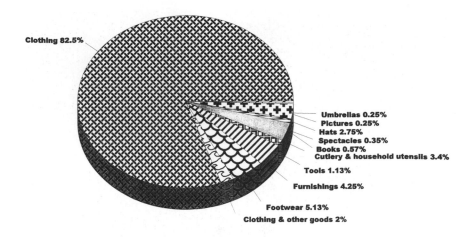

Source: J 90/504, Public Record Office, London.
Note: Sample size: 800 transactions.

Figure 5. Categories of Goods Pawned, Sheffield, 1816.

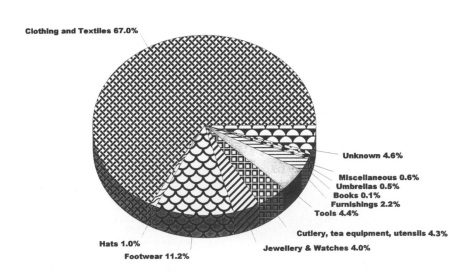

Source: C110/134, Public Record Office, London.

Figure 6. Categories of Goods Pawned, East London, 1832–3.

Figure 7. John Flude's trade card illustrates the central importance of clothing and accoutrements among pawned goods.
Bodleian Library, John Johnson Collection, Trades and Professions, Box 6.

pawnbroker John Flude, suggests the importance of apparel and accoutrements in his line of work – garments for men and women hang in his windows and dozens of shoe buckles are displayed in a street-side showcase (Fig. 7). Few pawnbrokers could boast a countrywide trade such as his, yet most regions were well served by these invaluable traders. One hundred years following the records created by John Pope, a business ledger from York illuminates the vibrant trade in an even wider array of goods owned by plebeian women and men in this northern cathedral city (Fig 4). The goods brought to Fettes' shop included basic apparel and some fashionable ware, plus assorted niceties like the pair of Bristol stone buttons, woman's new shoes and several pairs of silver buckles. George Fettes' York trade is followed by similar evidence in a sample from Sheffield, in 1816, reflecting the continuing vibrant exchange of goods for cash, with over 80 percent of pledges assured with plebeian clothing. The 1830s sample taken from a London-based pawnbroker shows a slightly lower rate of apparel pawned; but for the women and men of East London's Lime Street, Leadenhall Street, Hackney Road and Whitechapel, the garments and personal items in their possession continued to represent their easiest route to cash or credit (Figs. 5 & 6).

Each of these examples comes from a specific community with distinct social structures, with sometimes quite distinct political and economic conditions. Another of the obvious variations in the substance of these figures can be found in the size of the sample or number of transactions summarized for each period. The first three samples summarize smaller numbers of exchanges where the ratios of apparel to other goods are, nevertheless, very clear. In the last three tables the volume of trade and the surviving records are substantially larger; moreover, the underlying documentation is situated at the onset of industrialization where the dynamism of the age shows itself in the wider array of consumer items commonly owned. Yet here, too, there is clear and continuing indication of the use of clothing as a savings mechanism, with value easily realized through pawning and the used clothes market. Melanie Tebbutt captured the attitude still prevalent among nineteenth-century working-class men and women when she observed that they never looked on objects for their aesthetic or use value alone. They showed instead

a qualitatively different view of material resources, which they regarded as a tangible asset to be drawn on in periods of financial difficulty. When buying sales goods the poor habitually asked what they would fetch if offered in pawn, and frequently confessed they were influenced in their choice by the articles' potential pledge value... This belief in tangible assets was an important feature of working-class domestic finance, and frequently overwhelmed other considerations (Tebbutt, 1983: 16).

Were these budgetary tactics exclusively found only amongst the working poor? The historical record suggests otherwise. For generations, rich and poor alike availed themselves of the services of pawnbrokers and clothes dealers – Philip Henslowe lent relatively large sums on pledges of quite sumptuous garments. For example, Mrs Rysse pledged her damask gown 'layd with a lace of sylke and gowld' for £5 and Lord Burte received a similar amount for his cloak (Korda, 1996: 189). These gentlefolk employed their clothing for fiscal ends quite handily. But over several centuries, the wealthy and even the middle classes gradually devised more formal financial mechanisms through which to obtain loans and, at the same time, the traffic with pawnbrokers gradually assumed a more discreditable taint. From the late eighteenth century onwards, affluent property-holders could easily negotiate loans with the many banks springing up throughout England; while respectable artisans or small shopkeepers could turn to loan societies, organizations which proliferated after 1800 and charged lower interest rates than most pawnbrokers. Thus, pawning became less the norm for the genteel and respectable folk and was seen as the resort of the desperate, the indigent or the profligate. Nonetheless, for at least three centuries, clothing as currency circulated in neighborhood pawnshops and in the barrows, baskets and shop shelves of ordinary retailers and specialist second hand dealers, flowing into the vast confluence of used goods.

For the working poor, pledged items ensured income for the short-term, with interest charged for the privilege.[4] But articles were not always reclaimed, or were sold off in bulk at the end of a life of business, part of a voluminous commerce. The overwhelming prominence of apparel as the primary article of exchange is worthy of comment, even as new consumer wares came more readily to the hands of ordinary men and women, from spectacles to furnishings, umbrellas to saltcellars. The continuing and unique prominence of clothing in the second hand market is only partially explained by the growing volume of dress wares and the inherent mutability of these goods. Fashion also played a role, a role in the value assigned goods and in the animation of the second hand market.

Fashion, Value and the Consumer Market

Money functions as a medium of exchange and a store of value (Hogendorn, 1999: 56; Neale, 1976: 7). As the history I describe makes clear, apparel was uniquely placed to circulate widely as an exchange commodity, storing and releasing value as required. Much of the value in garments was founded on the quality of the fabrics used in their construction, the weight, weave, finish and substance of the cloth, plus the presence or absence of braid, lace, buttons or accessories. A related but less tangible aspect were the elements of style – cut, color, pattern, form and texture – which added cachet to commodities sold in certain markets, with certain buyers, within a finite time frame. From the time of its genesis, fashion's force in the market was a real phenomenon, working to liven the market. The power and scope of fashion grew in force over the early modern period, even as its expression varied from region to region, group to group. Gilles Lipovetsky contends that fashion itself is 'an exceptional process inseparable from the origin and development of the modern West ... [when] the renewal of forms became a social value'. Lipovetsky goes on to note that, 'With the birth of fashion, inconstancy in matters of form and ornamentation was no longer the exception but the lasting rule' (1994: 15). Inconstancy in the marketplace generated a premium for goods perceived to possess a stylish essence; whatever the quality of the items themselves, they represented traits that attracted or repelled, defining and refining the fashion circles in which these goods moved. Mary Douglas reminds students of fashion and the consumer process to be as sensitive to expressions of dislike as to paeans of approbation. She notes that 'hated garments ... [also] signal cultural affiliation' (1996: 82). In the historical context, there is as much evidence of dislike for certain styles as there is enthusiasm; each manifests the boundaries of groups distinguished by age, sex, social rank or affiliation, religious persuasion or political allegiance, suggesting the complexity within the marketplace. Fashion helped assign value and this facet of fashion reveals the difficulties inherent in alternative currencies of this sort. Only through the flexibility and scale of the second hand market could sellers secure something like full worth for their goods. This perspective refutes the exclusively top-down view, which subscribes to the trickle-down theory of fashion; it compels us to think again of the elements of style created by different age groups, religious communities, social networks and the generation of competing fashions (Lemire, 2000: 391–417).

The shifting currency of fashion is noteworthy for several reasons. First and foremost, elements of style interacted with the inherent value of the garment to determine its relative worth. That clothing circulated as a ubiquitous alternative currency is not in dispute; but the store that could be released was determined by several factors – the functional attributes of the item was certainly one of these factors. Equally significant was its attractiveness to some segment of the consumer market. This last ingredient distinguished second hand clothing from more objective mediums of exchange, since the capacity to recoup a full measure of worth for a given commodity depended on matching garments with consumers most likely to respond to the ephemeral characteristics of style. The second hand market worked to bring salable goods before consumers most likely to respond to the qualities of the goods in question. The movement of wigs from one market to another was a case in point. By the early decades of the nineteenth century the wearing of wigs in England was associated solely with elderly men for whom respectability was defined by these distinct hairpieces. Wigs pawned and sold, accumulated from years gone by, risked losing all value if brought by dealers to English markets, where no young man would be caught dead in an out-of-date rig with a geriatric character. In the case of wigs, these were collected and shipped to Ireland, where a ready demand continued to be found most likely in rural parts of the country. Similarly, in the late eighteenth century, corduroy breeches had usurped buckskin among all ranks of men in England, except grooms and gentlemen who hunted; left-off buckskin breeches were shipped overseas, to Ireland and other markets where corduroy was not yet in vogue. Fashion favored certain goods and shunned others. The skill among dealers lay in finding the right market and customers through which to release the latent value in their wares. So wigs and leather breeches were shipped out to distant markets, while later in the century thrifty shoppers in London hunted for frock coats in second hand shops and market stalls, the frock coat being, as Christopher Breward notes, 'a stable benchmark of decency through the 1880s' (1999: 36). In the mid-nineteenth century, frock coats were very much in demand by 'working people ... often working people's wives or mothers... They're capital judges as to what'll fit their men' (Mayhew, 1861–2: 27–8, 41). Elsewhere, overseas markets on the Atlantic received shipments of clothing which suited the particular priorities of that community, whether fishing port, slave plantation or regional center. In this tradition, sales of imported second hand clothing were announced in a local newspaper in Saint John, New Brunswick, in British North America, part of the supplies of clothing to arrive regularly from Britain in this region (*New Brunswick Courier*, 1832, 1834; Lemire, 1988: 5, n. 7).

Style mattered. It was a key if shifting element, a fact of which all clothes dealers were well aware and none more so than those in the second hand trade. Monmouth Street was favored by Charles Dickens for one of his detailed sketches, mixing speculation and observation, as he mused on the passage of garments through this curb-side emporium: 'great-coats with wooden buttons have usurped the place of the ponderous laced coats with full skirts; embroidered waistcoats with large flaps have yielded to double-breasted checks with roll collars; and three-cornered hats of quaint appearance have given place to the low crowns and broad brims of the coachman school'. Perhaps the waxing and waning of styles inspired Dickens to conclude that Monmouth Street was 'the burial place of ... fashions' (Dickens 1836: 35). It could equally be claimed that the second hand shops

Figure 8. The Pithay, in Bristol, was one of the many sites of transfiguration, where the utility and style of second hand garments found new expressions and new markets.
Courtesy of Bristol City Museum & Art Gallery.

in Monmouth Street, or Bristol's Pithay, were sites of transfiguration where utility and style found new expressions and new markets, where value was released as clothes were recycled through a recognized medium, well known and long employed (Fig. 8).

Conclusion

Material culture intersects with social and economic patterns altering with time and place. By the nineteenth century, the use of alternative currencies was in flux, less frequently called upon within the middle classes and gradually less readily understood. In 1593, without a qualm William Lord Vaux pawned his parliamentary robes to facilitate an immediate loan; no stigma was attached to these seemingly radical measures. In the 1630s, the young clergyman, Ralph Josselin, sold most of his clothes to finance a journey to Bedfordshire, where he hoped to find work. In the mid 1700s, Sarah Nowler supported herself as a pawnbroker in London's dockside district of Rotherhithe dealing in 'Men's and Women's Wearing Apparel of all Sorts'. James Boswell commonly relied on the second hand trade to balance his budget. Writing in the winter of 1762, he recounted, 'This day I cast my eye on my old laced hat, which I saw would raise me a small supply [of money]. No sooner thought than done ¼ I carried it to a jeweler's in Piccadilly and sold it for 6s. 6d., which was a great cause of joy to me' (Jones & Stallybrass, 2000: 29; MacFarlane, 1970: 17; Lemire, 1997: 108; Boswell, 1950: 109). The extensive resale, barter and pawning networks over this period cannot be equated with contemporary second hand exchanges in developed countries, where monetized systems are so highly developed and credit facilities so extensive. In the early modern era, these practices flourished in the absence of other alternatives, at a time when, as Joan Thirsk first identified, there was a heightened consumer activity even in the lower social ranks (Thirsk, 1978; Spufford, 1984). Equally, there was a pent-up need for mediums of exchange to enable the individual and market to interact. The extensive and generalized knowledge about cloth and clothing, combined with the increasing credit assigned fashionable wares of all sorts, permitted the growth of this phenomenon and ensured the ubiquity of this model until such times as other alternatives presented themselves.

Over the nineteenth century, within wealthy homes, the trade in discarded goods continued from the kitchen door, with some items described in hand bills, by those soliciting trade, in explicit terms as monetary equivalents. Among the growing middle class, the receipt of wages, salaries, and interest on investments meant that an outlay on material goods as a prophylactic against future want was altogether unnecessary. The middle class, now describing and defining mainstream culture, came to regard the ancient alternative currencies in a very jaundiced light. In spite of the antiquity of the second hand trade, transformations in commerce and industry offered more secure sources of credit and more precise financial tools. Yes, a smaller, high-end pawning trade continued to meet the needs of the genteel woman or professional man facing temporary or terminal financial embarrassment. But these exchanges were exceptional, respectable and discreet in sharp contrast to the still vast working-class commerce in used wares. The working class alone continued its reliance on the twofold functions of material goods: use value and potential in exchange. Those practices seemed increasingly bizarre to respectable observers. Dickens wondered at the behavior of men and women working in seasonal trades, like fishwomen and costermongers who invested in 'great squab brooches as convenient pledges, and the latter massive silver rings' (Tebbutt, 1983: 17). There was clearly planning in their purchases of such ostentatious items, planning which took into account the optimum trends within their communities. Like other working men and women, these hawkers appreciated the risks with which they lived and the value of a piece of clothing or flashy jewelery that would draw appreciative glances from their neighbors, and produce the required sum if pledged or sold. The ebb and flow of goods was a feature of life among the poor that arose not from improvidence, but as a defense against penury. Paul Johnson described such purchases within the nineteenth-century working class as 'a substitute savings bank for low-income households', recognizing the ambiguity of the consumption process itself, which afforded use, defined social and cultural properties, and secured future disbursements as need required (Johnson, 1983: 157; Benson, 1996). This pattern of consumerism was antithetical to a middle class which sought to create a permanent material world in their homes and in their dress, saving and spending in more structured, monetized forms. Nevertheless, the working poor continued along a different path which only gradually intersected and melded with fully monetized routes of exchange.

William Reddy described the disparate meanings to rich and poor of similar transactions, differences that arose simply because of the relative value of each contract in the lives of the participants. In the context of this study, we might use the example of a merchant, for whom the purchase of a coat would be a relatively minor matter, while for the clerk or the coal heaver it was a matter of great import. Reddy termed this 'asymmetry' and identified the consequences of this asymmetry in the relative forms and meanings given to transactions.

> This asymmetry in the stake each party had in given transactions, based as it was on a contrast in the use value of given commodities to each party, worked to give shape to a large proportion of European society by the early modern period. The poor's use of commodities was more varied and multidimensional than the rich's; it was comparatively difficult for the poor to reduce in any satisfying way this varied use to a single, quantitative monetary expression (1987: 66).

Such asymmetrical structures in transactions continued into the modern period, with each transaction, each purchase, each decision to consume for the laborer imbued with complexities unmatched in their urgency by those within the wealthier classes.

The discrepancy between middle-class and working-class practice was not simply mirrored in the different world of goods, but also in the different world of meanings assigned the artifacts of daily life. Thus, the fishwoman's brooch and the costermonger's ring served as more than decorative emblems – they were also investment and insurance, badges of style and social affiliation, an alternative currency fit for their neighborhood. Victorian commentators often shook their heads when they witnessed unaccountable purchases among the working poor: a coat with silver buttons, a fine bonnet or a silver watch. These may well have seemed like signs of profligacy to observers steeped in the dogma of thrift. But these acts may have also represented rational investments among a constituency engaged in a different type of economic practice. As we look back across the complexities of modernization, as we consider the steps in this process taken by generations, let us think again of the efficient and inventive mediums employed to give life to economic desires and to ensure survival; let us think again about the full meanings of the 'tufted Holland mantle', the 'breeches and knives', 'gauze shawl' and 'silver watch and chain' that traveled from hand to hand through generations of second hand trade.

Notes

1. Sumptuary legislation in sixteenth-century England speaks to plebeian demand and reflects the greater array of items owned and worn by men and women below the gentry in spite of prohibitions. For example, legislation from 1533 barred 'servants, yeomen and all persons with incomes of less than 40s. a year' from wearing hose from fabric costing more than two shillings per yard, barred silk ribbons outright from this group, as well as 'shirts, coiffes, bonnets, hats … embroidered or trimmed with silk, gold or silver'. The recurrence of similar legal bars confirms the ineffectiveness of these measures.

2. For other examples see Carole Frick, in this volume and Maria Bogucka (1998); Montserrat Carbonell (1998); Hilde van Wijngaarden (1998). Also, Patricia Allerston (1999); Elizabeth Sanderson (1996); Laurence Fontaine (2002), pp. 24–5.

3. For example, Court of Orphans Inventory, 885, Daniel Garnett, October 1673, CLRO; Court of Orphans Inventory, 1049, Ann Deacon, July 1674, CLRO; PROB 5/1804, George Thayne, January 1702, Public Record Office, London (hereafter PRO); and PROB 3/29/213, Probate Inventory of William Mackvity, July 1730, PRO.

4. The rates of interest charged by pawnbrokers preoccupied legislators over the centuries. Between 1800 and 1872, pawnbrokers were restricted to an official rate of 20 per cent interest per annum; however, Melanie Tebbutt clearly shows that interest rates for small repeated loans on pledges were essentially unlimited, since 'the smaller the loan the higher the interest, the heaviest rate falling on the very people who were the least able to bear it' (1983: 8–9). Nevertheless, for countless generations, pawning was the quintessential method of securing loans.

3

Cast-Offs: Civilization, Charity or Commerce? Aspects of Second Hand Clothing Use in Australia, 1788–1900

Margot Riley

The trade in second hand clothing in Australia has a history as long as white settlement itself. Traditionally, practitioners of second hand dressing are the poor and the dispossessed. Such people leave few official records and are rarely visually documented. Circumstances peculiar to the colonization of Australia, however, produced a range of written accounts and imagery that allow the sketching of an outline in this area of research. This chapter presents an overview centered mainly on Australia's oldest state, New South Wales, as a mirror of second hand clothing use around the country. Shaped by the records encountered, it focuses on select figures and events to begin tracing local participation in the practice of second hand dressing in colonial Australia.

Two hundred years ago Australia seemed as distant from the rest of the 'civilized' world as the moon. The myth of a Great South Land had long captured the imagination of adventurers and travellers alike. Australia was one of the last great land discoveries and early argonauts stretched the boundaries of the known world in the race to chart its seas, facing risks equal to those of the modern astronaut. In 1770 Captain James Cook traversed the Pacific Ocean and, on finding the east coast of the continent, named it New South Wales (NSW), claiming possession for England. Soon after, with the combined threat of French imperialism and the American Revolution of 1776, the British resolved to set up a strategic outpost in the Pacific. Enclosure and mechanization had led the unemployed to the cities, where economic and social pressures resulted in a crime wave through the winter of 1784–5. Prison populations swelled and, with exportation of felons to America no longer an option, Viscount Sydney proposed settling NSW with convicts. Once the Transportation Act was passed in 1786, the British Government began planning their mission of colonization.

First Fleet

'I think I hear you saying, "Where the Deuce is Sydney Cove, Port Jackson?"', wrote George Worgan, surgeon on the convict transport *Sirius*, in 1788. The First Fleet had sailed from Portsmouth harbour, England, on May 13, 1787: 'the Cape of Good Hope was the last country touched at ... where every article necessary for forming a civilised colony was provisioned and, thus equipped, each like another Noah's Ark, eleven ships steered away for Botany Bay [Sydney]' (Worgan, 1788: 1). Governor Arthur Phillip relocated the settlement to Port Jackson and the fleet arrived at Sydney Cove on January 26, 1788. Of the 1464 people who had undertaken the nine-month journey, more than half did so against their will. There were 736 convicts (564 males and 192 females) in addition to their jailers and the fleet seamen. The convicts came from all over England but most were Londoners; all had been convicted for crimes against property, the majority for minor theft. Their crimes were mostly forced by necessity but the theft of trifles for resale or barter for food and drink resulted in seven years transportation. During the period of convict transportation to the eastern colonies of Australia (1788–1840) 160,000 convicts were sent to NSW, Van Diemens Land (Tasmania), Victoria and Queensland. Of these, at least 6 percent were transported for theft of wearing apparel, a potent reminder of the value of clothes as a commodity and how ill-clothed the English poor were before cheap, mass-produced clothing became widely available (Hughes, 1988: 163).

The First Fleet brought remnants of the British rag trade amongst its passengers and in their baggage. The oldest convict, Dorothy Handler, gave her profession as an 'old clothes woman', as did Fanny Anderson. Elizabeth Hayward, aged 13, was transported for stealing a linen gown, a cloak and a silk bonnet from the man to whom she was apprenticed; the gown was later found in a pawnshop. The youngest boy, 9-year-old orphaned chimney sweep John Hudson, had been caught at a pawnshop with stolen clothing (Gillen, 1989: s.v.).

The prisoners were not issued with clothing prior to departure but were allowed to bring their belongings. Problems soon arose with the new 'slop' clothing requisitioned for convict use. The surgeon on the female transport *Lady Penryn* recorded that, 'a great part of the women's clothing was not come up from London when we sailed ... (and) was made of very slight materials, much too small and in general came to pieces'. As a result, throughout the voyage, the women were 'perpetually thieving the Cloaths from each other, nay almost from their backs' and 'plundering the Sailors ... of their necessary cloaths and cutting them up for some purpose of their own' (Bowes-Smyth, 10 Dec. 1787).

Disembarked at Sydney Cove, their landing wardrobes supplemented by an issue of slops, the convict women and children were observed to be 'dress'd in general very clean and some few among them might be said to be well dress'd' (Bowes-Smyth, 5 Feb. 1788). The efforts of the women to look their best was no doubt a survival instinct. Attracting the attention of the better class of protector could go a long way to determining one's future in the colony.

Convicts and Settlers

Surrounded by sea and unexplored territory, the early penal settlements operated as 'prisons without walls' and, arriving in a country without an existing manufacturing base, early Australians were not self-sufficient in clothing. Beyond what the first colonists brought with them, they were entirely dependent on government provisioning until the Second Fleet arrived, later supplemented by what could be imported or produced locally. The sale of convict issue slops was prohibited from 1801 but free settlers eagerly purchased them when alternative clothing was in short supply (Maynard, 1994: 32), and eventually everybody, including convicts, the free working class and indigenous people, was wearing very similar types of coarse, loose-fitting, ready-made 'slop' clothing. Whether these garments were new, second or third hand was probably more a matter of chance than anything else. As convict slops became standard working-class wear, the inability to distinguish between the clothing worn by convicts and free settlers diminished the traditional role of dress as a signifier of class and blurred social demarcation, lending a false air of egalitarianism to Australian dress that was later much characterized as being of broader significance to colonial society.

In Europe, people had access to networks of new clothes making facilities, 'slop' shops selling ready-made garments, second hand clothes brokers, pawnshops, and cast-off or stolen clothing via peddlers and rag fairs. In Australia, initially at least, settlers had to dress themselves without familiar patterns of clothing consumption. At the outset, trade in new and second hand clothing operated by auction, barter or theft. Later, convicts with the means to clothe themselves, and the families of civil personnel and free landowners who formed the small fashionable elite in colonial society were all subject to the vagaries of shipping. But, within a single generation, each colony had constructed a fully organized capitalist society, in which the shortfall between new and worn-out clothing could be filled by exchange or purchase of second hand goods from tailors, dealers, pawnshops, markets and hawkers.

Convicted of theft and transported to Sydney Cove in 1796, Sarah Bird is thought to have authored a letter that provides evidence of the entrepreneurial instincts of colonists:

> I did a little trade in the passage here in a number of small articles such as sugar, tea, tobacco, thread, snuff, needles and everything that I could get anything by ... I have sold my petticoats at two guineas each and my long black coat at ten guineas which shews that black silk sells well here; the edging that I gave 1s.8d. per yard in England I got 5s. for here. I have sold the worst of my clothes, as wearing apparel brings a good price (*True Briton*, 10 Nov. 1798 quoted in Clarke & Spender, 1992: 144–5).

Despite her denial of a protector, Sarah seems to have had unusual financial resources and freedom to buy goods on the voyage as well as the business acumen to put these to good use on landing. Assigned to labor for an employer, she continued to work the system to her advantage and within six months reported that she'd bought a house and was running her own business (Clarke & Spender, 1992: 144–5).

Paucity of local supply and irregularities in shipping made clothing a valuable commodity for barter and, as NSW had no currency of its own until 1813, cloth and clothes were often used in exchange. Convicts frequently swapped their clothing for liquor and sex, or gambled them away. The 1822 Bigge Report, inquiring into the management of the colony, recommended that convicts be issued with clothing only when needed as garments were being sold and the money used to buy spirits (Maynard, 1994: 23). The demand for clothing of all kinds can be gauged by the variety of garments listed in theft notices lodged after 1803 in the *Sydney Gazette*, Australia's first daily newspaper. The colonial appetite for fashionable dress was described by many early visitors and prompted one editorial to attribute the downfall of young women from poor families lured into service for the growing class of 'kept women', to the prospect of cast-off 'silk shoes and left-off suits' (*Sydney Gazette*, 20 May 1820: 4).

From its earliest days, the hub of colonial society was the marketplace. When the Second Fleet of convicts finally arrived in 1789, the ragged settlers gathered on the docks to bargain for surplus supplies. By 1792 they had the right to sell excess farm produce at a weekly market. Trading in the markets would become a means to prosperity for many emancipists (ex-convicts) and, in due course, for other disadvantaged groups, especially women and recently arrived migrants. Goods brought by merchant ships were auctioned on landing or at the importer's premises but unsold cargo and second hand goods found their way to the marketplace, making the Sydney Market a cross between Britain's rural markets and the flea markets of London.

In 1810 Governor Macquarie (1810–22) moved the market, by now a daily event, to the George Street site where it remained until the 1890s. Saturdays were given over to a fringe market, open until 10 p.m. and offering novelties, clothing and second hand goods for sale or exchange. Regulation of the markets by Governor Bourke (1831–37) caused some traders to set up a 'Paddy's' Market opposite the hay and cattle market in Campbell Street, in the area still known as Haymarket. After 1844, the George Street Market was open late on Wednesdays as well as Saturdays and for the rest of the century the markets remained the focal point of a night on the town (Christie, 1988: 22–51, 60).

Aborigines

I think we are in a fine stat, we bought nothing but thefs out with us to find nothing but thefs...

Ralph Clarke, *Journal*, 19 Feb. 1788

Through centuries of European trade and exploration in the Indian Ocean, South Asia and the Pacific, 'gifting' played a vital role in establishing good relations with indigenous peoples. Settling into Sydney Cove, both British and Aboriginal people would have expected 'gifting' on first contact and as a gesture of friendship. Aboriginal societies were linked by complex exchange systems extending over thousands of kilometers to access rare or locally unavailable raw materials. Governor Phillip's bartering intentions were clear from the trading goods requisitioned for the First Fleet; their importance ensured that 'articles of traffick' were divided amongst the ships, along with the tools, stores and seeds necessary for the colony's survival, so none would arrive without the gifts necessary for diplomatic encounters.

Exchange was further encouraged by the eagerness of the fleet's gentlemen officers to acquire natural history specimens and aboriginal artifacts, either for their own interest in 'artificial curiosities' or resale on the English collectibles market. Comments about what 'pleased' or was 'demanded' by Aborigines document the goods they 'valued' in return. These included hatchets, knives, fishing hooks and lines, some European clothing and food. Hats and bread, in particular, seemed 'exotic' to Aborigines and may have possessed a rarity value comparable to the 'artificial curiosities' sought by Europeans (McBryde, 1989: 169–82). However, after the preliminary niceties of exchange were observed, both sides resorted to thieving, as relations between the two communities quickly soured.

Introduction of disease and alcohol as well as lifestyle and dietary changes caused the health of Aboriginal people to deteriorate rapidly and, as the colonial frontier extended, Aboriginal social patterns altered irrevocably. With coinage short, alcohol, particularly rum, became the colony's currency and, as dispossession made its impact on indigenous subsistence regimes, food was also used as payment. By 1793: 'It was no uncommon circumstance to see [Aborigines] coming into town with bundles of firewood which they had been hired to procure or bringing water from the tanks; for which services they thought themselves well rewarded with any worn-out jackets or trousers, or blankets or a piece of bread' (Collins, 1798: vol.1, 297).

Traditionally, Aboriginal people wore little clothing apart from opossum and kangaroo skin cloaks, ornamental and carrying belts, headbands and fringes, employing skin decorations including body piercings, scarification and colouring as important symbols of initiation and tribal identification. Of all the textile and clothing items introduced through European contact, blankets found greatest favor with Aborigines because they resembled traditional cloaks, becoming even more desirable as European settlement caused a scarcity of indigenous animals and the decline of cloak manufacture. By the term of Governor Macquarie, initiatives to resettle and educate Aborigines had begun and, for Europeans, a starting point in civilizing indigenous Australians meant clothing their nakedness. Perpetuation of traditional bartering practices encouraged Aborigines to dress in cast-offs which hastened their descent from 'noble savage' to 'social pariah' and, from the 1820s, the sight of nude Aborigines in settled areas was thought to reflect badly on the respectability of colonial towns (Maynard, 1994: 64).

Those Aborigines who accepted European clothing usually wore only a shirt or a jacket. Aboriginal men seemed to dislike trousers, perhaps because these impeded movement and tribal attire included no leg covering. Aboriginal women also often preferred a man's shirt to European women's wear. For Europeans, coming from a culture in which leg display had serious moral and sexual implications, it was the uncovered legs of Aborigines that offended settlers' sensibilities most. Some Aborigines happily put on clothes when coming into town and seemed proud of their ability to move easily in the white man's world but most continued to remain nude or wear traditional dress when living away from Europeans. Lack of interest in and experience with European clothing often led to misuse by Aborigines. For white Australians, who saw dress and observance of its codes as a sign of civilization, clothing misuse confirmed the primitiveness of the blacks. Choice of dress was seen as a sign of an Aborigine's acculturation, with readiness to wear European clothing correctly and acceptance of 'nether' garments deemed as indicators of progress towards civilization (Maynard, 1994: 53, 66).

Bungaree was perhaps the best-known Aboriginal identity in early Sydney. Justly famous for his role as conciliator, guide and interpreter to explorers like Matthew Flinders, on whose epic voyage (1801–2) he become the first Aborigine to circumnavigate his country, Bungaree's life achievements rate one of the rare indigenous entries in the *Australian Dictionary of Biography*. In 1815, to create a central figure through whom to communicate to the local Aborigines, Governor Macquarie presented Bungaree with a brass gorget (neck-plate) inscribed with the title 'Chief of the Broken Bay Tribe', although Bungaree had no tribal authority. On Macquarie's departure from the colony in 1822, he gave Bungaree a suit of his own old general's uniforms 'to dress him out as a Chief' (Macquarie, 11 Feb. 1822).

Augustus Earle's oil painting (*c.*1826) of Bungaree shows him wearing what are supposed to be the Governor's cast-offs. Posed in the grand European manner Earle reserved for portraits of the colonial elite, but reduced to half-scale, Bungaree's 'kingdom' is depicted behind him as 'civilized', while Bungaree himself remains a 'curiosity'. Portrayed as an eccentric beggar king, his lack of 'civilization' is recorded in the incongruity of his dress as he greets the viewer in his well-known manner:

> King Boongarre [sic] ... bedizened in his varnished cocked hat of 'formal cut', his gold-laced ... coat (flanked on the shoulders by a pair of massy epaulettes) buttoned closely up, to evade the extravagance of including a shirt in the catalogue of this wardrobe; and his bare and broad platter feet, of dull cinder hue, spreading out like a pair of toads... Advancing slowly ... his hat gracefully poised in his hand, and his phiz wreathed in many a fantastic smile, he bids massa welcome to *his* country... (Cunningham, 1827: 43–4).

Earle's lithograph of this painting was the first portrait print published in Australia and found a market with colonists looking for souvenirs to send back home. Bungaree's celebrity inspired seventeen known portraits, making him the most illustrated figure in early Australian art history (Neville, 1991: 37–40).

In contrast to Bungaree, the pen and ink drawing of 'Tara [&] Perva' by J. Alphonse Pellion (Fig. 9) seems the only record of their existence. Pellion, a French artist and midshipman on tour of duty with Louis-Claude de Freycinet's round-the-world scientific expedition (1817–20), sketched the two youths whilst visiting their camp on the colonial frontier and, in comparison to Earle's carefully styled portrait of Bungaree, this image reads like a modern traveller's snapshot.

On first contact, Aborigines were often puzzled by the lack of facial hair on white males and, unfamiliar with European dress codes and gender-concealing apparel, sought visual clarification of sex. Subsequently, they were reluctant to adopt garments that masked their gender and scarification. In Pellion's sketch, Tara, posed full frontal, wears a cast-off, double-breasted tailcoat yet despite his appropriation of European clothing, the coat gapes at the neck to expose his initiation scars and, cut away in front, frames his

Figure 9. J. Alphonse Pellion, 'Tara [&] Perva', pen and ink sketch, 1819. Mitchell Library, State Library of New South Wales.

genitalia leaving us in no doubt as to his sex. Perva stands in profile, the cut of his jacket allowing display of his manhood whilst still providing upper body warmth. Some years later, the expedition sketches were 'touched up' and compiled for publication and, perhaps to make the finished plate (Arago, 1825: pl.100) more palatable to the European market, Tara and his two new companions are shown only from the waist up.

With the passing years, Aborigines gained experience in the ways of European consumerism and expectations of the new society and, they began to wear clothing in the accepted European manner. The evangelical desire of settlers to convert the indigenous population to Christianity also forced acceptance of European clothing habits on Aborigines. White women, encountering naked blacks, satisfied both their charitable impulses and their morality by giving them old clothes. Throughout the colonial period, British officials played an increasingly interventionist role in clothing Aborigines, which persisted long after transportation and government control over dress of the lowest class of white inhabitants had ceased (Maynard, 1994: 65). As indigenous dispossession escalated, Aborigines were relocated to government reserves where administrators continued to foster dependence through regular issues of food, clothes and blankets.

The Gold Rush

Gold has a magnetism that the welfare state has dulled. To win gold was the only honest chance that millions of people had of bettering themselves, of gaining independence, of storing money for old age or sickness, of teaching their children to read or write

Geoffrey Blainey, *The Rush that Never Ended*, 1963

Whilst NSW remained a penal colony, all gold finds were the property of the government. British authorities decreed gold prospecting could not begin until the convict strain had been sufficiently diluted by free and assisted immigration. After 1840, when transportation to the eastern states ceased, the population doubled every eight years and approximately 1.6 million people migrated freely to Australia in the nineteenth century. Gold was discovered in NSW in February 1851, and in Victoria later the same year, with progressive rushes continuing around the continent. The ensuing frenzy drew hundreds of thousands of people to Australia and disorganized the whole structure of colonial society (Stannage, 2001: 13–20).

Before prospectors experienced life in the antipodes, migrant ships prepared them for changes to come. Close proximity to differing classes prefigured the mix of humanity encountered on shore. Living conditions on board, including bad weather, lack of space, privacy and washing facilities, encouraged the wearing of comfortable, shabby clothing to endure the wear and tear of ship life. Nineteenth-century philanthropist Caroline Chisholm, believed the arrival of immigrants strengthened the lack of social deference and apparent egalitarian style of dress in colonial populations. By wearing cast-offs or old clothes in public, migrants transgressed established codes of dress, foreshadowing the more casual attitude to clothes in the socially dislocated communities for which they were bound (Maynard, 1994: 139, 160).

Disembarking in an Australia gone mad with gold fever, new arrivals were confused by the uniformity of dress. Ready-made clothes were worn by all classes of men in the colonies and became unreliable as indicators of 'who was who' in towns and on the diggings. The English artist William Strutt abandoned his job as an illustrator in Melbourne when the rush for gold began, adopting 'the digger's simple and comfortable dress of serge shirt, canvas or moleskin trousers, loose necktie and cabbage tree hat ... a first rate work-a-day costume in which of course I became almost immediately unrecognisable to my friends in town' (Strutt, c.1890: vol. 1, 317).

Prospectors were shocked at the high prices in the colony and many exhausted their capital before arriving at the diggings. Impromptu sales of the personal effects of 'new chums' (identifiable by their frockcoats, high collars and top hats) were a common sight on roadsides and riverbanks. Strutt illustrated one such scene in 1852 (Fig. 10) and later recalled:

> numbers of emigrants arrived in the colony with scarcely any money and in a very short time were compelled to sell even their clothes to obtain food. I myself have seen ... persons of respectability ... trying hard to sell articles ... spread out on the ground before them urging the passers by with a pleading despairing look... Many had stowed their boxes at so much per week ... but few indeed ever came back to claim them. The storage itself had absorbed the value. The custodian then advertised and sold them by auction. A firm profit usually being made out of these effects. I knew one man who boasted of having cleared 300 pounds out of such purchases! (Strutt, c.1890: vol. 1, 381–2)

William Kelly, a tourist en route to the goldfields, recorded Melbourne's short-lived Emigrant Rag Fair:

> in front of the Custom-house ... (which) proved to be a new and ingenious device, adopted by a newly arrived crowd of emigrants... An impromptu bazaar ... the boxes ... being arranged in lines as benches, on which the 'not wanted' were placed in double rows back to back, with upturned lids, strewed with the contents so that

Figure 10. William Strutt, 'Hard up! Compulsory Sale Melbourne, Dec. 1852', pen
and watercolour sketch from *Victoria the Golden Scenes sketches and
Jottings from Nature*, 1850–1862.
Reproduced with permission of the Library Committee of the Parliament
of Victoria.

in passing along each row the merchandise was fully exposed for inspection. There
was a really brisk and remunerative trade doing, much to the disgust of some
groups of unwashed Jews who regarded the whole proceeding as an unwarranted
encroachment on their peculiar manor ... A new feature was soon after introduced
with excellent effect – that of the auction system – Here again the envious Jews
stepped in ... to repress the practice of unlicensed auctioneering. They also went
(to) the length of erecting booths adjoining this antipodean Rag Fair, creating
rows and fermenting disturbances to such an extent that the Government were left
no choice but abolish the market altogether (Kelly, 1860: vol. 1, 137 9).

A rag fair was also set up opposite the camp at the first night stop on the
road to the goldfields.

Though coach services to the diggings were available, to save money many
prospectors walked, carrying their possessions on their backs. Domestic
arrangements on the goldfields were makeshift. Miners and their families

lived in tents or bark huts, working their claims six days a week. Many found digging backbreaking, hazardous work with few rewards and the numbers leaving the goldfields soon rivalled those arriving (Stannage, 2001: 33–49). Others set up businesses catering to the needs of the diggers and their families. Notoriously, the most successful group on the diggings were storekeepers, trading in new and second hand goods at inflated prices, as the price of everything, especially ready-made clothing, soared due to labour shortages, raising local costs and increasing demand (Maynard, 1994: 148).

Like most frontier societies, gold rush communities were largely composed of men. Laundry work afforded women struggling to make ends meet within a family unit, or abandoned by death or desertion, with a respectable living and a legal alternative to selling 'sly-grog' (alcohol). From 'taking in washing', some women made the natural progression to second hand clothes dealing. A local newspaper recorded competition between bidders at an estate auction conducted on the NSW goldfields:

> A primitive form of 'rag fair' was extended to Gulgong last Saturday ... offering for sale in the main street of a diggings township, article by article, the contents of ... clothing trunks. It was an edifying sight to witness (the local magistrate) ... bidding against Mary the washerwoman for the deceased parson's shirts and when his bid was successful to watch the keen glance of scrutiny he cast over his purchase (*Gulgong Guardian*, 9 Nov. 1872).

The Swagman and the Wagga

In the nineteenth and early twentieth-century Australian art and popular culture the 'swagman' (aka bagman, hobo or tramp) was as potent a national symbol as the kangaroo. Cast by local and visiting artists as a picturesque figure in the Australian landscape, an antipodean counterpart to the European gypsy, peddler or tinker, the swagman first appeared during the gold rushes when men who'd searched for gold walked off the diggings to look for work, their belongings rolled in a blanket or 'swag' and slung over their shoulders (Astbury, 1985: 43–78). By 1895, this itinerant bush workforce of stockmen and shearer 'swaggies' had been immortalized in Australia's unofficial anthem 'Waltzing Matilda' (vernacular for carrying one's swag). The last generation of swagmen took to the roads during the 1930s Great Depression.

The persona of the Australian swagman was represented as non-conformist, imbued with a swashbuckling quest for freedom as he shunned the tameness of city living and the responsibilities of home, work and

Figure 11. 'The Murrumbidgee Whaler. One of the old time swagmen still to be
seen in the country during the 1930s.'
Photograph by W. Hatton. Mitchell Library, State Library of New South
Wales.

family. This imposed aura of dashing independence more likely obscured the
necessity he actually faced, travelling the outback in the search of work or
food. The term 'Murrumbidgee Whaler' (Fig. 11) denoted the 'sundowner'
class of swagmen, who wandered the banks of the Murrumbidgee River,
NSW, surviving by fishing and begging. The distinction between a 'swagman'
and a 'sundowner' was clear; the latter habitually arrived at sundown, too
late to work for his ration of food and place to sleep. Customarily clad in
'bumming clothes', usually obtained as a handout from the station owner or
manager's wife, these were worn to maximum effect when begging.

Most swagmen owned a 'wagga', the wholecloth utilitarian Australian
quilt form of indigent and working class males known since the 1890s. Made
from four or five jute sacks sewn together with twine, the term probably
derived from the town of Wagga Wagga, NSW, where the Murrumbidgee
Milling Company – the source of the sacks – was located (Hucker, *c*.1995).

Also used by working-class rural families, the domestic 'wagga' was a kind of 'rag sandwich' made from two 'slices' of unbleached calico, recycled from flour, wheat or sugar bags, the filling comprised of anything wool, including worn-out blankets, pieces of old clothes, unrepairable socks and matted sweaters, stitched down to the backing layer. Tops were pieced from whatever was to hand with outdated tailor's suiting sample books a common source of patches (Rolfe, 1998: 11–12).

People living on remote properties relied on itinerant dealers to provide onsite access to goods otherwise necessitating a trip to town. Indian and Chinese hawkers made scheduled visits in horse or camel drawn vans to supply outlying areas with hardware, haberdashery and drapery goods, often taking second hand goods in exchange. This form of barter continued in the country long after cash was required to trade in shops (Maynard, 1994: 131–2).

Urban Shops

Australia experienced rapid economic development during the second half of the nineteenth century. Colonial towns developed in the pattern of British cities, housing a quarter of the population by the 1860s, with numbers swelling in winter when rural workers came looking for work. Arrival of the railways encouraged suburban living for the upper and middle classes but the quality of urban working-class life declined as populations grew ahead of city amenities. Gold hadn't generated an equal society and, given the fluctuating labor market and the deprived life of the underclasses, claims that the colonies were a workingman's paradise were no longer true. In general, Australian workers were generally no better off, nor better clothed, than their British counterparts. Sydney wasn't an old city but, as the population trebled to 400,000 in 1891, the environment was no healthier than British cities from whence people had emigrated (Fitzgerald, 1987: 2, 100).

Retailing also changed as the century progressed. Housewives still shopped at the markets and bargained with street hawkers but, by the 1870s, mixed businesses, auction rooms and small retail outlets were being supplanted by department stores and shopping arcades (Maynard, 1994: 132–3). While general dealers, salesmen, warehousemen and tailors are all listed in nineteenth-century business directories, evidence of shops dealings in second hand garments cannot be determined from listings alone, due to imprecise terminology.

At a time when documentation of the underclasses is rare, the existence of an exterior photograph of John Morgan's premises is a remarkable survival.

Linked to the contemporary description of the shop's interior, as inspected by the Sydney City and Sewerage and Health Board on 2 December 1875, it provides unequivocal proof of the class of trader to which 'John Morgan, Dealer', belonged:

> This house ... contains no furniture of any kind. Indeed there is no room for it, the entire available floor space being crowded with stock-in-trade of the proprietor, who is a dealer in old clothes. Piles upon piles of garments of all sorts are stowed away below and aloft which, like the house, appear considerably the worse for wear. These may possibly be renewed by some artificial process, but no renovation is possible for the house itself ... no further efforts to prevent this house from falling down should be permitted. (*Sydney City and Suburban Sewerage Board Report*, 1876: 26).

Photographs also confirm W.T. Baker, 'general dealer', and T.C. Johnson, 'tailor' as second hand traders. Situated in the same street as Morgan's dishevelled shop, but closer to the smarter shopping area of George Street, signage above the neat façade of Baker's store bears the legend, 'W. T. Baker... Ladies and Gentlemen's Left-off clothing'. The sign nailed by the front door of Johnson's premises reads, 'Tailor, gentlemen's clothes, cleaned dyed and repaired. Second hand clothes bought and sold. The highest prices given'.

Three photographs taken between 1901 and 1909 show the street frontages of 'Benjamin's Old Original New and Second hand Clothing Shop' and the backyard, where a woman, presumably Mrs Benjamin, is surrounded by laundry. The 1895 trade directory contains a listing for Mrs Benjamin, 'Clothier', and undoubtedly she had no shortage of clients as Sydney's least fortunate citizens frequented this area near the Haymarket. The City Mission House, Chinese Mission, Salvation Army Coffee Palace, several pawnbrokers and quite a number of dealers also operated in the vicinity. In a photograph of 'The Bargain Shop', at 185 Elizabeth Street, the proprietor, Mrs Leah Rugg, stands in the doorway surrounded by merchandise. Second hand clothes hang in the window and all around the façade, documenting the nature of the bargains to be found inside.

Louis Stone's novel *Jonah* (1907) is a tale of slum life in early twentieth-century Sydney. When a young couple in search of cheap furnishings attend a house sale, the ensuing description supplies a rare vignette: 'Mother Jenkins ... was the auctioneer's scavenger ... her second-hand shop in Bathurst Street had taught her to despise nothing that had an ounce of wear left in it. Her bids never ran beyond a few shillings ... forced up to price by a friend to increase her commission' (Stone, 1907: 134).

The Bathurst Street premises of Mr and Mrs Woolf, 'wardrobe dealers', buyers of 'second hand clothing and dresses, old gold and artificial teeth', are documented in another photograph. The 1894 trade directory first lists M. Woolf, 'second hand clothier', with only one other dealer and a pawnbroker nearby. By 1900, in the aftermath of the 1890s depression, three pawnbrokers, four second hand clothes dealers and five general dealers are listed. The Woolfs traded until 1955, when, in an era of post-war prosperity, Charlie Woolf began dealing in sporting goods. Bathurst Street remained a centre for second hand dealers and pawnbrokers until well into the late twentieth century.

Paddy's Market

The 'Paddy's' market concept derived from the traditional open-air fairs of Ireland, with their mixture of merry-go-rounds, sideshows, fast food stalls, produce and second hand dealers. There was a well-known Paddy's Market in Liverpool, the main embarkation port for Irish emigrants to Australia, and its reconstitution in a country that received thousands of convicts and immigrants from Ireland is not surprising (Christie, 1988: 88, 138–40). Sydney's 'Paddy's' Market was located opposite the Campbell Street Market in Haymarket and already well established by the 1840s. The Eastern Market in Bourke Street, Melbourne, was also known as 'Paddy's' Market, especially on Saturdays when it turned into a poor man's bazaar selling miscellaneous merchandise (*Illustrated Australian News*, 28 Mar. 1867: 6).

In addition to late night shopping at the George Street Market, trading hours were extended at Paddy's Market in the early 1870s, and thousands of Sydneysiders spent the evenings promenading between the two sites. Visiting in 1875, John Laing described Paddy's customers as 'belonging almost exclusively to the poorer classes of the community ... hard working men and their families, servant girls let loose until 10pm, factory girls freed from their week's labour, slatterns from the lanes and alleys and above all a large admixture of the larrikin tribe'. Bargains included, 'the better sort of second-hand wearing apparel, and articles of "Brummagem" finery, down to ... humble necessities for the kitchen' (Laing, c.1875: 120–3).

In the 1890s, the George Street Market site was redeveloped into a palatial shopping arcade and stallholders were rehoused with those from Paddy's and the Campbell Street Market in the new Belmore Market complex at Haymarket. Travel journalist Phill Harris visited one Saturday and watched as the old clothes dealers turned their section of the sheds into a Petticoat Lane (Harris, 1908: 350). Finally relocated to the opposite side of George

Street in 1909, Rex Hazelwood's photograph shows second hand clothes stalls at the Sydney Markets, *c.*1910, and vividly records the stock-in-trade of such dealers.

Louis Stone's *Jonah* provides another literary description of the markets at the turn of the century:

> On Saturdays the great market ... was a debauch of sound colour and smell ... (where) the smug respectability of the shops was cast aside ... There was no caprice of the belly that could not be gratified, no want of the naked body that could not be supplied in this huge bazaar of the poor; but its cost had to counted in pence, for those that bought in the cheapest market came here (Stone, 1907: 69–70).

And specifically:

> watching the Jews driving bargains in second-hand clothes, renovated with secret processes handed down from the Ark. Coats and trousers, equipped for their last adventure with mysterious darns and patches, cheated the eye like a painted beauty at a ball. Women's finery lay in disordered heaps – silk blouses covered with tawdry lace, skirts heavy with gaudy trimming – the draggled plumage of fine birds that had come to grief. But here the buyer and seller met on level terms, for each knew to a hair the value of the sorry garments (Stone, 1907: 71).

Jonah is attributed as one of the earliest novels to use the screen writing form (Green, 1991: xix), but it would be the 1917 silent version of C. J. Dennis's classic poem, *The Sentimental Bloke*, that would capture trade at a Paddy's Market second hand clothes stall on moving footage for the first time.

Conclusion

> The poor are often as in want of clothes as of food and to obtain them we must take trouble rather than expend money ... for many a poor person fails to find a place for want of decent clothes.
>
> *Manual of the Society of St Vincent de Paul*

Survival in the Australian colonies always depended on regular work and good health. In leaving home, migrants left behind networks of extended family and friends, and poor people without relatives were a problem in Australia from the start. By the late nineteenth century, branches of the major international voluntary religious groups were at work in Australia, soon joined by local charities like the Smith Family (1922). Traditionally, charitable groups have expended much activity ensuring that supplies of second hand clothing are kept on hand and early manuals outlined methods for gathering and distributing clothing to the poor. With the late-twentieth-century professionalization of charity worldwide, these methods have evolved into profit-generating merchandising strategies and second hand clothing has, once again, become a valuable commodity.

4

Second Hand Silk Kimono Migrating Across Borders

Terry Satsuki Milhaupt

Inside and outside of Japan's borders, the kimono survives within contemporary cultural consciousness as a symbol of a traditional Japan. Yet the heritage of kimono, as romanticized concept and wearable garment, continues to fade as younger generations of Japanese have relatively limited knowledge of and experiences with kimono. Although occasionally donned for ceremonial events, the kimono has all but disappeared from everyday life. Preserved through generations, the kimono is more likely encountered today as an object of display in a museum, as an antique item for sale at temple markets, or as an heirloom tucked away among a grandmother's treasured belongings.

While the T-shaped kimono has been the subject of much study, this classical garment has enjoyed a longevity in other forms yet to be explored. Made from a single length of cloth cut into seven sections, the kimono easily lends itself to fragmentation and reuse. Two body panels, two sleeve sections, two front overlaps, and a collar are stitched together with straight seams and minimal tailoring. When a kimono exhibits signs of wear, or when its color, design or sleeve length are no longer appropriate for its owner, it can be unstitched and resized into a child's garment, reconstituted with other garment sections to create a 'new' look, or refashioned into a totally different configuration.

The ease with which the kimono's simple format can be physically reshaped to conform to new cultural and historical settings has contributed to its seemingly effortless passage across geographic and generational borders. As a kimono traverses the domains of use and reuse, fragmentation and reconfiguration, exchange and resale, its meaning mutates with its physical appearance. Indeed, the kimono survives today in multiple forms with mutable meanings. Thus it is instructive to view the trajectory of a kimono in its secondary forms and meanings, rather than fixating on its 'timeless' qualities.

This paper discusses the reuse and reinterpretation of a silk kimono in three specific transformations – corporeal, symbolic and transcultural. In each case, a kimono is unstitched and reconfigured as it crosses borders between public and private, secular and sacred, or East and West. Through a process of disassembling and restitching, as well as use and reuse, secondhand silk kimono acquire new formats, functions and cultural meanings as they travel from one context to another.

The conceptual framework of what I term 'outside in' captures these multiple manifestations of the corporeal, symbolic, and transcultural and traces the metamorphosis of kimono as it migrates across borders. 'Outside in' refers to shifts in function, space, or value. The corporeal view exposes how the kimono's function shifts in relation to the body and focuses on the transformation of salvageable sections of outer garments pieced together and reused as an inner garment. The symbolic analysis situates kimono in relation to space and describes how a secular kimono from the outside world is transformed into sacred cloth within the inner sanctums of a Buddhist temple. A view through the transcultural lens follows the transformation of secondhand kimono as it crosses geographic and social divides in its migration from secondhand shops within Japan's borders to its use outside of Japan as an element of fashionable attire for the affluent. The transition from outside in is often preceded or followed by a similar movement from inside out. Each shift reflects the mobility of garments and the mutability of their meaning within disparate historical, cultural, temporal and spatial contexts. The individual biographies (Kopytoff, 1986: 64–91) of three types of reworked textiles explored in this paper – inner kimono, Buddhist vestments and Western-style garments – evidence the broader social practice of producing clothes with new cultural meanings from secondhand silk kimono.

My approach deliberately spans temporal (premodern through contemporary) and spatial boundaries (public to private, secular to sacred, and East to West, respectively) in an effort to expose groups of objects rendered invisible by more conventional approaches (Ulrich, 2001: 8). The objective of this essay is to situate second hand kimono within distinctive cultural settings from the sixteenth through twentieth centuries, and to recognize how these reinterpreted clothes inform our understanding of the economic, symbolic, and cultural value of cloth in society. Whether the motivations for recycling cloth derive from frugality, conspicuous display, reverence for a religious ideal, an aesthetic impulse to transform old into new, or a combination of these and other factors, the objects described below document the multiple values and meanings ascribed to fragments of silk kimono.

The Multiple Values of Patched Garments

Garments made of silk – a highly valued and much traded commodity in sixteenth-century Japan – circulated as forms of currency, payment and reward (Takeda, 2002: 71–72). Valued as precious commodities, silk garments were reused rather than discarded. Undamaged portions of garments were creatively recombined to produce 'new' clothes. In some cases, body and sleeve panels from two distinct garments might be combined to form a more visually arresting composition, or to conform to current styles. For example, a Noh robe (Art Institute of Chicago, 1992: 41) incorporates sections from two different sixteenth-century garments in a format known as *katamigawari* (or two different sides). In other cases, preserved fragments were reused to decorate other garments. In one notable type, intricately embroidered crests from a seventeenth-century Noh robe were cut out and applied to a nineteenth-century ground fabric. A reverence for tradition, rather than innovation, led to the repetition of formulaic compositions and designs in Noh theatrical costumes. The reuse of embroidered crests on a later garment may valorize this continuity of tradition, or may have been motivated by economic concerns.

Conversely, patched garments could embody their owners' wealth, rather than frugality. A sumptuous robe, previously owned by the warlord Uesugi Kenshin (1530–78) is a mosaic of highly coveted and expensive imported Chinese brocades. Clearly, its construction required access to substantial financial resources. Patched together from fragments, this robe symbolizes ostentatious excess rather than practical frugality. Two extant garments suggest that sentimental motivations, as well as economic concerns, generated a desire to create patched garments. In one case, early seventeenth-century fragments from a disassembled robe were pieced together to form a garment to be worn under a warrior's armor (*gusokushita*), closest to his body (Maruyama, 1994: 33). In another, fragments from a robe typically worn by wives and female relatives of the military elite served as the tight-fitting sleeves of a similar battle garment (Nagasaki, 1998: 56–7). Perhaps the warrior embarking on a military campaign derived an emotional layer of protection and comfort cloaked in a garment comprising fabrics donated by female relatives or loyal retainers.

The fragmentary nature of written evidence describing the social practice of piecing together old kimono dictates an approach that highlights the significance of the surviving physical evidence. The composition of this essay, therefore, resembles the American crazy quilts of the nineteenth century in which distinctively shaped pieces of seemingly unrelated cloth were carefully selected and stitched together to create a single unified design. In this essay, an assemblage of pieces of information, organized into three selectively defined sections, presents an integrated and composite view of reused and reinterpreted secondhand silk kimono. Rather than exclusive or absolute, the three crafted categories of exterior and interior views represent some of the myriad perspectives afforded by this rich and relatively unexplored topic.

Corporeal: The Shift from Outer to Inner Garment

The word *wafuku* (Japanese-style dress) gained currency in the nineteenth century when the need arose to distinguish Japanese clothing from the western-style fashions, or *yōfuku*, that had begun to infiltrate Japan's previously restricted borders. Over time *ki[ru]mono* (literally 'thing to wear'), or kimono, referred more specifically to the T-shaped garment with which we associate the word today. The kimono's antecedent was referred to as a *kosode* (literally 'small sleeves').

In the Heian period (794–1185) the *kosode* functioned as a type of undergarment for members of the aristocracy, as well as outer clothing for the lower classes (Nagasaki, 1993: 92). Anyone familiar with the eleventh-century Japanese classic, *The Tale of Genji*, will recall descriptions of women clad in multiple layers of garments, the colors of which were coordinated to evoke particular seasonal associations. The *kosode*, worn closest to the skin, served the practical purpose of absorbing perspiration generated by the numerous robes that enveloped an aristocratic woman's body. Over the next few centuries as power shifted from the aristocracy into the hands of the military elite who favored a less cumbersome form of dress, clothing styles of the upper classes tended toward the functional and less voluminous. By the sixteenth century, the *kosode* emerged as an outer garment for all classes. In its relation to the body, the *kosode* moved from inside, out.

Reversing the process, fragments of outer silk kimono were salvaged and transfigured into inner garments. In short, the garment moved from outside in. Most extant examples of inner garments, such as *aigi* ('between clothing') or *shitagi* ('under clothing'), date from the eighteenth through twentieth centuries. In general, the fragments are laid out in a geometric composition that reverses across the center seam of the T-shaped kimono. Narrow vertical bands of fabric decorate the collar and sleeve openings and the lower body panels from knee to hem. Visible when the outer garment shifts with the wearer's movements, these areas are often constructed of the same fabric. The internal design scheme varies from vertically oriented strips of cloth to the juxtaposition of triangles with horizontal and vertical bands of various widths. The selection and combination of shapes, motifs and colors mark each garment with its creator's distinctive sense of design.

In addition to enhancing the overall layout of the patched inner garment, fragments were likely selected for their nostalgic associations with a previous owner. In the example of an inner garment illustrated here (Fig. 12), the maker selected a somber color palette with motifs imbued with poetic allusions. Individual fragments decorated with light blue irises and plank bridges against a dark grayish-green ground connote a locale in Mikawa province known as Yatsuhashi (Eight Bridges). Familiar to a literate audience through the classic collection of poems, the *Tales of Ise*, the vignette of irises and eight plank bridges serves as a visual reminder of a traveler far from home, who composed the following poem:

Figure 12. Late nineteenth century silk under kimono made from recycled kimono fabric.
Private collection, New York. Photograph by author.

*ka*ragoromo	I have a beloved wife,
*ki*tsutsu narenishi	familiar as the skirt
*tsu*ma shi areba	of a well-worn robe,
*ha*rubaru kinuru	and so this distant journeying
*ta*bi o shi zo omou	fills my heart with grief (McCullough, 1968: 74–5).

The first syllable of each line of the poem forms the Japanese word for iris (*kakitsu[b]ata*). Fragments with the iris and bridge motif decorate the collar, sleeve openings and hem area of this late nineteenth-century inner robe. Rose-colored calligraphic characters, written in a highly stylized cursive script, flow in myriad directions against a brown ground in the upper front and back sections of the body panels. In the sleeves and mid-section of the body panels, cocoon-shaped motifs entangled within a black spider web encapsulate images of silhouetted figures and snow-laden pine trees. While the exact identity of the wearer remains a mystery, the muted color tones of this garment, coupled with poetic allusions to a traveler longing for his wife, suggest that this inner garment may have been made by or designed for a mature, married woman.

Private and personal in nature, this inner robe in the above example reflects the individual tastes of a particular woman. Although her specific identity is irretrievable, it is instructive to view garments of this type as a group. While they may represent the frugality of their wearer, they also embody deliberately selected fragments of garments, specifically chosen for aesthetic, sentimental, or symbolic characteristics. Comprised of the fragments and memories of other robes, this *aigi*, as the remaining shell of a woman's body, physically re-members the life of the now anonymous woman who fabricated and wore this simple garment.

Symbolic: The Transition from the Outer World to the Inner Sanctum

The social practice of piecing together clothes from the remnants of other garments may emulate the Buddhist practice of producing robes for monks and nuns from the used clothing of believers. Prescribed rules existed for the types of cloth suitable for use as monastic robes. The Zen master Dōgen (1200–53) devoted an entire section of his thirteenth-century treatise *Shōbogenzō* ('The Eye Treasury of the Right Dharma') to the subject of clothing (Yūhō, 1976: 88–106). 'Discarded cloths' were collected, washed, and sewn into patched *kesa* and *funzō-e*, two types of robes worn by Buddhist clerics (Lyman 1984: 25–57). Based on the Buddha's teachings, the *Shōbogenzō* states:

According to the traditional teachings of the Buddha a *kasåya [kesa]* made of discarded cloth, that is a *påmsüla [funzō-e]* is the best. There are either four or ten types of such cloth. The four types of cloth are those that have been burned by fire, munched by oxen, gnawed by mice, or worn by the dead (Yūhō, 1976: 94).

The ten types of discarded cloth are (1) cloth munched by oxen, (2) cloth gnawed by mice, (3) cloth burned by fire, (4) cloth soiled by menstrual blood, (5) cloth soiled by the blood of childbirth, (6) cloth discarded at shrines, (7) cloth discarded in a cemetery, (8) cloth presented as an offering, (9) cloth discarded by government officials, and (10) cloth used to cover the dead (Yūhō, 1976: 105).

In contrast to the humble types of cloth described in the *Shōbogenzō* as appropriate for reuse by Buddhist clergy, many surviving examples of altar cloths, vestments and temple banners were actually made from precious textiles. Silk garments of the finest quality entered temple collections as a form of payment to the clerics that performed funerary services in honor of the deceased. Monks and nuns cleaned, dismantled and reused the donated garments. In some cases, they fashioned the cloth into rectangular-shaped vestments, or *kesa*, for their own use. Symbolically, the act of dissecting the treasured garment into smaller pieces diminished its commercial value, in effect neutralizing its material value, and rendered it more appropriate for religious use. The vow of poverty imposed on clerics that required them to create their own garments from scraps of discarded fabrics, ironically also allowed them to wear some of the most precious and expensive recycled silks.

Garments offered to temples in honor of the deceased served a number of purposes. The efficacy of a donated garment to the donor, recipient, and departed is described in 'The Initiates' chapter of the epic *Tale of the Heike*. When the Imperial Lady Kenreimon'in took vows to become a nun, she presented one of Emperor Antoku's robes as an offering to the monk who performed the ceremony. The text explains:

> The Former Emperor had worn the garment until the hour of his death, and it still bore the scent of his body. She had brought it all the way from the western provinces to the capital with the intention of keeping it as a memento – of never letting it leave her side. But now, for lack of another suitable offering, she produced it in tears, telling herself that the deed might also help the Former Emperor attain enlightenment. The monk received it, unable to respond, and took his leave with tears drenching his black sleeves. People say it was made into a banner to be hung in front of the Buddha at the Chōrakuji (McCullough, 1988: 426–7).

In this account, an article of clothing was transformed from a memento (*katami*) of the deceased into an offering or form of remuneration for a monk's services. The donor also saw her donation as a potential means of attaining enlightenment for the deceased while the community of believers viewed it as an offering to the Buddha. Two banners preserved in Chōrakuji temple, Kyoto, exist today as vestiges of this account and according to temple tradition, the banners were remade from Emperor Antoku's robes (Nunome, 1992: 67, 253–4).

From the sixteenth century, more physical evidence documenting the practice of donating a deceased's treasured garment to a temple exists. Garments served as an offering to Buddhist clerics and temple affiliates who prayed for the peaceful repose of the departed's soul. In some cases, the donated garment was then disassembled and reconfigured into sacred textiles to be worn by monks. In other instances, the donated garments were transformed into altar cloths and temple banners to adorn the inner sanctums of the Buddha hall.

Monks, nuns and lay believers acquired merit for producing *kesa*. The composition of *kesa*, based on a prescribed format, consists of an interior section of pieces of fabric laid out in a grid-like pattern enclosed within a rectangular border (Kennedy, 1990: 121–9). Narrow vertical bands demarcate spaces between wider columns that range in number from five to twenty-five. Thin horizontal bands within each column separate long and short lengths of cloth. Square patches in each of the four corners represent the four cardinal directions. Two square patches that stand in for his attendants often flank the central column, a symbolic representation of the Buddha.

In an example of a *kesa* remade from a donated garment, now in the Metropolitan Museum of Art's collection (32.65.25), an eighteenth-century kimono from an upper class woman's wardrobe was cut up and sewn into a five-column *kesa*. Physically, the obliterated T-shape of the kimono is now a mosaic of small patches that form a rectangular Buddhist vestment of maple leaves and fans executed in paste resist dyeing, embroidery and shaped-resist dyeing (*shibori*) floating against a red silk *chirimen* crepe ground. The sumptuous materials and vibrant palette of this *kesa* belie its use as a surplice, possibly worn by a Buddhist nun during informal events. A cord and toggle secured the richly dyed and embroidered rectangular cloth around the torso in such a way that it concealed the physical shape of the wearer's body.

Some donated garments, transformed into altar cloths and *kesa*, emerged from their sacred sanctuaries in the late nineteenth century when Buddhist temples, in need of financial support, began to sell their treasures. Antique dealers and collectors, most notably Nomura Shōjirō (1879–1943), purchased many of these sacred textiles. He unstitched them, often removing inscribed linings in the process, and remounted the remaining fragments on two-panel folding screens in a layout effectively recreating the appearance of a single garment (Paul, 1984: 17–19). Functionally, Nomura's reconfigured garments pasted onto gold screens represent yet another transformation of second hand fragments, this time from ritual cloth to objets d'art. Nomura's series of 100 screens, completed in 1934, was never intended for sale. Rather, fragments of the original garment, transformed into a sacred cloth, ultimately survive again in the form of a garment, but one that functions as an item for museum display rather than as adornment for the body (Milhaupt, 2003: 324–6; 344–5; 348–9).

In an alternate 'inside to out' route from temple to marketplace, a donated garment might be kept intact by the temple for an appropriate period, then later sold to a second hand clothing shop. Proceeds from the sale supported temple activities. The Meireki fire of 1657, also known as the *furisode kaji* (or 'swinging sleeves fire') purportedly started when monks at the Honmyoji temple in Edo (modern-day Tokyo) attempted to burn the garment of a recently deceased young woman (Nagasaki, 1999: 42–3). The garment, originally donated by the young woman's grieving family, was sold by the priests to a used clothing store. Another young woman purchased it, and she, too, died at a young age. When the same garment was again donated to the temple, the monks decided to burn it in a *segaki* ritual where unwanted clothing was, through burning, intended to clothe those who had been reborn into the realm of starving, wandering ghosts. A strong wind suddenly arose and the burning robe blew into the sky, causing a fire that spread and eventually killed an estimated 100,000 people. The tale, an apocryphal account of the origins of the fire, nonetheless alludes to the role of Buddhist clerics as facilitators in the rebirth, recycling, and preservation of kimono.

Transcultural: The Migration of Kimono Across Japan's Borders

In seventeenth-century Japan, kimono also reached the second hand market through used clothing shops, pawn shops, and dealers that specialized in the sale of textile fragments. In the 1690 publication *Jinrin kinmo zui* (Illustrated instructions on human relations) a woman presents a garment to a pawnshop dealer (*shichiya*), who is shown calculating the value of the offered robe. At the time, an estimated 345 pawnshops existed in Osaka (Asakura, 1990: 137–9). Shops known as *furuteya* ('old hand shop') that specialized in the buying and selling of old garments and obi were located on Karasuma near Nijō and on Gojō street west of Muromachi in Kyoto. Other shops referred to as *kireya* ('cutting shops') sold textile fragments. While the *Jinrin kinmo zui* describes secondhand textile shops centered in the Kansai area, regional trade in used textiles also likely developed in response to market demands.

The mid nineteenth-century publication *Morisada Mankō* (Observations by Morisada) written by Kitagawa Morisada (b. 1810) describes a bustling market for used clothes located in the city of Edo (Kitagawa, 1996: 175). According to Kitagawa, every morning when the weather was clear, vendors selling used clothing lined the streets of Tomizawa-chō and Tachibana-chō. A lively secondhand clothing market also thrived in Asakusa. Kitagawa explicitly notes that in certain areas used clothing sellers placed their goods on straw mats, suggesting a more portable and transient mode of business, while others displayed them in stalls, indicating a relatively stable domestic demand for used clothing.

By the late nineteenth century, in addition to serving Japanese clients, the second hand kimono market began to cater to foreigners. Nomura (Iwanaga) Tei (d. 1916), mother of Nomura Shōjirō early on recognized the economic value of antique Japanese textiles in the international market, and she specifically targeted a Western clientele (Paul, 1984: 13). Tei's entrepreneurial skills transformed her textile business from a small stall located on the Kamo riverbank in Kyoto into a more permanent shop in central Kyoto by the turn of the twentieth century. Tei's son Shōjirō became a well-known dealer and collector of Japanese textiles who served clients both within Japan and abroad.

Modern painters represent another type of client, who had slightly different agendas. As second hand kimono made their way to European curio shops, artists purchased them to use as models in their paintings (Screech, 2002: 52–5). This late nineteenth-century vogue for 'things Japanese', fueled by international expositions and an increasingly global marketplace (Conant, 1991: 79–92), is referred to as *Japonisme*. The generally favorable reception of Japanese manufactured products by American, European, and British audiences contributed to a heightened desire to incorporate these exotic items into Western interior design, dressmaking and painting (Hosley, 1990; Fukai, 1994; Berger, 1992). Paintings of kimono-clad women by James Tissot (1836–1902), Claude Monet (1840–1926) and James Abbot McNeill Whistler (1834–1903) suggest the international availability of kimono. In a letter to his mother from Paris dated November 12, 1864, the English painter Dante Gabriel Rossetti (1828–82) recounts his visit to a Parisian shop selling Japanese goods:

I have bought very little – only four Japanese books – but found all the costumes were being snapped up by a French artist, Tissot, who it seems is doing three Japanese pictures which the mistress of the shop described to me as the three wonders of the world, evidently in her opinion quite throwing Whistler into the shade (Wentworth, 1980: 128–4).

In 1876, Monet painted his wife Camille wearing a costume possibly brought over for a theatrical production during the International Exhibition held in Paris in 1867 (Liddell, 1989: 194). In the painting entitled *La Japonaise* (Museum of Fine Arts, Boston), Camille reveals her back to the viewer as she strikes a theatrical pose. Among the Japanese fans that decorate the wall behind her, one depicts the surprised expression of a Japanese woman. Perhaps the Japanese woman in the fan is unnerved by Camille's flamboyant and unorthodox posture in what appears to be a kabuki costume, a performance art that had been restricted to male actors in Japan since the early seventeenth century. If Monet were cognizant of the male actor tradition within kabuki theater, the shocked expression on the face of the Japanese woman in the fan painting could be interpreted as Monet's response to ethnic and gendered cross-dressing. Or perhaps the incongruous appearance of a married woman apparently flouting cultural norms by wearing such a flamboyant costume disturbed the Japanese female observer in the fan.

Within Japan, time-honored codes bind those who wear kimono (Dalby, 1993: 163–213). Age, gender and status dictate the style, colors and motifs appropriate for a particular season or occasion. The flirtatious, fluttering sleeves of the unmarried woman's garment are cut off and shortened when she weds. The vibrant reds worn by children and young girls disappear from the wardrobes of married women, when more somber blues and grays dominate. Cherry blossoms decorate spring kimono, maple leaves and deer appear in autumn, and snow-laden bamboo adorn winter garments.

Heian period diaries of court ladies comment on a woman's aesthetic sensibility, as revealed through her selection of materials, decorative techniques and combination of colors (Bowring, 1982: 67) – distinctions recognizable only to an elite strata of eleventh-century Japanese society. Sumptuary laws regulating the types of material and colors of dress appropriate to certain classes, promulgated since the seventeenth century, led one scholar to describe a 'rule by status' system (Hall, 1974: 45). Indeed, government officials of the Edo period (1600–1868) enacted laws dictating how much could be spent on a new robe and who was allowed the privilege of wearing silk (Ikegami, 1997: 145–53). Those who dressed lavishly or conspicuously flaunted finery inappropriate to their status could be arrested for such behavior (Shively, 1964–65: 123–64).

Historical precedents continue to inform the sartorial choices of today's kimono cognoscenti who occupy an ever-diminishing social niche. Even if they may no longer recognize the traditional sources that guide their decisions on appropriate colors, patterns and sleeve-lengths, older generations of Japanese women still recognize a kimono fashion faux pas. This inherited memory continues to fade, however, as fewer Japanese are familiar with the protocol for wearing kimono.

Unconstrained by culturally determined norms of kimono fabric selection based on age, gender, status and occasion in Japan, two contemporary American designers transform old Japanese textiles into ready-to-wear clothing. Their company, Asiatica, considered by some as a pioneer in the 'kimono reform' movement, began recycling Japanese fabrics over twenty years ago (Wilson, E., 2002). In the late 1960s, Elizabeth Wilson, co-founder of Asiatica, began collecting Japanese textiles which were at that time readily available and relatively inexpensive *(Sōsaku ichiba*, 1997: 66–7). From the 1980s, Wilson and her partner Fifi White began to unstitch kimono and reconfigure them into blouses and jackets for resale outside of Japan. A popular Asiatica jacket design features an asymmetrically cut front hem that visually echoes the diagonal slant of the front neck closure. To unify the design, a pocket cut from a contrasting fabric is positioned on the back rather than front of the jacket. In a pewter-colored jacket of this style (Fig. 13), Asiatica's conscious blending of Eastern and Western design elements transformed the white, star-like swirls and black roundels, originally executed by Japanese dyers to decorate a T-shaped kimono, into dramatically positioned accents. The simple lines and loose-fitting structure of Asiatica's creations mimic kimono drapery and distinctively juxtapose the unusual patterns, techniques and colors of Japanese cloth.

With the globalizing exchange of kimono, culturally defined messages encoded within the motifs, colors and tailoring details of their T-shaped frame are transfigured and translated into foreign fashion statements. In the case of Asiatica, two American women established a successful business by catering primarily to a non-Japanese clientele. Their signature style, described by their loyal patrons as 'timeless', 'unique', and 'perfect for any occasion', appeals to a small circle of affluent American women who appreciate unusual clothing that incorporates Japanese designs and materials. Those who choose to wear these garments may place a higher value on individually crafted objects in our postmodern society of mass-produced unisex fashion. An imagined ideal of a static, exotic East may also contribute to the perceived 'timeless' quality of Asiatica's designs (Skov, 1996: 138; Kondo, 1997: 55–99). The notion that these garments are 'perfect for any occasion' may simply result from the loss of their Japanese

Figure 13. Silk jacket by Asiatica, produced in the 1990s from recycled kimono
fabric.
Private collection, New York. Photograph by author.

cultural referents within an unfamiliar, Western context. The meaning and
attraction of these garments evolves with the time and context in which they
are worn.

The continuation of this particular form of ethnic cross-dressing will be
conditioned by the uncertain future of the second hand silk kimono market.
When Asiatica was first established, kimono could be purchased by the bale.
Dealers who handled discarded kimono were relatively undiscriminating;
they sold by the pound or the piece. According to Wilson, the second
hand kimono market at that time catered primarily to two distinct groups:
foreigners and impoverished Japanese who could not afford to purchase a
new kimono for special occasions. Today, the dynamics of supply and demand
have radically altered the market. Fewer Japanese wear kimono, therefore
fewer survive. The supply of used kimono dwindles at an accelerated pace.
A limited number of garments re-emerge in the second hand market. Others

resurface in the storerooms of museums and collectors to be preserved for future generations as artifacts of a past era.

Additionally there is increased competition for the limited supply of second hand kimono. Japanese women, possibly propelled by nostalgic sentiments, have forged a renewed appreciation for what many still identify as their national dress. In 1993, Dalby wrote: 'Wearing kimono today combines Japanese pride, traditional sensibility, cultural connectedness, and conspicuous consumption' (119). For Japanese women today who wish to express these attributes without the burdens of the hobbling skirt, rib-crunching obi and movement-restricting contours of kimono, new alternatives are on the horizon. Japanese designers are boldly rejuvenating kimono into functional, less costly silhouettes (*Sōsaku ichiba*, 1997: 8–29; *Rokushō*, 1998: 74–7).

Increasingly, makers and wearers of second hand kimono operate inside and outside of Japan. In 1992, the mother-daughter team Noriko and Kyoko Takasa opened their shop, Silk Road, in Tokyo (Jeffs, 1998: 12). According to an interview with Angela Jeffs, '[Noriko] knew foreigners in particular would love to wear lovely old fabrics in new ways.' That only 10 percent of Silk Road's clientele is Japanese suggests that some may harbor resistance to the practice of incorporating their national costume into what is commonly perceived as Western-style clothing, even though the Japanese adopted this mode of dress over a century ago. Some designers with shops in Japan expanded their marketing efforts to an eager consumer base in American and European cities. One designer reports that 'belts and bands made from kimono fabric are very popular in Paris. It's interesting to note the differences in taste between Europeans and Japanese' (Karino, 2002: 5).

Centers of production and consumption, no longer localized but global-ized, enable worldwide participation in ethnic cross-dressing. The supply of antique kimono still emanates from Japan, but increased market demand for second hand kimono radiates from a core of women born and bred outside of Japan's geographic borders. Until recently, those who validated the practice of recycling kimono by purchasing garments which incorporated antique Japanese fabrics into new designs were predominantly non-Japanese. Thus, the secondary market for kimono is indebted, at least in part, to an outsider's appreciation for its continued success. European and American women may be more apt to transgress the cultural code that defines and confines the traditional mode of wearing kimono. Recognizing the potential encased within the T-shaped garment, they physically alter its shape, and simultaneously its projected meaning.

The vogue for second hand kimono now resonates with younger Japanese women, generations removed from the days when kimono was more frequently worn. From a consumption perspective, groups of Japanese women unfamiliar with or uninhibited by the 'kimono code', possibly a result of generational distance, appear to be primary consumers of updated kimono fashions. As one reporter observes:

> Kimonos aren't just for New Year's Day anymore. Young women are starting to wear kimono – often secondhand ones – on other special occasions as well. But perhaps most interesting is the way the traditional dress is being incorporated into contemporary fashion. Pieces of old kimono are literally being used to create original, modern clothes and accessories that express a neo-Japanese spirit (Karino, 2002: 5).

The manager of the newly established store Tansu-ya, commented to Karino: 'Old kimonos buried in closets find new life in contemporary styles' (Karino, 2002: 5).

The Multiple Lives of Second Hand Silk Kimono

Clothes, pieced together from fragments of used silk kimono, embody an individual maker's creative impulses and the wearer's projection of a desired persona within a specific context. Tracing the social histories of three types of dress reproduced from second hand kimono exposes their divergent patterns of use and preservation. All began as T-shaped garments for use within Japan. Reused under distinct circumstances, clothing made from kimono fragments has served a variety of needs.

When viewed from the outside in/inside out, cycles of fashion within each of the three constructed categories become apparent. From the use of kimono within the private sphere as an inner garment under voluminous layers of robes in the Heian period to a more public role as outer garment by the sixteenth century, the corporeal shift views kimono in relation to the physical body. Fragments of outer garments, pieced together in graphic layouts, later returned to the private realm, most notably as sections of inner garments in the eighteenth through twentieth centuries.

The symbolic perspective tracks the movement of secular garments worn in the outside world to the sacred space of a temple where they were remade into ritual textiles. Eventually, many of these sacred cloths were secularized when they entered the antique market of the late nineteenth century as Buddhist temples came under increasing financial pressure and sold many of their treasures. Today, a select number of altar cloths have entered the protected storage spaces of museums (modern-day temples of culture). As the Japanese economy continues to stagnate, many precious textiles are resurfacing in the international art market. The object's function – as garment, *kesa*, art market commodity, museum object – and shape changes as they migrate across secular and sacred borders.

The transcultural viewpoint observes the migration of second hand kimono across the East-West divide. American designers have traveled within Japan to obtain materials and translated those fabrics into high-fashion items for sale outside of the cultural borders of their original production and use. In recent years, Japanese women have marketed designs remade from second hand kimono to domestic and international clients. With each shift, the kimono acquires new meaning for its makers and users.

Clothing remade from second hand silk kimono has been ignored by much of the scholarly community. In part, this is due to a bias of our own times; a cultural aversion to objects that are 'used', rather than brand new, or that exist in 'fragments', rather than as perfectly formed and whole. Traditional scholarly approaches divided by region, medium, period and discipline further obscure our vision of objects that exist in the interstices, thereby hampering the study of fragmented objects. Until these various forms of second hand kimono are recognized as a subject worthy of scholarly attention, these singular objects will remain buried in storage.

By defining three types of dress made from used Japanese fabric, this essay attempts to bring the study of second hand silk kimono out of the closet. The heated debate – among museum curators, fashion designers and the wider audience who value kimono – over whether a kimono's life should be spent as a museum object, as reinterpreted fashion, or as a memento of a former life remains unresolved. As kimono become rarer and possibly extinct in their primary use, the dynamic stories of their secondary function – as inner robes, ritual vestments and western-style garments – is crucial to mapping the larger, layered history of the makers and users of Japanese cloth.

5

Parcels from America: American Clothes in Ireland c.1930–1980

Hilary O'Kelly

Through much of the twentieth century people in Ireland talked about magical parcels arriving from America. Sent by emigrant Irish women, these parcels of unfamiliar clothes, represented a system of materially assisting rural Irish families, and of maintaining a physical and emotional bond between two worlds. The parcels were normally received as a domestic and social benefit to the family and were interpreted at home and in the wider community as a sign of financial success in America; but they could sometimes achieve a contrary effect. The parcel could on occasion create an unease in relationships while almost inevitably the expense involved in creating a parcel would further impoverish the already hard pressed emigrant.

Made possible with the introduction of parcel post in Ireland in 1883, these parcels not only crossed the Atlantic but crossed from one culture to a very different one, because until the middle of the twentieth century there was a dramatic difference between Ireland and America. But since the late 1950s and early 1960s American culture has become the central influence on Irish society. Because of the power of American culture and influence in Ireland Fintan O'Toole has argued that it is no longer only returned emigrants who experience a sense of loss and incomprehension at the fact that everything is different from the way it was remembered. He says that: 'nowadays in Ireland, we are all returned Yanks, tourists to our own country' (Haughey, 1996).

This view reflects my own experience. Although born in America I grew up in suburban Dublin in the 1960s and 1970s, in a family with a car, a television and a nearby shopping centre (the first in Ireland). All the children

I knew had a supply of shop-bought clothes supplemented by whatever some mothers made or knit for them. America did not seem so very strange or far away, but I loved hearing about a time when things were different. I loved hearing adults talking about parcels from America bringing big fancy dresses with slips and underskirts that would otherwise have been way beyond the reach of the purse and the parish of the country girls who got them (Fig. 14). I loved hearing how the dresses made occasions for these young women and made their dancing years. Later on different sorts of parcels aroused my interest and I became equally fascinated to realize that not everyone had such positive recollections of those parcels. Some were outraged, shamed and disappointed by their contents.

Those parcels with their industrially manufactured clothes, in man-made fabrics with bright colors, fancy patterns and zips made quite an impact in rural Ireland when in the 1930s, 1940s and 1950s, clothing sources were limited with most clothes being made by the local tailor or dressmaker, being homemade or hand knit. Occasional garments were bought in the local drapery or nearest town, and for very special occasions, like First Holy Communion, confirmation or weddings, people would go to the city. A small number of wealthy people might visit an exclusive couturiere, like Sybil Connolly, while the very poor could buy second hand clothes from country

Figure 14. The seven children of one Kerry family in May 1964 all wearing sweaters knit by their mother except for the youngest and eldest daughter (second left back row). This young woman, according to her older brother 'is wearing a dress which arrived in our house in an American parcel. The dress was made of chiffon and was a mixture of red, green and cream colours.'

fairs or street markets. The styles available from these sources followed mainstream fashions but avoided extremes of cut, color or decoration.

It was not until the 1960s that shops selling inexpensive mass-produced garments appeared in Ireland and even then they were confined to the main cities and it took time for their impact to reach rural Ireland. The clothing in parcels from America operated outside this system of manufacture and consumption, offering a chance of social and sartorial distinction otherwise impossible to a rural population. But equally often the clothes in the parcels, as the only clothes available to people with their own sense of position and identity, represented a personal challenge.

The parcels represented an influx of foreign goods into Ireland, they represented the material culture of one country being consumed in another and in that process taking on different meanings mediated by personal and cultural tastes. This research assesses how American clothes differed from those worn in Ireland and how they were integrated into the existing clothing pattern and attempts an understanding of the value and currency represented by these clothes. Individuals could be transformed, either for better of for worse by these parcels and the research therefore suggests that by embodying new experiences in a monocultural limited social environment, by creating rites of passage and by challenging ideas of etiquette and morality, the parcels from America helped shape the experience and imagination of Ireland in the middle of the twentieth century.

The parcels were a corollary of emigration by women, from a country poor in cash and commodities, to a country with a cash economy based on manufacture and consumption. This research focuses on the West Coast of Ireland and on the middle of the twentieth century for several reasons: firstly, because the study is motivated by oral history accounts from the 1930s, 1940s and 1950s and the research is built around that; secondly, the main sources used were written or collated between the 1940s and 1970s; and thirdly, because this seems to be when and where parcels were most prominent and made their greatest impact.

Background

From Ireland the journey to America took weeks and even months by ship so that the people at home could only imagine what world their relations had gone to. The basis of their imagining came from letters home and through news gleaned from returned 'Yanks'. But more abstract imaginings were inspired in other ways, through the dollars and the parcels that crossed the Atlantic Ocean.

At first a tremendous impression was made on Irish country people by the dollars sent home in letters. Unused to handling or even seeing large sums of money it gave truth to the image of America as a promised land, one as they used to say 'with gold and silver out on the ditches and nothing to do but to gather it'. The serious economic and social benefits of American dollars in Ireland in the late nineteenth and early twentieth century are well documented in history. What this research suggests is that the almost wholly undocumented parcel from America was also significant in creating the image of America as a land of plenty and a land of opportunity and also as a place of progress and modernity.

As a person's response to the parcel and the clothes it contained was obviously affected by gender, age and social and economic circumstances this research is largely organized in terms of how parcels were received by men, by women, by children and by the financially better and less well off. The first written source on the subject was the Department of Irish Folklore in University College Dublin, which houses reports from the 1940s on the subject of dress. It also houses research carried out in 1955 on the subject of emigration. Both of these reports comprise the written memories of hundreds of elderly people on the subjects of dress and emigration elicited in response to questionnaires from the Irish Folklore Commission. Neither questionnaire enquires specifically about the parcel but the respondents mention it or ideas relating to it. In response to my specific request for any information on the parcel several members of The Irish Countrywomens Association and their friends wrote up their memories. Interviews were carried out with retired Post Office workers and case studies made of three women from the West Coast of Ireland in Donegal, Cork and Galway. A further rich source emerged in memoirs and novels of twentieth-century Ireland, particularly the book *Nineteen Acres* by John Healy in which he records not only the story of his own Co. Mayo family but also that of so many small holders on the West of Ireland.

The parcel itself according to my correspondents was usually a big cardboard box up to three feet long by two feet deep and was a testament to expendable ease and excess in America. Emigrants could afford not only to purchase these clothes once, but then could pass them on and replace them. Sometimes the parcels contained little extras like tobacco or tea. But whatever it contained lots of people remember the parcels having a very special smell: 'Not mothballs, not perfume, but between the two, it was tangy'. The magic of the smell was probably bound up with the promise of the parcel as Mary, born in the 1940s, was very wistful when she told me: 'I'd love to get that smell again'.

The retired postmaster in Co. Kerry, remembers delivering the parcels on a pony and trap; there would be a big heap of them at Christmas time he said and there would be a tax to collect on them: 'One old fella used to get a parcel, usually with tobacco tucked into the folds of the clothes, but there was no tobacco this time so he refused to pay the tax and threw it all back at me'.[1] Clearly the goods had different value and importance for different people, despite the great effort, in terms of time and money, expended on the parcel by whoever sent it, this man appears to have learnt, perhaps from experience, that the clothes in parcels were valueless to him and it was only worth paying for what he could smoke.

Parcels and Gender

The parcels, more often than not, were sent by a female, usually an aunt or a sister in America. Irish female emigrants outnumbered males and the Irish women were generally unmarried and often their passage to America was paid for by a female relative already there. The fact that so many women emigrated and so many were unmarried may account for the prevalence of the American clothes parcel in Ireland.

The interweaving of issues of cloth and caring and of women's work with economic worth and family values is wonderfully outlined in a story recorded by John Healy about the emigration to America of his four aunts:

> The night before [the eldest] Mary went – as I would learn in Brooklyn many years later, Grandma had spent sewing ten sovereigns and fifteen pounds in paper money into the lining of her overcoat 'and always wear it until you get there, agradh'. And Mary had never left it off her, night or day, until she reached Brooklyn. A year after she arrived and was settled in a job as a kitchen maid, she made up her clothes parcel and sent it home. In the coat for Grandma, sewed as Grandma had sewed them, were the gold sovereigns, for, as she explained, 'Anna would want them when it was her turn to come'. The same gold sovereigns crossed and re-crossed the Atlantic four times and when the last had gone they came back to Castleduff to soften what hard times were in Ireland then (1978: 18).

In *The Culture of Fashion* Christopher Breward discusses the idea of the female role of providing and quotes Erica Uitz saying 'that until relatively recent times, the reputation of an honourable woman in western and central Europe depended to a large extent on whether she could provide her family and her home with textiles, clothes and other necessities' (1995: 29). This duty extended beyond the mother as primary carer. The word 'spinster' adequately communicates the importance of unmarried women in the process of producing cloth and clothing. In Ireland, the enduring image of the rural house is of women knitting and spinning, so it is not surprising then that young women who grew up in this system carried that familial duty with them even to America.

In 1957 John Healy went to Brooklyn to visit his aunts who, despite the distance remained an immediate part of his family. His Aunt Kit was a great source of parcels because she had a son he says: 'who was the one age with me. That meant when Junior had finished with a suit or shoes or shirts, they were packed into a parcel and sent to Nóra for the children' (Healy 1978: 62).

Since their departure in the 1930s the aunts had continued their commitment to easing the hard times in Ireland and John Healy had a rosy image of his Aunt Kit in a fine house in Brooklyn, only to discover in 1957 that she and Junior, lived up several flights of steps in a small flat. The easy life implied by the parcel belied its real origins. The parcels had been significant in John Healy's life but he felt ambivalent about them, he clearly felt a bit compromised by some of the arrivals that were too flashy for small town rural Ireland. He remarked that:

> Junior's two toned brogues might be big in the snazzier spots around uptown New York but in downtown Charlestown [Co. Mayo] in the 1940s it took a lot of courage to walk up Chapel Street in those chocolate brown and cream brogues. Similarly you looked a bit of a latchiko [impoverished fool], going to school in hand-me-down American knickerbockers but you had to admit grudgingly in cold weather they were a help (1978: 62).

This seems to be the enduring response, or at least the most recorded response by men to American clothes. Even recalling a much earlier time an old man in Mayo in 1955 reported that: 'Often now Yanks left suits of clothes at home to their brothers, and they would not like to wear them for best wear, you would hear them say this old Yankee suit' (Irish Folklore Collection [IFC], 1955: Vol. 1409, 149). And Mrs Douglas an 80-year-old from Donegal in the 1950s said that men would not put on the very different clothes from America 'in case they would be laughed at' (IFC, 1955: Vol. 1411, 54). Even if the men did not like to wear whole suits, they might try single garments like a hat, but as one Kerry man reported even then: 'You'd notice the difference, different peaked hats and hats with ear flaps, you'd say 'that was a parcel from America'.[2] The American clothes were 'marked' clothes and depending on your circumstances represented positive or negative connotations, and sometimes a mixture of both.

In Ireland communities were small and opportunities and aspirations were easily and closely monitored, it was therefore easy to feel alienated for better or worse from your peers when dressed in shop-bought garments form urban America. If the sender of the parcel were a recent emigrant, or close relative of the recipient, the disparity in taste and appropriateness may have been small. However as time passed circumstances on both sides changed and despite the best of intentions less appropriate garments may have been selected for the parcels.

In general women's memories of the parcel seem more positive than men's. It seems that distinguishing themselves in fancy clothes was a trial for Irish men. But for women the sort of magic that could be wrought with the clothes in a parcel is central to Maura Laverty's 1942 novel *Never No More* where the parcel is transformative in a very positive way. She writes:

> From the time Lizzie Doyle first went to America, she sent home a plentiful supply of clothes to her sister Maggie. Her mistress, it seems, was a carelessly generous woman and when she had tired of her clothes, which was often, she passed then on to Lizzie. Lizzie kept the best of them and sent the remainder home to Maggie. These American frocks did something to Maggie Doyle, always a good-looking girl … she became a raving beauty when she dressed herself in the gorgeous frocks that Lizzie sent home…
>
> It was an American frock that first made Denis Carroll take notice of Maggie. He overtook her one evening on his way home from the town. The elegance of the soft green, velvet frock she was wearing made him think she was some visitor, but when she said 'good evening to you Mr Denis', he recognised the soft little voice of Maggie Doyle. Still, he had to look twice before he could convince himself that this glowing creature was the quiet spoken girl who had lived all her life in the little cottage at the very gate of his home (quoted in IFC, 1955: Vol. 1408, 15).

Apart from the glamour the story of Lizzie and Maggie elucidates the notion that clothes were useful, and would fit and suit for somebody, which was central to the American parcel. Aunts and sisters in America, even if unmarried had access to hand-me-downs and to relatively inexpensive ready-made clothes. If they were married with families they had whatever their own children wore which should certainly do some of the, usually numerous, offspring of the siblings at home.

This was certainly the case with one of my case studies. Catherine grew up in the 1940s and 1950s, one of eight children on a remote farm in Donegal, with no cash income apart from that derived from the sale of about two dozen turkeys or geese at Christmas. They had very little in the way of things but always had food on the table and turf in the fire. Very regularly, certainly more than once a year a parcel would arrive from her grandaunts in America. Anything that came in that parcel was very much appreciated and used. With so many children whatever came fitted somebody and was passed on to the next one till it was well worn. But as well as clothes for house and farm use the parcels also contained good winter coats. They would all go off to mass 'dressed' in them and feel very proud. She says the family were regarded as very well dressed in these coats that they would never have had the money to buy. She says her family were not unusual – lots of people around were getting the parcels as well and those that weren't were sort of envious. Living on the hills among other small farmers she said they didn't feel better or worse than others just grateful and delighted.

Parcels and Class

But that, it seems, was not how everyone saw the situation. The parcels created a sense of community among some people but division among others. A girl from a wealthier background, Katherine Hurley from the smart address of Conlach House in Co. Galway records in 1940 that:

> Parents of the 'middle-class' tried but tried in vain to dress their children as became their social rank but their incomes would not permit them to do so. They had to economise, earn the money to purchase clothes for their daughters clothes – coats, frocks, costumes, scarf's, jumpers, blouses, gloves, boots and silk stockings – while the daughter of the working man and small farmer got her clothes 'second hand' from her aunts or sisters in America, and these second hand clothes excelled in cut and finish; thus home knitting, sewing and industry were killed. The daughter of a labourer drawing the 'dole', and an expense on the Rates, was smarter dressed than the daughter of the 'Large Farmer' who kept up the country. This has caused much discontent in the 'farmer's home' (IFC, Vol. 756, 253–4).

Though Katherine Hurley describes herself as 'middle-class', Tony Farmar has discussed how: 'Many citizens took the view that a class system did not exist in the new Irish state, there was only "two-pence ha'penny looking down on two pence", no doubt compared to the systematic elaboration of the British class system, the Irish version is meagre and un-worked out but it has never been non-existent' (Farmar, 1991: 2). In a society highly conscious of social, religious and economic conformity, sartorial distinction was deeply felt. The divisivness, as well as the pettiness and lack of clarity in social and sartorial distinction, is captured in Katherine Hurley's summary: 'I must work so hard to earn money to pay rates to keep up men on the dole, while their daughters attend technical schools, dance halls, dress in stylish clothes they receive from their friends in America and laugh at me in my working attire'.

The experience of Mary, a little girl in Co. Cork is another case study and represents the story of these less well-off children. Born in 1948, Mary was the middle daughter on a small farm in West Cork. She said that: 'Without my Auntie in America we'd have been very poor, there's no point in saying otherwise'. Just about every stitch they wore came from America. She never remembers going clothes shopping as a child. Twice a year her auntie (who is pictured in Fig. 15 on a visit home) would write to say to expect a parcel. Living by the sea they could see the ships passing into Cork harbour and hope their parcel was on it. They would 'come flying home everyday to see if the parcel had arrived'. When it did there was huge excitement to find all the clothes, as Mary described them, with lots of lace and big bows. The dresses also often had half slips which was a great bonus making them both warmer and more special.

Mary says there were never shoes or socks in the parcels and she didn't always have shoes. She well remembers one hot summer when she had a gorgeous dress but had to wear it to Mass three Sundays in a row with a pair of wellingtons. Clearly the clothes did not always fit seamlessly into the existing wardrobes and such obvious discrepancies in an overall outfit would clearly 'mark' the better garment as a hand-me-down.

She says most of her neighbours got clothes from someone in America, usually an older brother or sister or aunt or uncle. She remembers that lots of the children in her class wore 'checky things' [plaids] you'd know were American and also brightly coloured clothes with huge collars and zips.

Figure 15. Mary, in pale dress and bow, with her cousin in plaid dress with zip, both garments arrived in a parcel from America sent by Aunt (far right) pictured here with her husband, beside their hired car, on a visit home to West Cork in 1951.

People were familiar with what was available locally and the design of these garments clearly marked them as, in this case, a welcome parcel from America.

But not all children's memories are wholly positive. One of my correspondents Kay was given a pair of red shoes by a neighbor, which she loved and wore to school in the mid 1950s. Her mother told her to say that she had bought them presumably to avoid any implication of charity. However when she did so the neighbor's daughter said, 'No that is not true, they came from America and my mother gave them to her for nothing'.[3] Poor Kay was mortified to be caught lying and to be caught trying to appear what might be described as 'better than she was'.

Parcels and Value

This practice of giving away the unsuitable or ill-fitting clothes that came from America is as old as the parcels themselves and it is an important aspect of them that their benefits were willingly passed on. The clothes came as part fulfillment of female filial duty and as quite a personal way of being remembered and representing yourself 'at home'. The clothes staked a claim on close ties and had more significant exchange value among kinspeople than they had realisable cash value.

In fact, the community in Buncrana, Co. Donegal were quite shocked when one woman would cycle into town to sell what she got in the parcels. Her parcels apparently came from a niece and the clothes were inappropriate for a country woman of her years.[4] Catherine, from a different part of Donegal, said no one would do that. By which she meant no one with any sense of things – she actually remembers a woman who did – but of whom she'd expect no better. Even if you could do nothing with the clothes you wouldn't think of selling them. These clothes were never intended as economic commodities. They were not even treated as formal gifts, they represented an extension of familial devotion and duty and were therefore given from person to person.

A primary value of the clothes was in their function of covering the family decently. As a child Catherine felt her family was grateful for whatever came in a parcel for children. But as an adult and perhaps a little better off in the 1960s and 1970s, a greater nicety of judgment was exercised in relation to the often new clothes sent to herself and her new generation of children. Several garments arrived that she said she just would not wear: 'It was the colours' was her first comment and the one repeated most often and by most people. They were so loud. Strong colors were not normal and therefore unacceptable in rural Ireland. She said well that you'd wear most things around the farm: 'Because you get through a lot of clothes on a farm. But you wouldn't go out in a whole lot of them'. One surviving dress was never worn because she said: 'Sure you wouldn't wear it and the no sleeves. You'd wear a wee sleeve but not none'. A distaste for sleevelessness may have been influenced by the Roman Catholic Church which requires women to cover their shoulders entering a church, and until the 1960s Church and secular notions of modesty and morality were intertwined in Ireland.

While until the middle of the twentieth century almost everybody appreciated the economic and use value of the clothes, their cultural value was less certain. Clothes embodying different social and cultural values and aspirations arrived in the parcels to be embraced by some and rejected by others. And even though the garments may have been, as they regularly were, altered or even latterly discarded, their presence in the family home, sent by respected relations, must have pricked if not directly challenged, people's long established social and moral codes.

By the late 1950s and early 1960s many of the circumstances central to the value system of the parcels were changing. Ireland was becoming a little better off, the differences between Ireland and America were slowly declining and the nature of fashion itself was changing. The emergence of a youth culture, an increased color palette and new synthetic fabrics all made a significant impact. With these changes occurring earlier in America the potential came for even more discordance between the sender and the recipient of the parcel perhaps articulated by a correspondent, Bea in Galway, who wrote of the 1950s and 1960s.

> Most of the clothes my mother would have felt were unsuitable, especially the clothes that were intended for her. They would be of flimsy and light material and I'm sure she would have probably considered them immodest as the dresses I remember would be transparent with matching slips. If nothing else she considered you would get your death of cold in them. She had great theories on the fact that Americans all wore fur coats and lived in centrally heated houses.[5]

In this instance the parcel appears to have acted less as a link between distant family members and more as the embodiment of a social and circumstantial distance between them.

The adults appear to have exercised far greater sensitivity to what was suitable for their own attire than they did for children. The essential quality in children's clothes was apparently serviceability rather than style or design. While the children may have been sensitive to detail the parent's attitude was 'Sure who'll be looking at you?' The children's garment most often received from America, even by children who never got anything else, was the Holy Communion dress. It came to many girls in different shapes and was sometimes disappointing being too big, too small or having only short sleeves. But whatever the dress was like it had to be worn. Apart from a blue Holy Communion dress Catherine's daughter received flowered corduroy flares that she adored. However her brother to whom they were passed on hated them. For a boy In 1980 they were not the thing. Even though he was told he only had to wear them around the very remote farm he managed to get the flares caught in the bicycle chain and then finished them off by tearing them.[6] No boy in Ireland wore flowery clothes in 1980 and it was deeply offensive to wear a garment doubly marked as female, once by a flowery design and twice by having delighted his sister to wear.

Sometimes the value of the clothes lay in their domestic necessity but sometimes the value lay in the expression of family duty and family sensitivity. For example, Catherine's late husband, like most grown men was probably happy to receive fewer clothes in these checked, striped and synthetic parcels. He got little apart from some nice shirts and ties. However he did get one pair of synthetic trousers with a pattern of decorated diamonds on them. He would never have worn them except once when the relations who sent them were visiting. He put on the trousers going to visit his sister – just into the car and out again and no one outside the family would have seen them.

If we take an overview then of this sartorial practice we see that in the process of parcelling up clothes in America and sending them to Ireland, the value that is intended by the sender is not necessarily that perceived or experienced by the recipient. In the first instance the value of the clothes was in helping the emigrants assimilate into a new culture – to fit in – when sent back to Ireland their value was social and functional and helped distinguish the family as 'doing well' in America.

Looking special may have been a bonus for women and for children but not, it seems, for most men in 'this old Yankee suit'. Looking special for women, could easily translate into looking bold or brash in Ireland; a sleeveless or see-through dress was immodest and therefore unwearable. One correspondent, Margaret, remembers gorgeous dresses in the late 1950s and early 1960s. But the parcels she got also brought gaudy jewelry and very red lipstick, which she was not allowed to wear. In fact, she says, her father got great value from it both pragmatically and in pointing a moral for his daughters; he used the lipstick to mark the pigs going to the market.

Another parcel represented a threat to parents while it thrilled their daughter Frances from Galway (who emigrated in 1955). She had 'a passion to leave Ireland' partly because a favourite sister was there before her and partly fuelled by the clothes an aunt and uncle used to send home from Boston. In this case the clothes act as what could be termed 'material imaginings': trips into a possible future and distant world. She remembers: 'And I always loved the smell of that box. The excitement when a box would come from America. I remember hunter-green pants. I was dying to wear slacks and it wasn't allowed. I used to put them on in my bedroom, but I would never come out of the bedroom, because my parents would kill me' (O'Carroll, 1990: 75). The imaginative value of these parcels was felt by women in Ireland in the earlier twentieth century, for whom the options other than marriage or the convent, were to go to work in towns or to emigrate.

Conclusion

The system of consumption of these parcels from America is forged by values specific to the participants. While it does relate to a fashion system and to monetary value it equally relies on the concept of use-value and exchange value.

The recontextualized clothing acted in a complex role as a material manifestation of the sender and their goodwill and economic success. It acted as a material presence of the departed Irish person in a community often small enough to remember them specifically. For the recipient the cloth, color and pattern of the clothes as well as their cut and decoration are all design elements that signaled their difference and marked them as parcels from America, the only alternative source of clothing available to the rural West Coast of Ireland. To some they were a delight and even a proud display of the success of relatives in America whose continued connection with the family could blur the exact social status of those at home. If the clothes were sometimes embarrassing – a reverse familial duty was exercised. And the loud, brash or flashy clothes were worn generously in covert collusion with the aspirations of the visiting donor, but in the fervent hope of avoiding the gaze of the locals. To some people the clothes in parcels were to be avoided either as alienating or as a sign of an element of want at home.

In conclusion then, what this research suggests is that American clothes in Ireland were very different and could both thrill and embarrass people; that American parcels were an essential part of the twentieth-century Irish rural experience and that their impact went beyond the central job of dressing people. The American parcel was about economy and utility but it was also about memories and dreams. The American clothes in Ireland created a deep memory link between the emigrant and their family at home. And to those at home the American clothes created a deep imaginative bond with their source. The research also suggests that as emigration has had the greatest social and economic impact on Ireland in the twentieth century, that the parcel, like the dollar, was significant in shaping the imagining of a better future and helping assuage the fears of reluctant emigrants in relation to their, often inevitable, passage to *an t-Oiléan Ur* – The Golden Island. As was so often said, sure: 'America must be a grand place and the fine clothes that come out of it'.

Notes

1. In discussion with Nuala Fenton, Co. Kerry, June 2000.
2. In discussion with Nuala Fenton, Co. Kerry, June 2000.
3. Correspondence from Irish Countrywomen's Association (ICA) June 26, 2000.
4. With thanks to Mrs Mary Coyle, Buncrana for this information.
5. Correspondence with ICA, Barna, Co. Galway, June 2000.
6. In discussion with the author, June 7, 2000.

Part 2

Trading Cultures

Introduction

Hazel Clark and Alexandra Palmer

The trade in used clothing is far from new, as both Frick and Lemire have indicated in earlier chapters, but by the end of the twentieth century it was international and complex. Each of the chapters in this section adds to our knowledge and understanding of the global dimensions of the contemporary trade in second hand clothes. The authors' research in Africa, India, the Philippines and Hong Kong respectively present individual cases, which resonate with one another on a number of levels, not least in each being former colonies. The historical trade in cloth and garments between Asia and Africa and the West is well documented (Hansen, *passim*; Martin & Koda, 1994). In this section we discover contemporary forms of the trade which challenge the conventional Orientalist discourse of the West dominating the 'other' (Said, 1978). Scrutiny reveals that second hand clothing markets in Africa and the Philippines are not mere dumping grounds for the West's discarded garments. As Hansen states in her chapter 'the specific meaning of this consumption depends on the context of interaction and the economic and cultural politics of its time'. Each chapter reveals ways in which the used garment has become a global commodity capable of facilitating metanarratives of modernity and of constructing complex meanings between subject and object. For the post-colonial subject western clothing became an appealing and increasingly available means of 'becoming modern'. As colonizers and therefore role models, Western countries represented modernity and progress. The places discussed in this section were still affected at the time of discussion by their former colonial dependency, economically and culturally.

Despite its long history, the economic power and global scope of the trade in used clothing increased in the early 1990s in the wake of the liberalization of many Third World economies and following the sudden rise in demand from former Eastern Bloc countries, as Hansen notes. While clothing was exported from the West and Westernized countries to Zambia or the

Philippines, India was transforming used clothes for export to the West. Hong Kong by contrast was an advanced city importing fashionable items previously worn in developed countries. But whatever the point of origin and the geographical direction of the export, the commonality is that used clothing must be transformed to be recommodified. This transformation could be literal, by original garments being unpicked or cut up and remade, as Norris describes with the sari, or by cleaning and repair. But also and of greater complexity and interest, a transformation in meaning occurs to facilitate a second life, as each chapter makes evident.

The export of used clothing from the First World to the Second or Third Worlds is not simply a representation of the dying breath of colonialism. Norris notes how Michael Thompson's (1979) 'rubbish theory' is based on the premise that for objects to move from the transient category of depreciating value to the durable category of accumulating value, they must pass through the covert category of 'rubbish' to enable their value to be radically reassigned. Each author emphasizes how such a transformation must take place in order for used clothes to become acceptable in another cultural context. The meanings of commodities are not fixed and new meanings are assigned relative to the consumer, not inherent in the process of production. Milgram reiterates this point in citing Spooner's (1986) 'lore of the dealer' where the provenance of goods relates to their point of entering the trade, rather than to the moment of production. In the Philippines the role of narrative is highlighted as an unfolding process in the remaking of meanings. In Hong Kong the meanings of used clothing are made very much with reference to the international fashion system and in the context of a post-colonial search for identity.

In these chapters the consumer is presented as having an active role. Buying and wearing second hand successfully means having what Hansen refers to as 'clothing competence', or the knowledge to put disparate items together with confidence. She points out how the women in her study gain the 'competence', necessary in any fashion context, through their consumption of used, not new clothes. Here the distinction between buying new and used clothes becomes evident. Choices made in relation to new clothes are usually controlled by the current fashion 'look' as defined within the fashion system and realized by the availability of fresh goods in the retail market. Second hand clothing requires greater interpretation and creativity be it by the importer or by the individual consumer. Hansen interprets this as a reactivation of unwanted clothes on local terms. Clothes have their meanings recrafted as Norris explains in the construction of culturally specific logic and personal narratives. Interpersonal connections at various stages of the exchange process have a determining effect. In each of the chapters the gendered nature of the trade is implicit. At the local level women dominate both as traders and as consumers. In the Philippines the *ukay ukay* trade has provided women with original livelihoods and similarly in India, although as Norris notes the *bartanwale*, used clothing dealers, hold lower roles in the retail pecking order than men. At the point of retail it is most usually women who are involved in selling used clothes to other women.

In the places discussed the trade and interest in second hand clothing is set against an urban backdrop. The city is not just a place where items are sold, but it provides the context that gives second hand clothes their contemporary appeal. City life is central both to the learning of new consumer practices and to the pursuit of modernity. Hansen's observation that clothing consumption in Zambia goes to the heart of local experiences of modernity and development is echoed in the other chapters. Second hand clothing from the West has enabled city dwellers elsewhere to dress well in quality garments with an eye to fashion. The relationship between fashion, modernity and the city continued to underpin the trade in second hand clothes in the 1990s. While the sartorial dominance of the West remained evident in the traded items, it was simultaneously challenged by the fact that new meanings were inscribed as part of the second life of the clothes. The trade is predicated on foreignness and difference enhancing allure, but it is not monodirectional. Western clothes continue to appeal in the post-colonial context, but equally the Orientalist discourse is reified and commodified in the import of clothing and textiles from India to the west, transformed in form and in meaning as the exoticized other. The city was both influence and influenced, adopting as it did, with the retail of second hand clothing, methods of exchange and sale more common to the premodern period. Even in sophisticated Hong Kong the informality and social nature of second hand clothing sales held in hotel ballrooms had as much in common with the markets of Lusaka and Banuae as with the upmarket designer label shops in the territory's shopping malls. Rummaging, known in the Bemba language in Zambia as *salaula*, the thrill of the chase, the search for the 'find' was the 'hands on' aspect that characterized the trade at a variety of levels, in the city and in the country, locally and globally.

This section, while dealing with specific examples, indicates the importance of second hand clothes in the construction of a modern personal appearance and challenges any perceived domination of the West in this process. What is revealed is evidence of second hand clothing assuming a global scale both economically and culturally, while contributing to the construction of fashion identities at the local level. The received meanings of old clothes are challenged in order that new meanings can be constructed.

6

Crafting Appearances: The Second Hand Clothing Trade and Dress Practices in Zambia

Karen Tranberg Hansen

Many American and European travelers who have ventured into African cities in recent years have taken notice of the vibrant markets in second hand clothing. The displays of a vast volume of clothing and the piles of T-shirts emblazoned with easily recognizable brand names, logos and inscriptions have struck many visitors as thoroughly familiar. Such recognition has reinforced the impression that second hand clothing markets are dumping grounds for the West's discarded garments. Non-local observers have paid passing attention, if any, to what people wear, attributing the dress practices of such markets as a faded and worn imitation of the West.

Seeing only the West in the piles of second hand clothing in markets in Africa effectively forecloses any further inquiry into how African consumers deal with the imported second hand clothes that they so eagerly have been purchasing in several countries. The specific meaning of this consumption depends on the context of interaction and the economic and cultural politics of its time. I have examined this process in detail and from many angles in Zambia (Hansen, 2000b). Once wholesalers place second hand clothing bales for sale at the end of the import chain in Zambia as *salaula*, the West's cast-off clothing has been reconstructed into a desirable commodity. Translated from the Bemba language, *salaula* means 'selecting from a bale in the manner of rummaging'. In effect, the term *salaula* names how people deal with clothing, selecting and choosing garments to suit both their clothing needs and desires.

To be sure, there is much more to this import than meets the eye as an undifferentiated pile of second hand clothing. This chapter showcases segmentation and differentiation in Zambia's second hand clothing market both in terms of spatial location and consumer demand. After providing a brief background about the international trade and the processes through which used clothing exports reach places like Zambia, I sketch some whole-sale, retail and distribution arrangements that link segments of this trade across the country. I then describe how the West's cast-off clothing is trans-formed into new garments on its journey from the textile recycler's ware-house to the retail space in Zambia and onward through dress practices, in how, when and where the body is put together with clothing. In conclusion I return to the challenge to explain the international second hand clothing trade in specific, locally informed terms. In the case of Zambia, this trade offers rich evidence of traders and consumers working actively at giving new lives to the West's used garments, in the process making *salaula* into their own creation.

The Second Hand Clothing Trade

In much of the West today, shopping for second hand clothes has become a pastime rather than a need. Fashion conscious shoppers, both young and old, female and male, turn to the used clothing racks for vintage or retro looks. Charity shops offer a retail space for experimentation with the unknown, the imagined (Gregson, Brooks & Crewe, 2000). Across North America and Europe, second hand clothing makes up niche or fringe markets for con-sumers who are on the lookout for very specific garments. There is a vigorous resale market for designer clothes in stores that rarely feature words like 'used' and 'thrift' in their names. Established fashion houses intermittently feature vintage styles on the runway. And for those who wonder about how to wear vintage clothing with panache, a recent book 'takes the mystery out of buying, wearing, and caring for vintage clothes' (Dubin & Berman, 2001).[1] These processes have caught the attention of scholars whose chief concerns with second hand clothing have been with the up-scale aspect or the creation of alternative lifestyles (McRobbie, 1989).

In many Third World countries, second hand clothing is both desired and needed today. Vintage style on the fashion runway is merely one twist, though a glamorous one, in a rapidly expanding global trade that on the one hand grosses exporters of second hand clothing millions of dollars and on the other, fulfills clothing needs and desires in many Third World countries. There is little substantive work on the other end of this connection: the incorporation of the West's used clothing into clothing practices in the Third World. And there is hardly any scholarly work at all on the needy and thrifty dimensions of practices involving used clothing, that is to say, its charitable guise (Hansen, 2000b: 100–26).

In the West today, the second hand clothing trade both in domestic and foreign markets is dominated by non-profit charitable organizations and private textile recycling/grading firms, often family owned. Its financial side has largely eluded public scrutiny. Thriving by an ethic of giving, the major charitable organizations look like patrons in a worldwide clothing donation project. Growing environmental concerns in the West in recent years have enhanced both the profitability and respectability of this trade, giving its practitioners a new cachet as textile salvagers and waste recyclers.

The charitable organizations are the largest single source of the garments that fuel the international trade in second hand clothing. These organizations routinely sell a large proportion of their donated clothing, between 40 and 75 percent, depending on whom you talk to. The textile recyclers/graders purchase used clothing in bulk from the enormous yield gathered by the charitable organizations, and they also buy surplus clothing from resale stores. The textile recycling business is very lucrative because every piece of used clothing has many potential future lives. Clothes are transformed, for instance, into filler in roofing felts, loudspeaker cones, car dashboards, panel lining; some end up as flock for mattresses, car seating or insulation; or as wiper rags for industrial use.

The bulk of the clothing that has been sourced in this way is destined for new lives in the second hand clothing export market which yields more profit than the rag and fiber trade. At their warehouses/sorting plants, the clothing recyclers sort clothing by garment types, fabric and quality before compressing them into bales. The standard weight is 50 kilograms yet some firms compress bales of much larger weight, usually unsorted. The bottom quality goes to Africa, and medium quality to Latin America, while Japan receives a large portion of top-quality items, among which brand-name denim jeans and sneakers are in popular demand (Mead, 2002).

Although the second hand clothing trade has a long history, its economic power and global scope were never as vast as they have been since the early 1990s in the wake of the liberalization of many Third World economies and following the sudden rise in demand from former Eastern Bloc countries. Worldwide between 1980 and 1997, the trade grew more than eightfold (from a value of US$207 million to US$1,693 million (United Nations, 1996: 60; 1999: 60). The United States is the world's largest exporter in terms of both volume and value, followed in 1998 by Germany, the United Kingdom, the Netherlands, Belgium-Luxembourg and Italy (United Nations, 1999: 60). United States worldwide exports more than doubled between 1990 and 1997 (from a value of US$174 million to US$390 million (United Nations, 1996: 60; 1999: 60).[2]

The countries of sub-Saharan Africa are the world's largest second hand clothing destination, receiving close to one fourth of total world exports in 1995 and one third in 1998 (United Nations, 1996: 60; 1999: 60). The export has grown in spurts, particularly during post-war periods when surplus army clothing flooded the market. The substantive increase of the African second hand clothing export market occurred after World War Two. General economic growth and increased welfare both in Europe and the United States and the mass production of affordable garments and apparel created a vast surplus of still wearable clothing. At the same time, rapid socioeconomic changes across much of the African continent made more and more people enter the clothing market as consumers.

Zambia: Preoccupations with Dress

From the early colonial days in Northern Rhodesia – as Zambia was called then – men and women eagerly appropriated Western-styled clothing as local dress. City life was central both to the learning of new consumer practices and to their pursuit. Clothing and apparel were among the first items on which urban workers spent their wages, and they comprised a major portion of the goods returning migrants brought home. That is to say that clothing consumption in Zambia goes to the heart of local experiences of modernity and development, depending on the discourse invoked. Past and present, people in Zambia have been eager to cut a fine figure, a desire which an increasing proportion of the population has been fulfilling by purchasing second hand clothing.

Zambia's second hand clothing trade dates back to the colonial period when imported used clothing reached Northern Rhodesia from across the border with the Belgian Congo, now the Democratic Republic of Congo. During the first decades after independence in 1964, direct importation of this commodity was prohibited, yet smuggling did take place from the Congo. When restrictive import and foreign exchange regulations were relaxed in the mid to late 1980s, the second hand clothing trade grew rapidly. The name *salaula* came into use at that time.

Zambia is classified in United Nations terms as one of the world's 'least developed countries'. Elections in 1991 replaced a 19-year-old one-party regime with a multi-party government set on liberalizing the economy and following structural adjustment policies advanced by the International Monetary Fund and the World Bank in order to improve the livelihoods of the country's population of nearly eight million. Approximately half live in cities (Hansen, 1997). The manufacturing sector had all but collapsed, including the textile and garment industry. Retrenchment in the public and private sector and wage freezes have been accompanied by a decline in the provision of health and education. The gap between poverty and wealth has increased while rural-urban disparities in standard of living have narrowed. Given the decline in purchasing power, the significance of second hand clothing is not surprising. Yet the enormous crossover appeal of this commodity can be explained not merely in terms of its affordability but above all by reference to the importance people in Zambia attribute to dressing and dressing well.

The preoccupation with the dressed body involves an aesthetic sensibility that brings discerning skills from a variety of sources to bear on creating an overall look that mediates experiences of pride and well-being. I have called this skill *clothing competence*, and I discuss it in detail in a later section of this chapter. In Zambia, dressing, and dressing up, is both an end and a means. Crafting oneself through dress provides that space between the performed and the desired that we may term fashion even for the case of second hand dress. Joanne Finkelstein whom I am paraphrasing for this constructive insight acknowledges that our first inclination is to think of fashion as instantaneous and volatile, that is, really fleeting and evanescent. Yet she argues 'the constancy of circulation, whether in ideas or material goods, indicates that the actual function of fashion is to give the appearance of change and novelty without actually precipitating any ruptures of the status quo' (1998: 5–6).

Wholesale, Retail and Distribution

Wholesalers in Zambia import second hand clothing from textile salvage dealers in the United Sates, Canada, and several countries in Europe. Among the wholesalers are long established trading firms with Indian family backgrounds, some Lebanese enterprises with commercial experiences from elsewhere in Africa, and a shifting number of local African-owned firms. The second hand clothing consignments arrive by container ships in the ports of Dar es Salaam in Tanzania, Durban in South Africa and Beira in Mozambique, from where they are trucked to wholesalers' warehouses. Lusaka is the hub of the *salaula* wholesale trade. One large firm has its headquarters in Chipata, a provincial headquarters on the border with Malawi. At the warehouse, marketeers, vendors, private individuals purchase bales of *salaula*. They in turn distribute and sell their goods in urban and rural markets, hawk them in the countryside, and transfer them in rural exchanges.

By the beginning of the 1990s the salaula sections of outdoor markets in both urban and rural areas had grown much larger than the food sections. In the mid 1990s the retail of *salaula* in cities and towns had spread from market places into urban high-income neighborhoods and downtown offices, and it had spilled out onto main streets. Today, *salaula* is available in most corners of the country brought out from Lusaka, Chipata or the Copperbelt by small-scale entrepreneurs or traders' hired hands who travel, for instance to commercial farms and other rural sites such as game parks and tourist lodges, where they sell their goods to workers on payday, and into the countryside where they exchange second hand clothing for agricultural produce, goats, chickens and fish.

Lusaka's Second Hand Clothing Markets

Zambia's geography of *salaula* retailing contains several distinct segments both in terms of retailing space and of customer appeal that are most evident in the capital city of Lusaka. When the second hand clothing trade began expanding in the late 1980s, Lusaka's second hand clothing retail scene shifted. Before that, township markets used to have a few second hand clothing traders who sourced garments at the door of expatriate households or had connections to people who brought used clothing to the capital from Zaire. During the mid to late 1980s Zairean traders began to bring bales into Kamwala, the oldest built-up market in the capital, and the first direct importers appeared on the scene. Imports grew rapidly in the early 1990s when all township and city markets included expanding *salaula* sections.

Salaula retail space is mapped out in changing cultural terms that testify to the troubled relationship between traders' and urban authorities. City and township markets have both inside and outside sections, the inside sections consisting of built-up stalls with roofs while the outside sections merely have demarcations on the ground. Open-air traders initially displayed their merchandise right on the ground, gradually building up their stalls. In the early 1990s, Soweto market had Lusaka's largest open-air section. This particular market had developed as a center of produce trade for farmers in the late 1970s on privately owned land. It was named after Soweto township in Johannesburg where the African population had been relegated to the periphery of town, far away from services and amenities.

Soweto market soon featured Lusaka's largest auto-part section as well as small-scale manufacture, repair and services. Traders called the large *salaula* section that arose on the bare ground around Soweto market Kambilombilo. The name stems from a rural resettlement scheme established on the

Copperbelt during the 1980s with the aim of turning unemployed urban youth into good farmers. The special meaning of the term derives from the fact that the youth who were brought there were left without any provision of services. The term Kambilombilo is used elsewhere for outside sections of markets, where traders are left to their own devices. At Kambilombilo, there is no infrastructure to speak of and no amenities.

Toward the end of 1994, traders in Soweto's outside *salaula* section and part of the built-up interior market were relocated to make space for the construction of a new city market. Some went out on the open field, establishing stands underneath tall pylons with power cables. Others moved to Kamwala market, where space became at a premium; many set themselves up upon the open field outside the built-up market next to the railway tracks. They called this section Gabon, a designation that is used in other open-air markets. The connotation is to perish in a disaster, like the Zambia National Football team who died in a plane crash after a match in Gabon in 1993.

As the *salaula* sections outside Lusaka's main markets expanded, traders spilled onto sidewalks and into main streets in the downtown area. The 1997 formal opening of the new City Market did not halt these developments. Complaining about high fees and lack of customers, vendors left their stands within the new market for the street. The new market did not fill up until 1999 when the city council supported by paramilitary and police demolished the street vendors' temporary stands in cities and towns across the country. An uneasy truce has prevailed between vendors and authorities since then, with vendors venturing out on the streets around rush hour and at night time. The effort to make street vendors return to established markets has caused unbelievable crowding and congestion at Kamwala and Soweto markets.

Although the new City Market has a *salaula* section, many stand-holders inside the new market also have outside stalls. Lusaka's main *salaula* section today is outside Soweto market under the power lines. On first sight, this vast *salaula* market meets the non-local observer's eye as a chaotic mass of second hand clothing hung up on flimsy wood contraptions, displayed on tables or dumped in piles on the ground. That view is deceptive. A variety of informal rules organize vending space and structure sales practices.

Both vendors and customers know these practices. A prospective customer looking for a specific garment will go to a particular part of the market. The vendors of men's suits, for example, one of the most expensive items in the *salaula* markets, tend to be located in a part of the outdoor market that is near to major thoroughfares such as a main road passable by automobiles. So are vendors of other high demand garments, such as women's skirts and

Figure 16. Second hand shoe vendors in Kabwe, 1993.
Photograph by Karen Tranberg Hansen.

blouses, and the best selling item of all, baby clothes. There are clusters of vendors selling shoes and, during the winter in the southern hemisphere, cold weather clothing (Fig. 16). These demarcations are not static as vendors sometimes change inventory.

The display on most second hand clothing stands is carefully designed. High-quality items are hung on clothes hangers on the makeshift walls. A clothes line or a wood stand may display a row of cotton dresses. Everything that meets the eye has been carefully selected with a view both to presentation and sales strategy. Sales are accompanied by lively discussions and price negotiations. The piles on the ground include damaged items and garments that have been around for a while without being sold. Such items are sold 'on order', that is, several pieces at a discount, and they are often purchased by rural customers who plan to resell in the villages (Fig. 17).

Near the high end of the *salaula* repertoire, and near the major roads of the market section cluster the 'boutiques'. Boutiques in the *salaula* markets sell specially pre-selected items, coordinated to form matched outfits that are stylish. Such stands tend to be operated by young vendors who 'pick', in the language of the market. Once other traders open bales, the pickers descend on them, selecting choice garments they buy on the spot. Then they

Figure 17. Scrutinizing *salaula*, Kabwe, 1993.
Photograph by Karen Tranberg Hansen.

make up, for instance, women's two-piece ensembles, men's suits and leisure wear. Most of the boutique operators I met were young men who were very skilled at choosing their stock with a fine eye for what might sell, a great sense of style, and a flair for making stunning combinations. Yet I also met boutique operators who were women. Some of them had tailoring skills and they sewed clothing to order from their own homes.

Transforming Value

Sorting and compressing second hand clothing into bales in the European or North American textile recycler's warehouse strip used garments of their prior social life (Appadurai, 1986). The value Zambian consumers attribute to salaula is created through a process of recommodification that involves several phases (Kopytoff, 1986). Transactions between overseas suppliers and local importers initiate the process through which the decommissioned value of the West's unwanted but still wearable clothing is reactivated on local terms. Through subsequent transformations the meanings shift in ways that help to redefine used clothes into 'new' garments. These transformations begin in communications between exporters and importers and in on-site visits, continue at the wholesale outlet and in public markets, and they are made public in how consumers put themselves together with *salaula*. In addition to processes through which the register of meaning of clothes shifts, there are also physical and material changes involving alteration, mending and recycling.

The sorting and grading of second hand clothing prior to export is guided not only by the West's garment distinctions but also by specifications from the importer's end in Zambia. When ordering consignments, the big wholesalers reckon with changing cultural and seasonal demand that place a local mark on the clothing universe. These local marks are the seasonally varying terms for what sells, when and where, and the culturally shifting terms for what is proper dress. Style designations influence the local marks as well as fabric and what is considered to be 'the latest', is reviewed just in the same manner as would be done in any other market globally.

Once imported bales of second hand clothing have been stacked in the warehouse and customers specify the type of bale they want to purchase, the transformation process continues. Customers assess their non-returnable bales with exacting care before completing a purchase. They scrutinize the plastic wrap and inspect the straps to determine that the bale has not been tampered with. Wholesalers who import bales larger than the standard weight sometimes open, sort and rebale items. Some importers are said to remove choice items, and clothing pre-sorted in this way is rumored to end up in formal stores. The purpose of the customer's scrutiny in the warehouse is to ascertain that the bale has arrived 'fresh' from its Western source, untouched by dealer interference, thus offering a range of 'new' items.

A variety of practices pertaining to the retail of salaula continue the transformation of the West's used clothing into 'new' objects. The process of redefinition hinges on the meaning of the term *salaula*: selecting from a pile in the manner of rummaging. Practices that express this are evident, for example, on 'opening day', when a bale of bulk garments is cut open for retail and its contents are counted and individualized into distinct objects of exchange that are assessed for quality and price. At this moment, when the clothes are ready to enter into another cycle of consumption, it is important that they have not been meddled with. Both traders and customers prefer to open bales publicly. A bale that is opened in the market in full view is considered to contain 'new' garments. If it were opened privately at home, a trader might put aside choice items, causing customers to suspect that they are being presented with a second cut and not 'new' clothing.

The desire for 'newness' is particularly evident in the boutique section of the *salaula* markets where traders piece together outfits from garments they carefully select when bales are opened. When I began this research in 1992, boutique vendors in Lusaka displayed their clothes laundered, ironed and neatly pressed. But in recent years, clothes in the boutique sections have been hung up 'fresh' from the bale, that is, with wrinkles and folds. Second hand clothing straight from the bale displayed with folds and wrinkles is considered to be 'genuine'. In the opinion of traders and customers alike, pre-washed and ironed clothing leaves the suspicion that the clothes are 'third hand', meaning previously owned and worn by Zambians.[3]

Clothing Competence

The shop window of Zambia's second hand clothing trade, the big public markets, creates an atmosphere much like the West's shopping malls where consumers can pursue almost unlimited desires with an abandon not possible in the formal stores, where they are often dealt with offhandedly or are pressured to purchase. *Salaula* markets thrive on the importance most Zambians attach to personal interaction and the attention they pay to keeping up pleasant interpersonal relations. In fact, these markets are important sites for both economic and social pursuits.

Consumers in Zambia go to *salaula* markets for many reasons. White-collar workers of both sexes in Lusaka's city center often spend their lunch hour going through the second hand clothing stalls as a pastime, sometimes making purchases at whim. Others go to find just that right item to match a particular garment. Some women who tailor in their homes search the *salaula* markets for interesting buttons, belts and trim to accent garments. And some go to purchase garments with the intention to resell. But the vast majority shop from *salaula* for clothing for themselves and their families. They come into the city center from residential areas like those in which I examined clothing consumption and where roughly two-thirds of all households supplied most of their members' clothing from *salaula*. Only the *apamwamba*, as the high income group is referred to in Zambia with a Nyanja term meaning literally 'those on the top', has an effective choice in the clothing market. This group sources clothing everywhere, including from *salaula*. For them, shopping 'from *salaula*' is a pastime.

Consumption is hard work. A vital dimension of the demand side is cultural taste and style issues that come together in the creation of a total look. When shopping from *salaula*, consumers' preoccupation with creating particular appearances is inspired by fashion trends and popular dress cultures from across the world. They draw on these influences in ways that are informed by local norms about bodies and dress. Above all, women must cover their 'private parts', which in this region of Africa includes their thighs. This means that dress length, tightness and fabric transparency become issues in interaction with men and elders at home and in public. My observations about the creative tensions between local dress norms and external influences are by no means unique to second hand clothing consumption in Zambia but parallel what takes place in Africa and beyond, the specificities depending significantly on their shifting local contexts (Durham, 1995; James, 1996; Tarlo, 1996a). This is to say that the work of consumption is situated in histories 'whose conjuncture has to be examined, alas, case by case' (Appadurai, 1997: 42–3).

The attraction of *salaula* to clothing-conscious Zambian consumers goes far beyond the price factor. Consumers want clothing that is not common. 'Clothes from *salaula* are not what other people wear,' one woman said to me when explaining why clothes from *salaula* are viewed as 'exclusive'. The clothing sensibility such statements convey hinges on social constructions of gendered and sexed bodies, comportment, personal grooming and presentation. It manifests itself in a visual aesthetic that is created in context. This meaning/value/sensibility is not inherent in the garments themselves but is attributed to them in social interaction. In effect, how much these constructions matter depend on context, for example, home versus work. It also has to do with the structure of the interaction in terms of gender and authority, for example, a situation involving people of the same sex and age or one where young people interact with people of the opposite sex of a senior generation. Occasional religious explanations of proper dress make reference to the Bible which is claimed to forbid women to wear trousers, short and tight clothing, and makeup. Thus, traditional standards regarding what parts of the body may be viewed, in contrast to Western permissiveness, is maintained through careful style selection.

The desire for uniqueness, to stand out, while dressing the body on Zambian terms entails considerable skill in garment selection based on quality, style and value for money, but also on the garment's potential to fit specific occasions and contexts, and in the overall presentation and comportment of the dressed body to produce a 'particular look'. In order to highlight that shopping from *salaula* does not mean that anything goes, I have called this skill, *clothing competence*. The underlying sensibility in the preoccupation with clothing is a visual aesthetics that on first sight cultivates endless variation yet on closer analysis also is in the service of continuity. The two dimensions do not cancel out each other. What is more, their simultaneity keeps the options open.

To flesh out these suggestions I describe some examples of adult women's dress practice. Distinctions by context are helpful here such as whether a woman is at home or at work, in an office setting, whether she is moving in public and for which purpose, for example shopping in an open air market in the city center or in a residential area, visiting a supermarket, or traveling by public transportation. There are special occasions as well that call for particular attire, among them, church attendance, funerals, kitchen parties and weddings.

Take Mrs Miyanda, a schoolteacher investing in a trip to one of Lusaka's largest *salaula* markets to shop for clothes for her children, a shirt for her husband, and 'the latest' for herself (Hansen, 2000b: 194–6). While her dress practice when working around the house is plain, involving almost any worn dress or skirt and blouse combination with a *chitenge* [colorful printed cloth] wrapper on top, her dress for other occasions is carefully put together, strategically calculated to produce a particular effect, that 'total look' that makes people take note. Behind this dress practice is a daily rehearsal involving careful choice, influenced by how she wants to be seen, where, when and by whom.

Mrs Miyanda's desire for uniqueness produces considerable variation in how she dresses for work. Like most other women whose dress practice I observed closely Mrs Miyanda never wears 'the same' dress to work, at least according to her own account. She arranges and rearranges her garments. One ensemble is succeeded by another and so on, leaving the impression of infinite novelty and indeed of ephemerality as one outfit leaves space for another. But this process is a strategic gesture, a sleight of hand that showcases rapid turnover while indeed conservation/continuity prevails. In fact, Mrs Miyanda rotates her garments and makes new combinations of dresses and skirts. Her rotation might occasionally include dresses in a cut and style that in the West might be considered to be evening wear. She also wears *chitenge* outfits to work, something that I rarely saw in the 1980s. And as an active member of the Seventh Day Adventist Church, she wears a church uniform for service on Saturdays, a blue dress with white trim and a white headscarf.

The inclusion of Mrs Miyanda's evening dress and her *chitenge* outfits among the garments she wears to work testifies to the many lives that clothes go through in their involvement with their owner's changing life. Once the demonstrative moment for display has passed, garments continue utilitarian lives. When she tires of garments as dress for school, she decommissions them from public work scenes to work around the house where they might be worn until they stop being useful. Some of them might be worn by young adults. But young women do not always agree with adult women's liking of *chitenge* outfits; they consider them to be for old women, mothers or even for grandmothers, according to essays on dress written for me by women students in the final grade of secondary school.

Conclusion

When the West is everywhere, Africa is not visible. As I argued at the outset, when explaining why second hand clothing matters in Zambia, reference to the Western origin of this commodity is not particularly helpful. What begins as charity with donations of used clothing in the West becomes a whole industry that draws in countries like Zambia not as passive receivers of the West's surplus clothing but actively involved in shaping the nature of the trade. The relationship revolves around a process of recommodification in which the meaning of second hand clothing is redefined in local terms. My emphasis has been on how the local value of imported second hand clothes is created through a variety of transformation processes that strip the imported commodity of its prior life and redefines it, readying it to enter new lives and relationships.

Zambia's salaula markets meet the non-local observer's eye as a chaotic mass of second hand clothing. This deceptive view hides many layers of market segmentation, both in terms of where used clothes are available for sale and of how they are displayed and sold. As we saw through Mrs Miyanda's shopping trip, a variety of informal rules organize vending space and structure sales practices. Both vendors and customers know these practices. The clothing competence consumers demonstrate when shopping 'from *salaula*' brings discerning skills to bear on creating a total look with a pleasing visual aesthetic that is culturally acceptable.

Shopping from *salaula* is not a process of random clothing selection but a strategic exercise that draws on specialist, practical and localized knowledge. Retailers and customers who create and share this knowledge operate within a frame of a culturally accepted dress profile. Against this backdrop, *salaula* markets make available an abundance and variety of clothes that allow consumers to add their individual mark to the culturally accepted clothing profile.

Notes

This chapter draws on research I undertook in North America, Europe and Zambia between 1992 and 1999, and published in 2000. My ongoing research in Zambia continues to influence my understanding of the second hand clothing phenomenon.

1. The quote is taken from the description inside the book's dust cover.
2. I am drawing on statistics from the United Nations *International Trade Statistics Yearbook* which lists exports by value in US dollars and does not provide information

about volume/weight. The figures are not very accurate as not all countries report to the United Nations and those who do report most likely underestimate the scope of this trade.

3. For additional insights into these constructions, see Hansen (2000b: 171–3). A similar practice has been observed in the Gambia. Gambian consumers 'prefer to buy clothes they know have originated in the West, not those previously worn and donated by the Gambian elite' (Field, Barrett, Browns & May, 1996: 372).

7

Creative Entrepreneurs: The Recycling of Second Hand Indian Clothing

Lucy Norris

Introduction

In recent years, Western markets have been overflowing with furnishings and clothing made from Indian sari fabrics. Independent traders working in street markets, festivals and small boutiques sell a variety of cushions, bedspreads and wall hangings, alongside various items of clothing in Western styles, such as halter-neck tops, skirts and trousers. By mid 1999, British shops selling furniture and furnishings were festooned with Indian fabrics and designs made up into Western consumer goods. High street stores were selling mass-produced clothing featuring embroidery in a 'Gujarati style', appliqué designs using Indian fabrics and jeans with gold thread borders attached, following a 'trickle-up' influence from the rising popularity of the clothing found in street markets across the country. These tastes were no doubt also fueled by the growing number of backpackers and clubbers traveling to India directly who were buying such clothes in tourist havens across the country. However, unbeknownst to most consumers was the fact that the material origins of many of the products found in Western street markets lie in the entrepreneurial recycling of second hand saris, which has in turn directly influenced the design styles of the high street.

This constitutes the opposite trajectory of two common aspects of scholarly research concerning the global trade in cloth and clothing and the relationship between the developed and developing worlds. Firstly, a burgeoning literature approaches the study of new Indian cloth as a product manufactured and produced for the export market, and the power relationships inherent in the trade during the pre-colonial, colonial and post-Independence periods (e.g. Guy, 1998; Mukerjii, 1983; Roy, 1996). Secondly, the trade in second hand clothing is either considered from a socio-economic perspective within Western societies (e.g. Gregson & Crewe, 2003; Lemire, 1988, 1997; McRobbie, 1989; Stallybrass, 1998), or conceived as a flow from the developed world to developing countries in Africa, Asia and South America (e.g. Hansen, 2000b).

This chapter investigates the complex trajectories of discarded Indian clothing, ejected from the wardrobe to be transformed into new coverings for bodies, objects and places both in India and across the world. This research forms part of fieldwork undertaken in Delhi and North India amongst middle-class urban women, the Waghri dealers and manufacturers between June 1999 and July 2000. It focuses on the recommodification of clothing through the entrepreneurial strategies of dealers in contemporary markets in India, looking at the factors which influence the various outcomes once garments are initially disposed of.

The Commodification of Old Clothes

The buying and giving of cloth and clothing constitutes an essential part of everyday life amongst all Indian families who can afford to do so. Whether purchased for daily activities or gifted at births, weddings, anniversaries or religious festivals, the flow of cloth through the household makes visible the construction of networks of relationships between kin and close friends. Special trousseau items are kept as inalienable objects by most women, (see Weiner, 1992) bundled together and locked in wardrobes to be handed down to daughters and daughters-in-law. However, a strong aesthetic of smartness and newness prevails among the middle and upper middle classes; favored cottons soon start to fade in Delhi's climate, silks tear and stain, and older clothes seen on earlier occasions no longer have the impact they once had when worn to a party. The problem arises of what to do with these unwanted clothes.

Most clothing constitutes a resource to be reused and recycled as fit, a process of transformation which draws upon value systems beyond those most concerned with the operation of thrift within the confines of economic maximization. Cloth is also valuable due to sentimental attachment, its role in constructing the family through networks of inheritance and handing on, and its usefulness in the fulfillment of obligations to others. Such qualities inherent in the cloth result in strategies of reuse which aim to capture and conserve these various values to maximum effect.

As clothing is outgrown, torn or stained, fades or wears out, it is put aside until a suitable use appears. Even among the upper classes, very few pieces gain value as antique textiles, although some contain real gold and silver thread, and can be burnt to reclaim the precious metal. Among the middle classes, clothing is usually handed down to younger relatives wherever possible. If it is tattier, then it is offered to servants as part of a continually negotiated obligation to provide for them. Although domestic recycling is less common as more women work full time, favorite pieces of cloth are cut up and reused in quilts, as dress trimmings and furnishings, while soft cotton cloths become rags, dusters and pot holders. Cloth is never simply thrown away, and will be used up until it literally wears out.

Despite such accustomed trajectories, large amounts of clothes are thought to be more of a problem these days, and constitute a burgeoning resource for which new avenues must be found (Norris, 2004). This is probably due to the move to smaller flats for nuclear families, the increasing distance between relatives to whom one used to pass them, and the built-in obsolescence of the fashion system. For the burgeoning middle class, experiencing the consumer boom since the economy was opened up in the early 1990s, the 'traditional' strategies of the rural gentry, petty urban aristocracy and educated elite cannot keep pace with the perceived increase in surplus goods.

An increasingly popular option is to commodify clothing through a system of bartering. Clothing is exchanged for *bartan,* kitchen utensils. The female old clothes dealers, *bartanwale,* literally 'those who deal in utensils' sit on the footpaths in suburban areas. On the road a few feet in front of them is a dazzling display of shining *bartan,* stainless steel plates, beakers, small bowls, storage jars and various cooking pots and pans and perhaps a small rack, sparkling in the sunlight (Fig. 18). Women stop and ask how many garments the *bartanwale* want for a pot or dish that has caught their eye, and the bargaining begins. Once a preliminary agreement is made, they arrange a time to come to the woman's home to view the items. Once there, they remain seated on the doorstep, while the clothes are brought out to them. Passions become heated as favorite clothes are disdained by the dealers, and each tries to get the upper hand. After each garment and each pot is thoroughly examined, a deal is struck, and the *bartanwale* demand half a sari to bundle up their pickings, hauling them up over their shoulder.

Women claim to be exhausted by the process, but are pleased to have new pots for the kitchen. Pots are commonly given with clothes as part of women's dowries, and both remain within the female domestic economy; shining pots are frequently displayed on open shelves in the kitchen. Exchanging tatty clothing for a new pot replaces a disintegrating store of value with a more durable form of wealth, and brings women great pleasure. At a

Figure 18. The *bartanwale* spread out their shining utensils on the footpath to tempt women to barter their old clothes in exchange. May 2000, Delhi. Photograph by Lucy Norris.

symbolic level, weaving is a metaphor for the creation of the universe, and uncut cloth symbolizes the thread of continuity and the life cycle; pots are thought to be both containers of and embodiment of divinity in their many forms and ritual uses, and are also symbols of fertility. They are therefore an appropriate form of wealth for women on a multiplicity of levels.

Appadurai describes barter as 'the exchange of objects for one another *without* reference to money and *with* maximum feasible reduction of social, cultural, political, or personal transaction costs'; it is the effort to exchange things without the constraints of sociality nor the complications of money (Appadurai, 1986: 9). The advantage of barter as a means of transaction is that it allows for the movement of objects between regimes of value through the exchange of sacrifices (Gell, 1992). Both parties negotiate the deal knowing that at the end they are 'quits', and no further relationship between them will exist (Humphrey & Hugh-Jones, 1992). The trader's relationship to other members of the society corresponds to the nature of the exchange. Exchange has certain moralities associated with it; 'embedded' exchange is socially rich, but disembedded exchange such as barter is anti-social. Those with whom one bargains should embody all that is 'anti-social' about the process, so the outcaste itinerant trader is the epitome of the exchange itself.

The *bartanwale* are analogous to Simmel's stranger, who is both far from the community yet near by virtue of his presence (Simmel, 1971).

The Market in Second Hand Clothing

Most middle-class Indian women believe that the *bartanwale* simply take their unwanted clothing and sell them on to the poor. This imaginary trajectory creates a largely unproblematic fall in value from once treasured sari, suit or shirt to anonymous garment, cast-off and cast out. Such unwanted clothes appear to have minimal value to all but the most needy. As Thompson clearly demonstrated (1979), in order for objects to pass from the transient category of depreciating value to the durable category of accumulating value, there must be a third, covert category of 'rubbish', through which such goods must pass if their value is to be radically reassigned. Once singular garments become piles of 'stuff' they are stripped of their unique identities, and become amalgamated into heaps of material laid out in a market, waiting to be transformed into a new product. A key feature of the means through which the value of clothing is renegotiated through the mechanisms of the marketplace is its apparent secrecy, removed from the realm of the visible in the worldview of the middle classes. The existence of a thriving community of old clothes dealers is largely unknown to middle-class Delhiites, who treat the *bartanwale* with undisguised disdain. Such lack of knowledge and their disregard for the women sitting on the pavements are key elements in the ability of the dealers to remove unwanted garments beyond the pale.

The role of the Waghri traders is similar to that of barbers and washermen in Indian society as necessary removers of dirt, pollution and exuviae. Clothing, once taken off the body and divested, retains the essence of the person; it cannot simply be treated as 'rubbish', and also needs to be properly got rid of. Through barter the identity of the individual who once inhabited the garment is stripped away. The subsequent processing of used clothing in order to commodify them assists in the removal of bodily traces from the garments, according to the sensitivity of the subsequent consumer. Those outside the indigenous socioeconomic and ritual hierarchy, foreigners for example, prove to be a popular target for dealers. Yet, although the origins of such cloth may not be particularly problematic for many non-Indian consumers, more subtle and complex manipulations of value are required for the elite home market. Middle- and upper-class Indian buyers require a high investment in material and conceptual transformation in order to remove or conceal the potentially polluting nature of used clothing, while the poor are less able to discriminate through need.

The *bartanwale* with whom I worked are Waghris who have migrated to Delhi from Gujarat and northwest India, and a large community lives in a suburb on the outskirts of the city. Most of the local population of 40,000 people earn a livelihood through dealing in used cloth in some capacity. The landscape is decorated with a multitude of clothing festooned from lines and draped across walls. Hundreds of pairs of faded blue jeans or coats regularly adorn the barriers of the main road. Through open doorways one sees piles of clothing bundled up in knotted old saris, or pairs of worn old shoes. Rows of tiny shops selling *bartan*, steel utensils, plastic tubs, glass bowls and china cups display their contents in serried ranks stretching yards out into the street. In this one suburb, the whole trade is visible – utensils are bought for the daily *pheriya* (doing 'the rounds'), cast-off clothing is brought back to the home in the evening, and sold the next morning in the Ghora Mandi, the market and economic hub of the community. Local buyers then wash and mend them, or creatively adapt them where they can. While the poorest struggle to survive at the margins of the business dealing in scraps day-to-day, more resourceful, established entrepreneurs are able to maximize the value of different clothes by transforming unwanted clothing into new products. The increasing numbers of traders leads to more competition and lower returns, but this is precariously balanced by both the growing surpluses of clothing in middle-class wardrobes to be teased out, and the development of new markets for used cloth.

Earning a living is undoubtedly exhausting for those *bartanwale* with the least resources behind them. It is almost always the women who ply the trade, leaving young children at home with elder siblings. But unlike the usual suburban trade in rubbish and scrap carried out by male traders, *kabariwale*, this doorstep trade undoubtedly benefits from its significant character, that is of women dealing with women, which increases the chance of access to the domestic sphere and intimate possessions.

Every day the women get up long before dawn to take the previous day's clothing to the Ghora Mandi to sell, arriving from 3.00 a.m., and staying until 9.00 or 10.00 a.m. until they are all sold. They then return home to prepare for the *pheriya*, travelling via the *bartan* shops to negotiate for more stock. By mid-morning they clamber into rickshaws or take a bus, often suffering abuse from city bus drivers who refuse to allow them on with their overfilled baskets of *bartan* carried over their shoulders. Traveling could take up to two hours in Delhi's traffic, traversing the length and breadth of the city. Many complained of police harassment for having no license to trade, and are forced to bribe them Rs 20 or 30 on some days.[1] The women were often suspected by local residents of tipping off their husbands resulting in local robberies and kidnapping. Late in the evening they return home with bundles of clothes and unsold *bartan*, to cook for their families and do the household chores.

The poorest families live hand to mouth, unable to amass clothing or *bartan*, with no access to running water to wash garments, no sewing machines or space to mend clothing, constantly begging every day for more credit at the *bartan* shop. Hajkumadri, a stainless steel dealer, displayed his account book, where all the local women's credit and repayments were recorded. He claimed that most women would try to buy a daily minimum of Rs 100–150 worth of steel as stock from him, using the money just received from the market, depending on how much they had left at home. There are over 160 steel dealers in the area, and some women run up accounts with several at a time. The better the quality of steel (and plastic) available to the suburban housewife and the wider range of utensils on offer, the more attracted she will be to stop on the roadside, and the more likely a garment dealer would obtain good quality clothing in return. Each piece is therefore aggressively scrutinized in the *bartan* shop for dents, scratches and ill-fitting lids before being purchased by the *bartanwale*. Hajkumadri estimated that women would get perhaps Rs 250 worth of clothing for a *bartan* worth Rs 100, but the *bartanwale* consistently claimed the returns were much less.

At dawn, the Ghora Mandi is full of women sitting cross-legged on the ground in rows. The buyers are all men, trawling up and down, singing out what they are looking for, bargaining for pieces, trying to evade the women thrusting unwanted items into their paths. Along the crowded pavements rows of men stand cleaning their teeth with *neem* twigs, drinking cups of tea and hawking. Music blares out across the market from the adjacent temple loudspeakers every morning, and a constant commentary announces the name of each dealer who donates a small sum as they leave. With arms draped full of clothes and more bundled up, the buyers eventually depart the frenzied market, clambering into rickshaws piled high with purchases, or trudging off down the road. This is the node of what is probably the largest used-clothing market in the subcontinent. Approximately 1000 to 1,500 dealers enter the market on any day, depending on religious festivals and the season. Sucking in unwanted clothing bartered across the country, the market re-energizes the latent value of cloth, it filters and sorts it, and acts as a powerful centrifugal force, ejecting tens of thousands of items every day.

One group of *bartanwale* made a trip to Agra, where the *pheriya* trade was far less developed. A few extended families got together to hire a big Tata truck, piling the open back high with huge baskets of *bartan* (worth Rs 70,000), children, bedrolls and stoves. Staying in a temple *dharamsala* (guesthouse), they would scour the better-off districts for clothing, returning several days later laden with garments. On a smaller scale, traders from the areas outside Delhi would also make weekly or even monthly trips to the Ghora Mandi with their bundles of clothing, hoping to find an urban market for items less desirable in the neighboring rural areas. The *bartanwales'* willingness to travel keeps different styles of clothing in circulation, maximizing the chance of selling them on for the best return where they are desired the most.

Buyers and Dealers

The women in the marketplace usually have between 50 and 100 garments in front of them; they always sell their own, as they alone know exactly what they paid for them in stainless steel, and what they must get in return. They try to attract the buyers' attention as they walk past. The buyers in the market are usually men, from families who have struggled up to the next rung of the economic ladder, and whose work is adding value to the particular type of clothing they buy before selling them on. Such operators are highly strategic, seizing opportunities as they arise and maximizing new niches in the market through personal contacts and sheer hard work. The possibilities for expansion depend upon business acumen, a willingness to take risks and forego immediate returns. A crucial factor is the materiality of the cloth itself, which determines the uses to which they can be put, reflected in their price. The relative values of types of clothes are described below; each material has a fairly established trajectory, but newcomers are constantly attempting to add to the options available and gain the edge over their competitors.

The easiest level to begin trading at is that in old cotton saris and *dhotis*. Most *bartanwale* have one or two old pieces in each transaction which cannot be mended and whose value lies in the softness and absorbency of the natural fibres, which makes them suitable for rags, dusters and polishing cloths. A six-yard sari can become six one square yard polishing cloths for the machine industry; *dhotis* are torn into three pieces, while shirts become smaller dusters. These are then sold on to hardware shops, factories and the machining industries. Petty traders need invest little: Gautam bought a few *dhotis* every day for Rs 2 to 3 each, which he tore up into strips and sold as dusters to a local factory for Rs 3 to 4 each, earning a few paise profit on each one (100 paise = 1 Rs).

There are over a hundred wholesale rag dealers in the area. They often act as middlemen themselves, selling on to others who have large *godowns* (warehouses) stocked to fill larger contracts in the international rag market.

Strips of old clothing are graded by the middlemen into bundles depending on fabric strength, size and fibres, the highest quality ensuring maximum absorbency and minimum shedding of lint. The biggest players in the market buy up rags from as far afield as Calcutta, Madras, Andhra and Gujarat, exporting container loads to the Middle East and beyond. Delhi is claimed to be a major centre in the worldwide rag market, turning familiar personal clothing into wipes for paint factories and machine tooling workshops across the globe, all expedited via the *bartan* trade.

The commonest use for the goods at the Ghora Mandi is as clothing for those unable to afford either new garments in the shops or the imported second hand clothing available in the local markets. Small dealers specialize in particular garments, depending upon the resources at their disposal to make the items worth more through washing and mending. Raghbir was a typical buyer. Travelling ten kilometers every morning to the market, he bought up to seventy-five old saris every day, which he took home for his wife to wash and darn. He chose mainly synthetic ones, occasionally artificial silk (with no borders), and sold them every Sunday at the Lal Qila (Red Fort), making Rs 3 to 5 profit on each one.

A large part of the market deals in *shalwar kamiz;* especially favoured are the synthetic suits which last longer and are easier to maintain. They are often in better condition, not faded but still bright. With both saris and suits, the range of colors, styles and fashions is enormous. A jeans dealer was apparently making a higher profit buying for Rs 5 to 10, washing and ironing them and selling them on for double. Another man dealt in old shirts, buying them for Rs 6 or 7 each, while his wife washed and repaired them. He then sold them on for Rs 8 to 10. With a high turnover of 150 to 200 shirts a week, the family could make up to Rs 2,000 a month. Profits per garment are low, less than Rs 3, but the harder wives and daughters in the household work, the higher the turnover.

The buyers will be able to sell on desirable clothing to their customers for a good profit, capitalizing on the fact that end-users can buy much better quality outfits second hand than they would ever have afforded new. Although most end-users will be the poor, it was often suggested that lower middle-class women might buy them on the quiet, perhaps claiming they were hand-me-downs from a relative to enquirers. Lemire (1988) also writes about the need for good second hand clothing for the working classes of pre-industrial England, who could not afford clothing in the period before large-scale production made 'brand new' clothes affordable. In Indian markets, better quality used garments from middle-class households may offer better value in terms of economic cost, status and quality than poorly made new garments.

Most of this clothing is then resold in the large Sunday Markets found across north India. Behind the Lal Qila in Delhi is a long established flea market, the Chor Bazaar. Rubbish dealers, the *kabariwale*, spread their treasures out on the ground: a mixture of old watches, clocks, household utensils, old furniture, scrap metal and books. At the far end of the market a couple of hundred Waghri men and women sit on tarpaulins on the ground behind piles of washed, ironed and neatly folded clothes. While sellers might try to attract the attention of passersby through calling out, it requires some effort to scrutinize the folded clothing, and this part of the market is noticeably quieter than the rest. Although a few daring, middle-class bargain hunters might visit the *kabari* market for amusement, they never venture to the end of the wasteland where the Waghris sit. Here, the clothes are only ever bought by the poor, the low-paid maids, rickshaw drivers and unskilled labourers in the city. A few Waghri sell used Indian clothing at the weekly *haat*, suburban markets. Second hand markets are also found around the old railway station next to Shahjahanabad, in Paharganj, the Qutub Road, and older parts of the city where recent immigrants have always arrived, akin to those found in London's East End.

Returning to the analysis of the Ghora Mandi the most valuable saris are changing hands at 3.00 a.m. every morning. Women place silk saris and those with decorative *zari* borders on the top of their heaps, shining in the half-light, and the earliest buyers are those snapping them up. Prices vary according to the area of decorative surface, and the amount of gold and silver used in the *kinari* (borders) and *pallu* (the decorative end-piece). One or two buyers call out for real gold and silver, paying a few hundred rupees for them and later taking them down to the *kinari* bazaar (borders' market) to be sold separately or burnt for their metal content. The usual purpose of unwanted silk (and good quality artificial silk) saris is as a raw material to be refashioned into soft furnishings and tailored clothing for the Western market.

All of the buyers are middlemen, building up stocks in their homes around the periphery of the market to fulfil contracts with large manufacturers or selling on directly to the family businesses in the neighboring district that transform them (Fig. 19). Although each *bartanwali* claims to rarely receive the finest silk saris for pots, common estimates suggest that at least 10,000 people go out on *pheriya* every day, so there are always some available. These garments are of the types that are often given as part of a trousseau or as significant ritual gifts to be worn for functions. They are usually high quality, but irreparably stained. When originally bought they can cost from a few hundred to several thousand rupees; one buyer suggested that a Rs 2,000 sari probably sells in the Ghora Mandi for about Rs 100, 5 percent of its original price.

Figure 19. Bundles of silk saris are stockpiled in small houses surrounding the Ghora Mandi, waiting for bulk orders from manufacturers of Western clothes and soft furnishings. May 2000, Delhi.
Photograph by Lucy Norris.

The buyers in the Ghora Mandi tend to earn profits in the region of Rs 15 to 25 per silk sari if they sell them on in bulk, although some highly prized individual pieces would fetch more. Few lower level dealers specialize in types within the general category of 'silk saris', and houses bulge with multicolored bundles of saris in every style: satins, *tanchois*, tissues, tie-dyed *bandhini*, Benarasi brocades and south Indian silks. One or two have found niche markets for particular types. A Muslim trader specialized in printed silk saris which he sold to a manufacturer. Those with the tiniest floral sprig were worth up to Rs 100 each, whereas larger patterns fetched only Rs 50 to 60, being less versatile for pattern cutters to make new products from. He bought 300 to 400 a month from the market and other dealers.

The most successful dealers are those who have acquired influence and control in a variety of interconnected fields, eliminating the middlemen.

Sushil was in his early twenties and beginning to deal in silk saris. Keen to meet tourists with whom he could deal directly, but who rarely found their way to northwest Delhi, his house was full of the most gorgeous silk saris, many of which he offered for several hundred rupees each. Through family contacts, he claimed to bypass the local Ghora Mandi and obtain clothing directly from dealers across Rajasthan, extolling the quality and beauty of saris formerly belonging to the royal princesses of minor desert courts. His father was the president of the *Bartan* Trader's Association, and a prominent member of both the local *panchayat* (community council) and the Ghora Mandir (temple) administration, so the family had influence and contacts in every sphere of business undertaken in the district. Sushil was making a name for himself as a dealer and *bartanwale* came to him directly.

Transformations

A short cycle rickshaw ride away from the Ghora Mandi, the neighboring suburb is a definite rung up the ladder of success. The area is modestly prosperous, comfortable, lower middle class in character. The traders are all Gujarati Waghris, who have been developing the business of recycling Gujarati embroidery since Independence. Tarlo documents the manner in which embroidery was traded for *bartan* across the states of Gujarat and Rajasthan, and sold to collectors and foreign tourists (Tarlo, 1996b).

The Delhi community of the Waghris is part of this network of dealers and manufacturers that extends across west and north India. Many dealers are still using primarily new and old Gujarati embroidery to make cushion covers, bedspreads and wall hangings made from scraps of embroidered clothing for the export market. The whole extended family is usually involved in manufacturing, and many employ several tailors on a piecework basis. In the last fifteen to twenty years, these manufacturers have turned from primarily using Gujarati embroidery to the growing abundance of decorated saris to be found in the nearby Ghora Mandi, creating an extended repertoire of designs for soft furnishings, each constructed according to certain sari styles.

Silk saris are cut up into pieces, according to their basic construction: the top and bottom borders (about five yards long), the decorated end, *pallu*, and the central field, often containing regularly repeated motifs. The type of construction, weave and texture is considered, along with whether borders are striped or tapestry woven with motifs and whether design elements in the *pallu* and field are small and repetitive or big and bold. Although the saris have initially been selected for their material properties of silkiness and *zari* content, it is the particular combination of design elements used in each type of sari which becomes a determining factor in their reuse.

Coarse black backing fabric is cut to the desired size and pieces of sari are laid out over it in a design. Benarasi brocades are most commonly used, as they tend to have bold *zari* borders with definite stripes, heavily patterned *pallu* in *zari*, and regularly recurring flower *butti* (motifs), animals and geometric shapes in the field. The remaining, plainer silk parts of the sari may be sold to others to be made up into scarves (*chuni* and headsquares), used as lining material in recycled clothing, or if in poor condition sold as scraps (*chindi, katran*) to the local rag merchants. Cushion covers and bedspreads are made up of a patchwork of these elements stitched together on cotton backing. A popular design is of a series of concentric bands of sari borders around a central square, laid down diagonally within the square or rectangle of the object. Borders of different colours and *zari* patterns are mixed together to create dazzling effects.

These traders are now the main manufacturers of these products in north India. The Ghora Mandi cannot supply enough silk saris to meet demand, and so the traders have capitalized on extensive networks across north India to buy up more raw materials, that are turned into their finished products. Ashok Kumar was one such trader, who has buyers working for him in second hand markets in Ahmedabad, Bombay, Surat and Benaras. The latter are both centres of production, and good sources for *zari* sari borders. Smaller traders in small- and medium-sized towns across India sell their used clothing to middlemen, who lug heavy bundles of second hand silk saris across the Indian rail network in bulging carriages to reach the major cities, and finally Delhi. There they are made up and sold back to traders in tourist destinations such as Goa, Bombay, Jaipur and Agra, and exported to Nepal and beyond. In Delhi as elsewhere, petty traders, usually Waghris, sell a few cushion covers outside the main attractions, and peddle them on the main streets such as Janpath and Connaught Place, while shopkeepers make a living in the poorer parts of town such as Paharganj selling them as souvenirs to backpackers. One dealer suggested that a sari cushion cover might wholesale for Rs 20 to 25, but tourists on Janpath might pay from Rs 50 to 60; however, new visitors unwilling to bargain probably part with many times that amount.

These products are ubiquitous, on offer to foreign tourists wherever they are to be found across India and south Asia as a whole, and they are now being imported in vast quantities into the West by entrepreneurial Western travellers-turned-traders. Sold through 'ethnic' trading shops, market stalls and festivals, these items have become hugely popular, although few end buyers realize they are essentially recycled goods. The entrepreneurial necessity of manufacturing goods from recycled materials is sold on to customers as age-old authenticity if mentioned at all.

In the UK, cushion covers can be priced from £15 for these cheaper versions, and often significantly more. In 2001, a double bedspread was on sale in Glastonbury for £195. As with many products fortuitously developed to recycle available cheap resources, the supplier of recycled sari cushions relies on what is available ad hoc, and the saris, brought in by the Waghri traders, constantly exercise their creativity. The overall style of 'Indian' ethnic sari product is now well defined, and the potential of design elements in various types of saris are understood and exploited through forms such as patchwork and stripes by their producers. However, each of these pieces is a unique combination of original materials that cannot be exactly replicated. The recent fashion for Indian furnishings has led low- to middle-market UK high street chain stores to sell 'sari cushions', featuring identical diagonally striped designs, originally developed according to the reuse of sari borders. However, large retailers in the West such as Pier One cannot rely on serendipity and happenstance: they need to be able to guarantee consistent quality, and large quantities of similar, if not identical, colours and designs to fit in with their seasonal marketing strategies, catalogues and displays. It would appear that new sari borders are bought in bulk, perhaps even commissioned, and made up to copy the 'original' recycled product, guaranteeing thousands of cushion covers that have no tears or pulled threads, and no chance of a surreptitiously hidden stain in a corner. The catalogue *The Pier* described their 'sari cushions' as 'made from Indian sari borders ... made from individual pieces of fabric; patterns may vary' (*The Pier* catalogue 2001). Each was priced at £29.95.

The aesthetics of patchwork and quilting as a recycling practice and the object forms chosen, such as cushions, throws and covers, have for long been common to Indian and Western culture. However, a more radical transformation of silk saris is involved in their being remade into Western fashion garments, a subject that cannot be covered here. At the lower end of the market, such clothing has been available for budget travelers in tourist destinations for decades, developed as a hybrid product between local manufacturers and foreigners wanting cheap garments that used exotic materials to create western styles.

Conclusion

The decision to get rid of unwanted garments in the wardrobe creates exchange value. This was often referred to by middle-class women as the joys of getting 'something for nothing'. By removing the body from clothing and detaching it from the person, clothing is immediately transformed into cloth, a new resource to be utilized. Clothing must become rubbish in order for such transformations to be successful; their conversion into new consumer goods with high value depends on their being largely conducted in secret, enabling them to move between regimes of value. The materiality of cloth is crucial to processes of recycling and the creation of value through its vulnerability to destructive actions such as cutting and remaking. The agency of the material object combines with the resourcefulness of the entrepreneurial dealers to create global networks of hybrid people and fabrics.

Notes

1. During the period of fieldwork between July 1999 and June 2000, £1 was worth approximately 67 to 70 Rs (Indian rupees).

8

'Ukay-Ukay' Chic: Tales of Second Hand Clothing Fashion and Trade in the Philippine Cordillera

B. Lynne Milgram

Introduction

In Cebu, they call it 'ukay-ukay' [second hand clothing]. In Baguio, it's called 'wagwagan.'[1] It's a paradise for bargain hunters looking for cheap but fashionable, even branded clothes.

Philippine Star '"Ukay-Ukay" Imports'

The primary thrill of shopping the *ukay-ukay* way is finding the elusive bargain amid an unpromising pile of garments... My teenage daughter was looking for a trench coat to wear during the cold Baguio City rainy season. So last summer while touring the Cordillera we visited the *ukay-ukay* shops. There we found jackets and coats that were going for incredibly low prices... My daughter eventually found a long coat with an Italian label for P200 [Philippine pesos]. She also spotted a leather jacket for P300 but it was one size too small... One find led to another.

Rina Jimenez-David '"Ukay-Ukay" Memoirs'

At first glance, newspaper stories like these provide us with nothing more than facts about popular shopping trends. Yet the story that knowledgeable readers can glimpse is far more complex. Such narratives relate how traders and consumers in the Philippines claim ownership over the West's discarded clothing to refashion modernity on their own terms. Since the early 1990s, the growing export of used clothing from North America and northwestern Europe to 'developing' countries may initially appear to be a continuance of Western exploitation and a threat to the position of local garment industries (Hansen, 2000b: 2). Without doubt the importation of second hand clothing into countries such as the Philippines has partially displaced sales of locally manufactured textiles and garments (Cabreza and Pazzibugan, 2002: A1). But to consider the flow of this commodity into southern countries as the late twentieth century's avatar of the linear modernization narrative – simply another marker of northern domination – overlooks the new spheres of self-expression and work that second hand clothing facilitates in a rapidly changing economy (see also Hansen, 1999: 343; 2000b: 2). *Ukay-ukay*, meaning to dig through, is the term generally used throughout the Philippines to describe how people choose garments from the imported second hand clothing currently sold throughout the country in permanent shops and in open markets. *Ukay-ukay* provides consumers with more choice to fulfill their 'clothing needs and desires' and gives traders, especially women, new profitable and respectable livelihood opportunities as clothing 'brokers' (Hansen, 2000b: 2; Ginsburg, 1980: 121). For both consumers and traders, *ukay-ukay* thus enables an alternative engagement with modernity and the agency to effect change beyond the local level.

Focusing on Banaue, Ifugao Province, northern Philippines, I argue that rather than being marginalized by the influx of second hand clothing, consumers and traders recraft this transglobal commodity into locally significant economic and cultural forms through the personal stories they construct in both market spheres and in dress practice. They draw on their earlier reconfiguration of imported goods during two colonial regimes to dispute the global homogenization narrative that depicts tales of development in terms of before and after. Some of the current scholarship that explores meaning in material culture draws on the 'dialogue' metaphor to situate their approach (e.g., E. Bruner, 1986a, 1986b; J. Bruner, 1987; DeMello, 2000; Stewart, 1996). Within this framework, analyses incorporate the diachronic aspect of narrative to argue that the stories people generate around objects indirectly account for, organize and shape personal experience – these stories about things provide a form of reflection on the meaning of one's own life and a path of action to realize that meaning (Hoskins, 1998: 2, 6; Rosaldo, 1993: 129–30). As Cory Silverstein (2001: 21) argues, personal narratives account for linkages among events by providing 'patterns for and patterns of' action within pre-existing structures in given cultural and historical contexts.

The research applying narrative to the understanding of objects, however, focuses primarily on material culture that is locally produced (e.g., Causey,

2003; Errington, 1994; Hoskins, 1998).[2] By exploring how people in the Philippines generate and transform meaning through the trade and consumption of imported second hand clothing, my study expands the former research as *ukay-ukay* is produced in sites different from those in which it is consumed. Consequently, the ideas about imported second hand clothing and the practices in which it is enmeshed are constantly changing. People thus situate their interaction with this commodity within a narrative framework because the inherent mutability of narrative can easily accommodate such shifts in attitude, values and behavior. Rather than cultural differences being increasingly eroded through the global circulation of Western second hand clothing, I suggest that Philippine consumers and traders narrate a personalized logic through which to receive, use and market these goods. By using personal narratives to fashion the in-flow of goods – their reception and domestication – people recraft meaning in imported objects thereby shifting attention from determinist ideas embedded in the out-flow of goods from the West and the meta-story of inevitable Western domination of values.

I use narrative here as both an analytical tool and an explanatory model to understand the nature of the connections people create through cross-cultural consumption and exchange. As women comprise the majority of informal-sector traders in the Philippine Cordillera and continue as the main provisioners for their families, I focus on this dynamic group. I suggest that women's tales of the trade and consumption of second hand clothing domesticate the logic of the market and the meaning of this ubiquitous commodity to recognizably local signs of status and value at the same time that they transform them. To illustrate this argument, I first review some of the literature analyzing material culture within a narrative framework. I then discuss the nature of the second hand clothing industry in the northern Philippines, and explore the channels through which traders and consumers conduct business in, and assert personalized ownership over, this globally traded commodity.

Narrative, Material Culture and Dress

Recent anthropological research on material culture has clearly demonstrated that objects play integral roles in the construction, maintenance, and transformation of social relations and identities (e.g., Appadurai, 1986; Collerado-Mansfeld, 1999; Milgram, 1999a; Miller, 1997; Myers, 2001; Phillips & Steiner, 1999; Schrift, 2001). These studies suggest that objects are essential as 'foils for self-definition and an anchor for the self-historizing subject' (Hoskins, 1998: 7). Southeast Asian ethnographers, in particular, have drawn on the narrative framework to demonstrate the integral role of material culture to the constitution of history and to social and economic life. As Janet Hoskins (1998: 24) argues, people use a variety of objects as metaphors to reify characteristics of personhood that must then be narratively organized into an identity (see also Errington, 1994; Kuipers, 1990). Renato Rosaldo (1986, 1993) illustrates this point with regard to Ilongot men's hunting practices in the northern Philippines when he argues that the Ilongot, in fact, seek out experiences that can be told as stories. 'These narratives, once acted out, "make" events and "make" history. They contribute to the reality of their participants' (J. Bruner, 1986: 42–3, quoted in Rosaldo, 1993: 129). In his work with woodcarvers in northern Sumatra, Andrew Causey (2003: 224) similarly demonstrates that the narratives accompanying the sale and purchase of Batak souvenir carvings provide avenues through which Western tourists and Toba Bataks define and negotiate their respective relationships in such exchanges.

Looking at First Nations material culture in colonial Canada, Cory Silverstein (2001: 23) suggests that in any given cultural or historical context, there are pre-existing plots or 'master narratives' that guide action for all those who share particular social and cultural practices. Within these master narratives, there also exist sub-plots that Silverstein terms 'cultural scripts'; these cultural scripts suggest frameworks and roles for the 'possible lives' of the actors who perform them (J. Bruner, 1987: 15, quoted in Silverstein, 2001: 21, 23). These broad frameworks – master narratives and cultural scripts – consist of plots, characters, settings and material culture from which individuals creatively construct personal configurations of roles (Silverstein, 2001: 23). As components of one's behavioral environment, these forms thereby serve, albeit flexibly, as cultural indicators to suggest 'appropriate' actions for individuals' and 'appropriate' interpretations of others' actions pervading most fields of human experience (Silverstein, 2001: 23; Stewart, 1996: 34). On the level of the individual, narratives provide 'recipes for structuring experience' within a purposeful framework of episodal units; on the level of the community, they provide coherence to collective shared beliefs and values; and rooted in historical contexts, personal narratives function, as well, both to constrain and to critique social action (J. Bruner, 1987: 31; J.H. Miller, 1990: 69; Polkinghorne, 1988: 11, 14, quoted in Silverstein, 2001: 23).

Kathleen Stewart's (1996:34) work in the American Appalachians, for example, demonstrates how people use stories to help create the world they experience; this narrated 'space at the side of the road' is like a 'scenic representation of the forces of a lyric image with the power to give pause to the straight line of narrative ordering of events from beginning to end'.

People thus use talk both 'to guide and deter truth's rigidity' (Causey, 2003: 6). In this way, narration as action can accurately portray the way things happened (Rodgers, 1995: 16–18). The value of such stories is not in repeating well-known facts, but rather for individuals to tell of recently lived episodes in order to exhibit their control over these new and often unexpected experiences (Rosaldo, 1986, 1993: 129). In so doing, the different parts of the plot are 'narrativized' into a sequential whole – that is, described, discussed and thus controlled by those taking part in them (Marin, 1984: 198–201). Such stories of peoples behaviors, embedded in cultural contexts, fulfill several functions: they help individuals define what it is they have experienced, enable introspection on past events and help to map the boundaries of what is possible in future interactions (Causey, 2003: 28; see also Hoskins, 1998: 6). Ilongot men's performance in public oratory clearly illustrates how 'stories significantly shape human conduct'; Ilongot men demonstrate their masculine prowess through narrative performance by telling 'themselves stories about who they are, what they care about, and how they hope to realize their aspirations' (Rosaldo, 1993: 129–30, see also 1986: 109–21).

Dress, a dynamic form of material culture, is one of the primary means through which we enact and interpret roles in the cultural scripts of everyday life. The extensive scholarship on dress, culture and identity perceptively illustrates this point by tracing the multiple avenues through which textiles and clothing 'mediate between self and society' across spheres of production, distribution and consumption (Hansen, 2000b: 4; see also Eicher, 1995; Entwistle & Wilson, 2001; Guy, Green & Banim, 2001; Niessen, Leshkowich & Jones, 2003; Weiner & Schneider, 1989). Jones and Leshkowich (2003: 6) argue for example, that by exploring the varied ways that people dress in different circumstances, we can reveal the 'relationship between individual choices, themselves subject to varying degrees of constraint and agency', and broader issues, such as 'nations' and 'markets that are invested in individuals performing in particular ways'.

Hansen's (1999, 2000a, 2000b) important study of the international trade in second hand clothing refocuses this insight on dress by applying it to used clothing (see also Lemire, 1997; McRobbie, 1989; Roche, 1994). She argues that clothing (including second hand clothing), is a special commodity that 'goes to the heart of widespread understandings of [people's] well-being... Its consumption traverses a wide field of social practice across class and between rural and urban areas that both gives effect to cultural normative values and helps to transform them' (Hansen, 2000b: 14–15). Edward Hawes research on how viewers perceive objects displayed in Museums, provides an entry to understanding the ways in which material culture such as dress can activate associations within narrative frameworks for action. He (1986) suggests that certain objects act as visual or sensory shorthand that triggers bundles of emotions and memories arranged within narrative frameworks. Applying Hawes' findings to dress in colonial Canada, Silverstein (2001) demonstrates that the donning of a specific dress style within narrative structures results in the internalization and enactment of social roles associated with that type of dress. Certain types of garments and styles of dress provoke instantaneous identification with familiar roles in cultural scripts such as that of a tomboy or a spoiled girl, and people choose their dress to identify with and participate in these roles (Kaiser, 1990: 71; Trautman, 1991: 146, quoted in Silverstein, 2001: 33). In the northern Philippines, trading, shopping for and wearing second hand clothing emerges then as one avenue through which people personalize cultural scripts of modernity. It opens up 'possibilities for agentive creation of identity through the manipulation of appearance' (Jones & Leshkowich, 2003: 7).

People construct *ukay-ukay* narratives, moreover, to recreate for both the teller and the listener, not only the facts about this type of clothing, but also the complex justifications for it within the Philippine context. Their stories about used clothing must subvert its earlier association with that of inexpensive garments purchased out of necessity by the poor to one of a desirable commodity that signifies prestige and value; and people constantly alter their justifications as they learn of other discourses of changing trends that, in turn, further inform their respective narratives. Through their tales of fashion and trade, people in the northern Philippines use second hand clothing as a point of departure from which to craft locally rooted, yet globally engaged identities posed between self, society and livelihood. Valuing the present they openly reconfigure, adapt and borrow from the past – their pre-existing master narratives.

The Setting for *Ukay-Ukay* in Ifugao, Upland Philippines

Ifugao is located in the Gran Cordillera Central mountain range that extends through much of northern Luzon. The main economic activity here, as throughout the Philippines, is wet-rice cultivation carried out in irrigated pond-fields, and in many areas, such as Banaue, the high elevation (1,500 m.) and cool climate limits cultivation to one rice crop per year. With no mixed agricultural production base and little agricultural surplus for sale, most families thus combine cultivation with non-agricultural income-generating work such as producing crafts for the tourist market, working in the tourist service industry, operating dry goods stores, and most recently engaging in the sale of second hand clothing.

Men and women both work in extra-household income-generating activities; and the region's socioeconomic systems of bilateral kinship and inheritance, ambilocal residence and primogeniture means that women own land and inherited wealth and have ready access to different economic opportunities. Most women are prominent in the management of household finances and hold power in this sphere by controlling the allocation of household cash resources. Men, however, predominate in public positions in politics and in religious office, and although men participate in domestic tasks, women still assume the bulk of childcare and domestic responsibilities (Kwiatkowski, 1998; Milgram, 1999b). Men and women thus continuously renegotiate gendered roles and power relations as they redefine their work and positions in Ifugao's commoditizing economy. Throughout the Cordillera, moreover, the differences among women, depending upon factors such as social class (landed elite, tenant or landless) and education, means that some women may have more of an advantage than others to gain social prestige and accumulate capital through their engagement in new enterprises such as *ukay-ukay*.

The accessibility of second hand clothing from countries such as the United States, Canada, Australia, Japan and northwestern Europe started to grow in many parts of Southeast Asia, generally, with increases in development aid following the end of the Second World War. In the Philippines, as Hansen (1999: 347; 2000b: 249–51) points out for Africa, the boom in the second hand clothing export market to these regions occurred in the early 1990s fueled by a large surplus of usable clothing in the West and the economic liberalization of many 'developing' countries that enabled increasing numbers of people to enter the market as consumers of Western imports (see also Haggblade, 1990: 508). In the Philippines, more dramatic increases in all manufactured goods coincided with government measures to loosen the stringent import restrictions in the last half of the 1980s with the new democratic government of Cory Aquino in 1986 (Chant, 1996). Charting the global trade of second hand clothing, Hansen (2000b: 99–155) outlines that the bulk of the used clothes that enter the West's export trade originate in sales from charitable organizations; a complex network of international clothing recyclers and brokers then channel the clothes to European and Asian collection centers for subsequent distribution.

The practice of wearing western-style clothing, imported or locally manufactured, has been firmly in place throughout the upland northern Philippines since the American colonial period (1898–1946) in the early twentieth century. With the recent availability of more reasonably priced used clothing, many people have found it an easy and logical transition to fulfill some of their clothing needs by substituting *ukay-ukay* for new garments. Indeed, newspaper headlines such as '"Ukay-Ukay" Memories' (Jimenez-David, 2002: A9), 'A Guide to the "Ukay-Ukay" Safari' (Subido, 2003: H2) and 'One-woman "Ukay-Ukay"' (Cuenca, 2002: 4–5) testify to the increasing popularity of used clothing in the Philippines and demonstrate how the media creates thematic story lines to highlight the widespread acceptance of this commodity.

Second Hand Clothing in the Philippine Cordillera

In 1995, the period of my initial fieldwork in the upland Cordillera provinces, second hand clothing was not widely available for purchase. Local residents could buy new Philippine-made Western-style garments or ready-to-wear (RTW) clothing at some grocery stores that usually stocked a few types of items, but the choice was often limited. While some Cordillera residents would purchase their clothing needs by making the ten-hour road trip to Baguio City, the regional administrative capital, many others tended to make the majority of their clothing purchases at their town's weekly market. In Banaue, the lively Saturday market provides a forum for itinerant traders, predominantly women from the lowlands, to set up temporary street displays of their products (e.g., cooked food, dry goods, fresh produce, kitchenwares). By late 1998, many of the Saturday marketers who formerly sold a wide variety of Philippine-made ready-to-wear clothing, had started to specialize in or augment their RTW stock with second hand clothing. By early 2000, a number of shops along Banaue's main road had opened selling only *ukay-ukay* and the stores selling RTW that had opened in 1999 had either closed or had converted much of their stock to second hand clothing. Indeed, Evangie Pindug,[3] a businesswoman who formerly sold RTW from her centrally located shop confirmed that in late 1999, in order to continue her business and fulfill local consumer demand, she had to convert her RTW stock to used clothing. *Ukay-ukay* shops are currently a visible presence in Banaue's retail landscape.

The dramatic growth in the trade and consumption of second hand clothing in the Philippines generally, and in the Cordillera, in particular, means that local traders negotiate business transactions with regional suppliers and international brokers through now well-established channels (see also Hansen, 2000b). Containers of second hand clothing originating in countries such as the United States, Canada, Australia, Japan, northwestern Europe and Hong Kong, as noted, are shipped to the Philippine ports of Manila and Cebu. Clothing brokers, some of whom are also involved in wholesaling new ready-to-wear clothing, distribute the shipments through their own network of regional suppliers to larger towns in the north, central and southern Philippines. In northern Luzon, Baguio City functions as the main collection and distribution hub for traders in the Cordillera provinces as well as being a major retail center. Indeed, by early 2002, the trade in *ukay-ukay* throughout the Philippines had grown to such an extent that the federal government, lobbied by retailers selling newly manufactured ready-to-wear clothing, threatened to impose a ban on used clothing imports and to enforce restrictions on local *ukay-ukay* businesses (Lacuarta, 2002: 7). Due to the equally vocal protests of consumers and second hand clothing dealers, however, these sanctions have not yet come to fruition (Manila Standard, 2002: 2).

The manner in which second hand clothing is packaged and shipped to the Philippines visually highlights its origin. Standard-sized boxes (72 × 42 × 48 cm.) packed in and arriving from Hong Kong contain assorted pieces of clothing for adults – men and women – or for children; and most of these garments have been sourced from the Hong Kong branches of charitable institutions such as the Salvation Army. Sacks or bales weighing either 50 or 100 kilograms contain used clothing originating in countries of northwestern Europe, Japan, the United States and Australia and contain one garment-type only such as T-shirts, men's pants or shirts, women's dresses or pants, bed linens and blankets or children's wear (infants to six years old, or six to twelve years old). Both boxes and bales are priced according to the quality of the garments they contain (A, B, or C grade) with traders preferring to purchase the top quality stock if they have the required capital. While the purchase of mixed garment boxes from Hong Kong enable smaller Cordillera retailers to obtain variety in their stock with minimal capital outlay, it also means that they risk receiving garments of mixed quality, regardless of the quality classification of the box. Larger retailers who have the capital to purchase both boxes and bales of clothing can maintain good stock variety and can potentially reduce the incidence of poorer quality goods because bales, most often, but not always, contain goods consistent with their designated quality category. To obtain the most marketable mix of garments then, traders customarily purchase used clothing in both forms (boxes and bales) depending upon consumer demand and upon the business capital they have available (Fig. 20).

Given this lack of control over stock quality, traders customarily negotiate a mutual understanding with their suppliers through a *suki* or favored relationship. The *suki* bond, a type personalized association, is marked by 'subjective values and extralegal sanctions which encourage individuals to meet obligations to others' (Davis, 1973: 211). Such economic personalism is essential to Philippine traders, as well as to consumers, because it is only by

Figure 20. A woman shopping for second hand clothing in a *ukay-ukay* shop in Banaue, Ifugao, northern Philippines. A box of assorted garments from Hong Kong is in the foreground.
Photograph by B. L. Milgram, 2001.

forming personal networks of obligatory relationships that both groups can overcome the barriers posed by a lack of trust and a weakness of institutional credit facilities such as the absence of written contracts (Davis, 1973: 211–12). Women, in particular, operationalize the *suki* bond by continuing, as they have always done, to adapt, reinterpret and transform their skills in reproductive activities to their business practices (Milgram, 2001). Their personal narratives about their engagement with new commodities such as second hand clothing thus chart a plurality of routes through modernity differentially drawing on customs rooted in past practice – their master narratives – and in kinship and community scripts but within thoroughly contemporary situations.

Shopping for Second Hand Clothing in the Philippine Cordillera

The research on dress has demonstrated, as I have noted earlier, that clothes fulfill a need to inscribe the self as an individual and as part of, or in relation to, a group (e.g. Barnes & Eicher, 1992; Entwistle & Wilson 2001; Guy et al., 2001; Hansen, 2000b). One of the ways in which dress asserts its power as a symbol of affiliation and identity is through peoples' stories about their clothes. People talk about shopping for and finding the right outfit at the right price and they talk about each other's clothes. This talk, I argue, has a practical effect; it actually shapes the understanding, reception and use of dress – a point that is particularly relevant to consumers' exercising control over second hand clothing, an imported dress form with its own distinctive set of associations and history.

On one of my visits with Mary Tayad, a *ukay-ukay* trader who has been selling second hand clothing since early 2000, she explains, for example: 'In my business today, I must be skilled not only in buying and pricing, but also in knowing the changing tastes of my customers. Now, I have to keep up with recent trends in fashion as well as with calculating my profit.' Mary's comment perceptively identifies that consumers in Banaue take pride both in finding a bargain and in dressing in accordance with their personalized style sense. Mary also points out that her customers know the type of items to purchase whether they are looking for contemporary styles or for durability and value for their money. Indeed, in Banaue, the word 'bargains,' has emerged as the most common term for second hand clothing and perceptively captures the feeling of pride and the skill that consumers exercise when shopping for and obtaining a good deal. Traders often refer to their customers as *barato,* meaning that shoppers drive a hard bargain in obtaining the best prices for goods.

Consumers, moreover, regale each other with stories of their bargaining conquests while traders, in turn, relate their own version of these tales. A consumer explains that recently she had been fortunate enough to find, at one shop, three elements she could coordinate into her desired outfit: high heeled shoes, narrow-leg pants and a short-cropped top. Her quest to purchase these at a price within her budget, however, entailed three return visits to the shop and extensive conversations with the vendor about her family background and about why these garments were so suitable to her purpose. A trader similarly recounts: 'If we offer the item for one-hundred pesos, they [the shopper] say can you give it to me for seventy-five pesos; the item is very special to me and besides, our families are long-time friends. So then I add ten pesos and we have a sale.' Through such narrative interchanges, traders and consumers nurture and expand their *suki* links with each other. Traders foster these interpersonal networks as they depend upon finding their customers first in pre-existing relationships grounded in kin and community networks. Consumers, in turn, shop first at their relatives' businesses expecting the best bargains, a discount or credit. For both groups then, bargaining narratives reproduce and expand pre-existing social connections as well as providing metaphors of control over an often unpredictable sphere of provisioning.

Philippine consumers are aware of the newest styles as they see them advertised on television and worn by their favorite actors. When students who are attending urban universities in Baguio City or Manila return to visit relatives in the rural areas of the Cordillera provinces, they bring with them knowledge of the most contemporary fashion trends and, indeed, return wearing the newest clothes they can afford to purchase. In my conversations with traders, they emphasize that: 'Our customers look first for signature clothes such as Levis, Nike, Adidas, and the alligator symbol [Lacoste] which are always the most popular finds. Our customers want a bargain, but they also want to wear garments that are widely recognized.' Traders like Mary confirm that they can always charge higher prices for garments that bear brand names and these are the hidden treasurers for which traders search in every box and bale of *ukay-ukay*[4] (Fig. 21).

During my visits with *ukay-ukay* traders, I frequently encountered young adult consumers, especially, patiently digging through the mounds of clothing

Figure 21. A woman shopping for second hand clothing amongst the street displays at the weekly Saturday market in Banaue, Ifugao, northern Philippines. At the left, the trader calculates the amount of the sale. Photograph by B. L. Milgram, 2003.

displayed at the Saturday market or through the boxes and racks of clothing in the town's shops in order to find just the right item. Matching colors, finding the correct fit and coordinating a fashionable mix of garments are priorities for teenage shoppers, in particular (see also Hansen 1999: 356). One shopper explains: 'Now the style is fitted, not baggy T-shirts like before although my brother still likes the oversized T-shirts.' A student, home on a break from university in Baguio City, proudly points out that: 'I like the pants that are fitted at the top, but that flare out at the bottom.' She explains that after seeing the style in which the lower sections of pants below the knees had been decorated with different fabric fringes and appliqué, she started to similarly decorate her pants with pieces of her mother's traditionally woven cloth: 'My friends in Banaue have started to sew our locally woven textiles to the bottom of our pants in this style. And we like to wear these decorated pants with the tighter-fitting T-shirts.' 'This year,' another female teenager points out, 'we are all asking for the "hanging top" or the "topper" with three-quarter length sleeves.' A teenage boy patiently explains that this season he is looking for pants with six pockets from Japan. Traders explain that they always try to purchase bales of garments from Japan because these garments are small in size and thus are the best fit for the Philippine body.

Even at Ifugao's indigenous ceremonial occasions (e.g., weddings, mortuary rites), the place of *ukay-ukay* is duly noted. At such public events men and women materially indicate their respective roles in society by wearing their traditionally designed clothing such as handwoven cotton skirts, loincloths and blankets (see Milgram, 1999a). While both men and women perform different parts of the ritual service, men tend to predominate in the oral recitation of odes to the appropriate ancestor spirits. At one wedding I attended, the host, showcasing his local oratory prowess, issued a challenge to male storytellers and dancers from 'all single men wearing "bargain" blue jeans'. Nine men took up his call, their clothing visually marking their social and sexual identity. Their used denim jeans provided a modern-day platform from which they could further distinguish themselves by appeasing the ancestral spirits through customary narrative performance. The type of clothing they chose to wear constructed messages about themselves and about their positions within the social collective.

Making a Living in *Ukay-Ukay*

From their first foray into *ukay-ukay*, traders strategize to successfully navigate the uncertainties of informal-sector businesses characterized by lack of control over stock quality, fierce competition, changing tastes of consumers and shifting fashion trends (see also Hansen, 2000b: 165–71). The distinctive clothing ensembles that Ruth Talango, a female trader, customarily wears on busy shopping days illustrates one way that traders seek to catch consumers' attention. Ruth moved back to Banaue from Manila in early 2003 to care for her ill mother; to earn income, she opened a second hand clothing store but in a very competitive retail clothing market. On Saturdays, she dresses in particular outfits that will showcase the best of her stock and encourage conversation. I visited her on a number of occasions when she wore a casual flannel outfit, jersey and pants, that featured cartoon characters printed over the entire surface of each garment. Ruth explains that she tries to stock mostly denim clothing (pants, jackets, shirts, skirts) as these products are saleable throughout the year; but she augments this stock with a specialization in children's wear and in flannel garments which are often in demand during Banaue's cold winter months. As women often shop with their children, Ruth will feature such clothes in a special display or don outfits like the one I saw her often wear in order to engage both the adult's and the child's attention and questions – in this case about the printed characters featured on her garments. Such strategies, she hopes, will facilitate sales. Leslie Langau, another trader who has been selling second hand clothing since mid 1999, explains that her biggest challenge is ensuring consistent stock quality:

> I cannot be assured that each box or bale that I purchase contains the quality or number of items that I expect. When I open the box and see miniskirts, short pants, swimming suits or women's fancy dresses, I know that these are not saleable; most women here wear pants and keep only one or two dresses to wear to church on Sundays.

Such economic vulnerability means that traders continue to rely on their *suki* connections with their customers and suppliers to facilitate the sustainability of their businesses. Narratives are integral to the *suki* relationship as the repeated stories of one's personal allegiances, in part, function to make that bond manifest. By nurturing *suki* links both with local consumers and with urban suppliers, *ukay-ukay* traders cultivate clients while ensuring a steady volume of stock and access to credit (Milgram, 2001). The trade of second hand clothing, a transglobal commodity that speaks of modernity, in fact, circulates in Ifugao through channels rooted in local customary and cultural practice.

Also, primary among traders' tactics to ensure business success is as Spooner (1986: 197) suggests 'the lore of the dealer.' Using the example of central Asian carpets, Spooner argues that such lore is generated by the history of the trade rather than by the conditions of production as goods are given a name and a narrative of provenance depending upon the point at which they enter the trade that is not necessarily their country of origin. *Ukay-ukay* traders do not deal with producers but through a globally-linked chain of wholesalers and distributors (see Hansen, 2000b). Thus dealer information is the trade lore generated in negotiating such commercial transactions (Spooner, 1986: 198). *Ukay-ukay* businesses involve not just the supply of clothes, as in the case of other commodities, but also the supply of information about them.

Traders know what goods are desirable. They listen to their customers who insist that it is not only the cost of 'bargains' – one-third to one-quarter the retail cost of new clothing – that gives *ukay-ukay* its appeal, but the belief that the quality of imported garments, even used ones, is more likely to be better than locally manufactured goods. Indeed, women and men would often comment on the T-shirts that I wore confirming that the colors of my shirts will not run when washed as 'these shirts are from your place'. Traders are certainly aware of this 'allure of the foreign' (Orlove & Bauer, 1997). As they open each box or bale of clothing, a treasure hunt ensues for designer label clothing that is always in demand. The consensus is that the best quality T-shirts come from Australia, especially for teenagers, both girls and boys, while the best quality children's wear is from the United States; both Japan and the United States are renowned for the quality of their bed linens and blankets. *Ukay-ukay* thus encapsulates the close association between 'foreignness and progress' the latter associated with Europe and the West. As such, used clothing in the Philippines emerges across the economic spectrum as 'a key token of modernity' that people use to situate themselves at the forefront of their changing world (Hansen, 2000b: 23; see also Langer, 1997: 16; Orlove & Bauer, 1997: 13).

Traders' narratives or lore then often capitalize on this predisposition by assuring customers that the garments they have chosen indeed originate in the 'favored country of the month'. Garments obtained from boxes are differentially desirable depending upon the strength of the link traders can forge between her or his stock and the wear of the most fashionable in Hong Kong. On the outside packaging of bales, however, the country of origin is often clearly written. Thus garments obtained from bales may readily assert their superior position if they originate in one of the desirable countries. In some of the more expensive or high-end shops, traders may conspicuously display empty bales that proudly sport their labels, 'Japan' or 'Washington' attesting to the origin of their contents. In the Philippines then, the narrative of provenance for *ukay-ukay* is very much a part of its caché.

Traders also use narratives to help them deal with their tenuous control over stock quality. By relating stories of one's great *ukay-ukay* shipments, traders verbally construct a sense of power over such uncertainties and in so doing demonstrate their favored status with their *suki* suppliers. A trader, Susan Pindug, for example shares her story about the bale of blankets she purchased in 2002 for 20,000 pesos. She explains:

> There were only 24 in the sack and I hesitated to open and sell it but my *suki*, Carmen said for me to try it. They were very nice and from Japan. Right away, the dentist bought five pieces; my neighbor, a teacher took two and another trader came by and also bought two, then I took two. I sold only nine blankets and was able to cover more than my buying price as well as getting free ones for the family. I went to 'Shoe Mart' in Manila and saw that the selling price there is 5,000 pesos each. Sometimes you hit the jackpot – business is a gamble.

Heather, another trader, relates that in December 2000 she had a 'prize' box from Hong Kong: 'The box contained children's toys as well as a DVD of children's cartoons and some video tapes; I was able to sell the contents very quickly and make a good profit on my investment.' Still another dealer tells of her good luck with a box of women's handbags and shoes, a type of stock-specific box for these types of items. In this box she found Louis Vuitton bags, 'only slightly used'.

A new vocabulary, moreover, has developed to attract customers and ensure them of the value of the goods offered. Some vendors currently display signs over part of their stock that read 'Selection'. Such declarations indicate that the vendor has personally pre-selected or 'cherry-picked' these garments from other vendors' stock to ensure high quality, and these garments are priced with accordingly higher prices. At the other end of the spectrum, new terms such as 'Take All' or 'Giveaway' indicate different types of sales that traders are currently offering to move items that have been slow to sell. 'Take All' signs thus invite inquiries from consumers to learn of the different conditions of particular sales; such engagements in co-narratives may instill a sense of obligation on the part of customers and encourage them not to leave the store empty-handed. In mid 2003, with increasing competition, some Banaue traders have taken steps to further distinguish their stock by dividing their stores into a high-end line of second hand signature or designer brands which are clearly labeled and a lower-end line of garments for quicker sales. Vendors are experimenting with different wall-mounted arrangements of such designer-brand pants, shirts and jackets that can clearly reveal their distinctive signature labels. These displays, they feel, attract consumers' interest in the signature garments, and enable traders to engage in a lively narrative with customers about how he or she had been able to secure such a fine piece of clothing. To initiate and guide the novice shopper through this expanding world of *ukay-ukay*, the newsletter for the University of the Philippines Baguio published a one-page *ukay-ukay* dictionary explaining the new language of this industry (Ti Similla, 2002: 12).

The stories consumers and traders tell about the garments they purchase and sell suggest specific cultural scripts that provide an intellectual and emotional context for these clothes. By creating their own narratives, people verbalize their motivations for purchasing such goods and relate what these goods mean to them. People thus read familiar stories into the appearance of others, as well as actively selecting personal dress in order to themselves participate in such narratives (DeMello, 2000: 12; Silverstein, 2001: 33). By assembling selected garments into a style that either displays their knowledge of wider clothing practice or subverts the received meaning of such goods, Banaue's consumers and traders assert 'local authorship over the West's used clothing' (Hansen, 1999: 357), and in so doing effect the creolization of goods that serves their personal and community identity statements (Fig. 22).

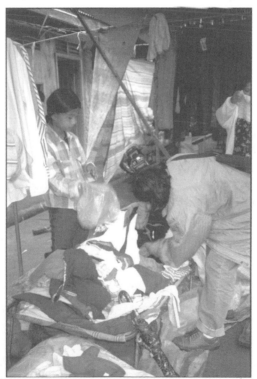

Figure 22. A woman digs through mounds of second hand clothing at the weekly Saturday market in Banaue, Ifugao, northern Philippines. Photograph by B. L. Milgram, 2003.

Conclusion

In her recent article on globalization, Anna Tsing (2000: 330) argues that although the flow of information, technology and goods is valorized the carving of the channel is not. In the northern Philippines, the agency of both consumers and traders to innovatively use and market second hand clothing resonates with Tsing's position. The personal stories they construct to negotiate the scripts of social and economic change dispute the nineteenth century European metanarrative that assumed a single direction toward a modernity and fixed and stable meanings for objects. Rather, one way that people attribute meaning to objects is through narrative – through 'unfolding processes [not] static structures' (Errington, 1994: 161). In the Philippines, traders' and consumers' personal narratives about second hand clothing reconfigure global commodities into localized modernities.

I realize, moreover, that traders and consumers in Ifugao operate within broader social and economic constraints as second hand clothing was initially parachuted into the economy uninvited. Yet, once it arrived, both groups proceeded to claim their own channels through which to realize dress and livelihood opportunities. Consumers play active roles in their own 'making' (Daunton & Hilton, 2001: 4) by wearing locally woven cloth side by side with second hand garments, decorating imported clothing with pieces of traditional cloth and then relating the details about how they composed such ensembles. Similarly, traders do not transcend customary practice, but rather join it to the present by marketing globally traded commodities through kin and community networks. In so doing, both groups create new stories for old, or used, objects (Errington, 1994: 160).

As Hoskins (1998: 6) argues, 'a coherent narrative constructs a unified image of the self out of the disparate, messy fragments of daily experience.' In repeating and embellishing successive versions of stories about themselves and objects, *ukay-ukay* traders and consumers revise and refine their own sense of connection between events, especially with the current economic changes; they tell their lives in ways that suit the predicaments in which they find themselves and '[they] edit, revise and "construct" these narratives for other audiences as well as to represent [them]selves' in the manner they want to be perceived (Hoskins, 1998: 6). At the same time, personal narratives are influenced by the context or parameters of the master narrative in which they are told, by the audience and by cultural notions of storytelling (Rosaldo, 1986; Silverstein, 2001: 24).

By exploring the diverse and often contradictory interpretations of the rhetorical value of objects such as *ukay-ukay*, we can begin to understand some of the ways in which people deal with social change. Individuals narrate stories about how they receive and domesticate objects symbolic of such change; in so doing they operationalize avenues through which to engage in and, in part, control such shifting conditions (Hoskins, 1998: 11–12). In Ifugao, people's involvement in and stories about *ukay-ukay* thus make visible and audible how local practices of consumption and trade are 'worked out in the contingent and compromised space' between market demand and the 'cultural intimacy' and expectations of family, community and customary practice (Li, 1999: 295). Regarding social change through the lens of *ukay-ukay* narratives highlights that in the Philippines, being modern or global is never questioned, only what form that modernity or globality should take.

Notes

1. *Wagwag*, meaning to shake and sell or to dust off, is another term describing how people shop for used clothing in the Philippines. It is a term distinctive to the second hand clothing industry in Baguio City, the administrative capital of the northern Cordillera provinces, and the primary collection, distribution and retail hub for imported used clothing.

2. For a detailed discussion of the cross-cultural consumption of material culture, but not necessarily within a narrative framework, see for example Hansen (2000b), Howes (1996), Steiner (1994) and Thomas (1991).

3. All personal names of individuals are pseudonyms.

4. It is interesting to note that Karen Tranberg Hansen (1999: 357) did not generally find the same degree of popularity for designer brands in used clothing among ordinary consumers in Zambia. Zambian consumers were most concerned that the garments not be manufactured in Zambia. Hansen notes however, that by 1997, some shops had begun to feature designer clothing and she suggests that this might indicate a growing trend.

9

Second Hand Fashion, Culture and Identity in Hong Kong

Hazel Clark

Wearing second hand clothes became an international fashion phenomenon in the 1990s as consumers who could afford new garments began to purchase and wear used clothing, traditionally associated with the poor. Something was resonating around the world to transform 'old' clothes into, what the fashion system deemed 'new looks'. Although the popularity of second hand clothing was part of a global fashion phenomenon affecting advanced economies, what was consumed and how it was consumed differed in detail from place to place. The interaction of the global and local dimensions of the export and import of second hand clothing has been described in preceding chapters. This chapter continues this theme by focusing on Hong Kong, where second hand clothing became popular in the 1990s, unexpectedly in as much as there was no explicit need and there was also certain cultural resistance to wearing used garments. The rationale was fashionable rather than functional and it is examined therefore in this chapter in the context of the global fashion system, and of the parallel 're-fashioning' of Hong Kong from a British colony to a territory of mainland China.

Before the 1990s, only poverty and necessity had sanctioned the wearing of used clothing in Hong Kong. Superstition made the indigenous Chinese population reject used garments, which were associated with the deceased, as well as with hard times for the economy. Yet curiously second hand clothes became fashionable in Hong Kong just before the 1997 'handover' to China. I propose that this happened due to the powerful impact of the global fashion system combined with a search for authenticity and identity that coincided at a profound historical moment, made manifest through practices of consumption. In doing so I draw attention to the 'glocal'[1] dimensions of the fashion for second hand clothes at the end of the twentieth century.

Hong Kong – Identity and Consumption

Settled by the British in 1841 and established as a colony with a 99-year lease in 1898, Hong Kong was 'handed back' to mainland China in 1997, with the ground work for that change having been laid in the early 1990s, politically, socially, economically, and culturally. What was being returned to China was not the 'barren rock' first ceded to the British, but an affluent and fashionable city and an international center of business, banking and trade.

The development of Hong Kong's colonial identity was gradual; the first significant population increase did not take place until the 1940s and 1950s. The Japanese invasion of the mainland and the civil unrest preceding the founding of the Peoples' Republic of China in 1949 stimulated substantial waves of migration, which were key to Hong Kong's development of business and manufacturing, especially in the garment industry. Textile entrepreneurs and skilled tailors from Shanghai brought the wealth and expertise necessary to establish the mass-production industry and the bespoke trade.

By the 1950s Hong Kong was producing and exporting large amounts of fashionable clothing to the West. The clothes were not available in the colony, other than as factory discards, and the majority of the population would not have been able to afford them, even if they had been for sale in local stores. Many Hong Kong immigrants from the mainland were suffering financial hardship, but nevertheless considered it important to keep up appearances, especially to preserve their social status (Bond, 1996: 360). Clothes were passed down within families where second hand items provided something 'new' to wear. For instance, the 'one and only suit' was circulated amongst groups of male friends, for formal occasions like weddings and funerals. (Ng, 1992: 6). In working class areas pawnshops signified by a bat holding a gold coin in its mouth, and street markets were commonplace and provided sources of cheap clothing. In Wanchai, North Point, Causeway Bay, Mongkok, Tsuen Wan and Shamshuipo, a dress could be picked up for as little as $HK10.00 or $HK20.00 ($1.00–2.00 (US)) from one of the ubiquitous local markets, where used clothing was on sale alongside surplus items from local garment factories. For those who had experienced poverty being well turned out in new clothes was an important marker of status and of self-esteem. Imports from the West, especially from America were attractive as being considered fashionable and modern, and because they had not been worn locally.

One observer recollected an incident from his childhood, just before Christmas in 1958 when a box of relief goods from wealthy Christians in the United States was opened in public in a church on the outlying island of

Cheung Chau. Gathered around were staff from the church, an excited crowd of young Cheung Chau residents, and the youngster from Mongkok, across the harbor in urban Kowloon, who told the tale. The quality and styles of the clothes delighted those present who rushed to try them on. Thick corduroy jackets, heavy flannel trousers, a denim suit, a bright colored brushed thick cotton shirt in blue and red, and plenty of multicolored checkered woolen scarves were included in the parcel (Chim, 1998). Although used, the clothes were desirable for their difference, as representations of 'Americanness' and as signifiers of modernity. At the time local women were still wearing the fitted Chinese style dress, known in Cantonese as the *cheongsam* for best, and both men and women were wearing *samfu*, the loose trousers and top, for everyday. Western-style fashion was seen as highly desirable and came with the authority of having been fashionable in places that dictated global fashion, namely the USA and Europe.

As the economic gloom lifted in the 1960s, due in part to the development of the clothing industry, the overall standard of living improved in Hong Kong and the need for used clothing declined. In a more buoyant economy, second hand goods carried the stigma and recent memory of poverty. Fewer people needed to rely on charity and fashionable Western-style clothes were more widely available and affordable to the majority. This was assisted by the emergence of local brands a number of which would become success stories, such as Giordano, one of several labels that chose foreign sounding names to obscure their local origin and thus increase their fashion credibility and desirability by appearing to be 'foreign'. There was an ongoing desire by Hong Kong people to buy into international fashion. In the 1980s and 1990s popular fashion brands such as Versace, Dolce & Gabbana, or Prada were available in the high-end fashion stores and soon after as much cheaper copies in the street stalls, allowing virtually all those who wanted to be able to demonstrate their modernity and fashionability through their association with the latest style or brand.

Global labels were a mark of recognition and credibility that contributed to the construction of a social identity in Hong Kong. Devotion to a brand also eased the anxiety of making choices as the items on sale had been pre-selected to constitute a given fashion 'look'. Teenagers were particularly drawn to international brands and they had high levels of disposable income to purchase expensive imports. According to a 1990s survey the average teenager received a substantial $HK846.00 (approximately $105.00 (US)) monthly allowance.[2] Much of the money was spent on brand name goods, especially fashionable clothing and accessories (Manuel, 1995). From a cultural perspective, the strength of conformity in Chinese society, evident in Hong Kong, created a keen motivation for individuals to identify with their peers. Research findings led Donald Tse to note, 'that Chinese consumers would place more emphasis on the opinions of their reference group in making purchases than would American consumers. And we would expect that Chinese consumers would be more likely to use name-brand products to identify with their peers than would American consumers' (Tse, 1996: 361).

Communication through fashionable global brands took on a particular cultural significance in Hong Kong because of the colonial context, as Ackbar Abbas has noted,

> One of the effects of a very efficient colonial administration is that it provides almost no outlet for political idealism ... as a result, most of the energy is directed toward the economic sphere. Historical imagination, the citizens' belief that they might have a hand in shaping their own history, gets replaced by speculation on the property or stock markets, or by an obsession with fashion or consumerism. If you cannot choose your political leaders, you can at least choose your own clothes (Abbas, 1997: 5).

Consumer practices and choices, as Abbas argues, cannot be dismissed lightly in Hong Kong where consumption is a highly informed signifying practice. The places where one shops and what one buys are important in defining the self in relation to others. David Tse has also noted the significance of shopping as a form of social interaction,

> Compared to American consumers (and other representatives of Western culture); Chinese people would be less receptive to consumption as a terminal goal. Chinese would be equally receptive to consumption as a life reward; Chinese would be more receptive to consumption as a source of daily satisfaction; and Chinese would be more receptive to consumption as a tool for building social relationships (Tse, 1996: 356).

Hong Kong people do not typically form great attachment to material things. Part of this is pragmatic, lack of space making storage difficult for most people. Clothes and other consumables are quickly discarded when the fashion changes. But unlike in the United States or Britain, the thrift or charity shop is not commonplace in Hong Kong, certainly not as a source of 'individual' items. Not only was there a traditional stigma attached with wearing used items, but also fashion tended towards conformity rather than individuality. Historically therefore, the Salvation Army and Oxfam were the only two international charities running second hand stores in the colony. Privately operated shops selling used clothes and textiles tended to be dealing in the antique variety as on the well-known Hollywood Road on Hong Kong Island.

In the 1990s the Salvation Army had only seven shops in this colony of over six million people, located in the mainly working-class residential communities of Tai Hang Tung, Chuk Yuen, Ngau Tau Kok, Yue Wan, Stanley, Tin Hau and Yau Ma Tei. (In her chapter Lynne Milgram mentions how the Salvation Army in Hong Kong was also exporting used clothing to the Philippines.) Oxfam, which opened its first shop in Hong Kong in 1977, was more centrally located. Discounted rents allowed it to occupy two prime retail locations, one in Jardine House, in Central, on Hong Kong island, and the other across the harbor in the Silvercord Centre in Tsim Sha Tsui, Kowloon's large shopping and tourist area. The merchandise included non-essential items such as compact discs, books, accessories and recently fashionable clothes, targeted at a more diverse range of consumers than the Salvation Army shops. Their locations indicate that the Oxfam shops would have appealed to a diverse population including expatriates. The latter comprised Americans, Britons, other Europeans, and Australians who regularly recycled furniture and domestic items usually via household sales as they moved in and out of the territory. But appropriation of used items was not commonplace amongst the majority Chinese population. The association of old things, especially clothing, with former wearers and with times of poverty reinforced their unacceptability. The consumption of second hand clothes in Hong Kong therefore had no real precedent beyond need.

In the 1990s many international fashion trends were nostalgic and also playing on issues of 'authenticity' by including signs of ethnic cultures. Others, Grunge[3] for example, incorporated used garments in a bricolage of items that first appeared as a mode of dress in subcultural style in the 1970s (Hebdige, 1979: 103). The evidence of a 'patina' of wear, whether actual or implied, became incorporated into global fashion looks and in parallel with the fashion for wearing second hand and vintage. Clothes that had or gave the sense of having 'cultural biographies' (Kopytoff, 1986) became prized in the 'nostalgia for the present' (Jameson, 1989) that characterized fashion within the wider politics of mass consumption before the millennium (Appadurai 1996). This provides some underlying logic for the interest in second hand clothes in Hong Kong, against previous cultural norms. Rather than seeing consumers merely as slavishly following global fashion trends, the interest in second hand clothes was perhaps as much a reflection of a growing sense of uncertainty surrounding the change in sovereignty. Choosing used clothes, either in the second hand or vintage category, was a material way of engaging with the past, which was seen as in effect being erased for Hong Kong people. Even though many citizens welcomed the 'handover' the future was very uncertain. At such times the past is the only known quantity. Hong Kong was experiencing a very heightened version of the global uncertainty provoked by the millennium. If we take Abbas's premise that Hong Kong people used consumption as a powerful means of demonstrating choices that had been denied to them historically in their self-determination, then the fashion for second hand clothes in the 1990s gains greater logic that at first appeared. So the unprecedented interest in second hand clothes in Hong Kong in the 1990s can be viewed on two levels, one because of the powerful impact of the global fashion system, and the other in relation to a local search for authenticity and identity. We now look in more detail at both levels via three different categories of consumer I have identified as being actively involved in buying and selling used clothes in Hong Kong in the 1990s: the emerging young quasi avant-garde, who were particularly drawn to American and Japanese culture; the higher income group who would usually prefer to wear globally fashionable brands; the well-off who had the means to be at the 'cutting edge' of international fashion trends.

Consuming Second Hand Fashion in Hong Kong

The Young and Quasi Avant-garde

One of the earliest fashionable second hand shops was Man and Earth, which opened in the Western district on Hong Kong island, probably in the mid 1990s. The merchandise was planned towards a distinct fashionable look. Photographs of the shop and its interior suggest that it was based more on a Grunge or anti-fashion look (Figs 23 & 24). The premises were in one of the characteristic tall narrow buildings. Its stock included imported items such as old Levi jeans, headscarves, army surplus overalls and great coats, the metal framed granny style glasses made popular by John Lennon, and other accessories including boots, bags and badges. The interior was sympathetic to the style of the merchandise and had a sense of the unfinished about it; with its crumbling plaster and ad hoc furnishings it gave the sense of a contemporary bazaar. Upstairs, the owner lived in an apartment with a canopy bed and Oriental tapestry and second hand printed fabrics casually covering the floor. The enterprise was short-lived because the building had a demolition order. But there was also apparently pressure from the tenants of neighboring businesses and residences who objected to the 'hippies' that the shop attracted.[4]

Man and Earth served an alternative niche market of artistic types, students and the young avant-garde, who were searching for something 'different' or unusual. Within the next few years more similar shops opened (Daswani,

Figure 23. Man & Earth shop front, Western district, Hong Kong island,
photographed mid 1990s.
Photograph by Teresa Ho.

2000; Leung, 2001). What distinguished these enterprises from charity shops was the fact that they were buying in used fashion items from overseas, especially from the United States and Japan, not recycling clothing obtained locally. In the mid 1990s used fashion shops could be found in the highly popular Causeway Bay shopping area, in Granville Circuit in Tsim Sha Tsui, and also in parts of Mongkok. Small and boutique-like, they were often tucked away in vertical malls such as the Beverley Commercial Centre in Tsim Sha Tsui, Kowloon, and the Kimberley Centre, and Eworld Trade Centre in Causeway Bay.[5] As the shops were not evident at street level, part of their appeal was that to know about them meant being in the fashion 'know' locally. Owned by young entrepreneurs, not large global conglomerates, the merchandise, space and the environment were the antithesis of brand name stores. These shops typically opened and closed late and performed a social

Figure 24. Man & Earth interior showing customers and merchandise,
photographed mid 1990s.
Photograph by Teresa Ho.

function; they were locations to be in and to be seen in, not merely places
to shop, demonstrating the role of consumption as a leisure activity or 'life
reward' (Tse, 1996) in Hong Kong.

Another of the early second hand shops was Beatniks, opened by Rensis
Ho in Granville Circuit in 1995, before used clothes had become generally
acceptable in the colony. 'At that time Hong Kong people weren't ready
for second-hand clothing. Now it's very trendy', Ho commented in 2001
(Leung, 2001). But two years on there had been such rapid change that in
1997 he sold the shop to escape an increasingly competitive business. It
continued under new ownership selling 'bread and butter' vintage items,
imported from the USA, like Levis 501s and T-shirts. The merchandise was
now carefully chosen to reflect current fashion trends. As co-owner Kee Lau
commented, 'I actually sit down with our supplier and talk about certain
trends. Say the fashion designers are doing 80s. So at the same time, we'll try

to put out 80s clothing' (Leung, 2001). These types of shop were predicated on importing styles of clothing from overseas that would represent the place of origin. Another, Midwest, which opened in 1993, based its whole image around Americana. Typical stock included 'square dancing shirts', which were 'reasonably priced' at $HK180 (approximately $23.00 (US)), 1970s cowboy and Boy Scout shirts, and more unusual items such as a zippered 1980s break-dancing jumpsuit or a 'bona fide 1950s Mexicana souvenir shirt'. The owner chose his stock with an eye to his customers' demands for specialized and higher quality items while playing on mythic connotations of the Wild West and the American Dream (Leung, 2001).

Japanese youth culture was very influential on the young and fashion conscious in Hong Kong in the 1990s, its trends being disseminated via the media. By the second half of the 1990s seven or eight shops had opened selling recycled Japanese fashion. (Clothes imported from Japan having the added practical advantage of better fit, being made smaller for Asian body types.) The owner of Recur, Ms Lau Pui-yu, made regular trips to Japan to source items from the 1970s such as penguin trousers, striped skirts and floral blouses, old LCD wristwatches, plastic framed sunglasses, and wallets with colorful beads. Recur was located in the Kimberley Shopping Centre in Causeway Bay, a mall popular with younger consumers. The Japanese owner of another shop, Funktionally that opened in Tsim Sha Tsui in 2001, chose a Japanese style interior and employed Japanese sales staff. Although it attempted to 'look Japanese', Funktionally sold quintessentially American clothes such as Polo shirts and rugby tops sourced from dealers in the USA. This mixing of different 'global' cultural styles added to the shop's appeal.

Such shops introduced a consumer experience that was literally quite foreign to Hong Kong. 'Shops like Me & George have few trappings and a more haphazard selection, closer to a market bazaar than boutique. Patience, time and imagination are vital to sift through yesterday's trash to find nuggets' (Leung, 2001). These were attributes uncommon to Hong Kong fashion shopping, which typically involved knowing exactly the brand and the item wanted and often needing to find it in a hurry. Imagination was rarely necessary when the task was to buy the latest and most fashionable thing. Shopping in these boutiques more resembled being in the street market than in the high fashion store. And although they offered the potential lure of the 'unique' find, retailers did not promote the cultural biography of particular items. In fact some shops obscured the origins of their merchandise with euphemisms like 'vintage' and 'antique', or even 'samples' as used by Me & George.

Selling imports was more acceptable than selling items obtained locally because the origins were remote and anonymous. The fact that the items were from a different time and place provided a reverse exoticism in that they had already been 'tried and tested' elsewhere in the global fashion arena. Also, the younger consumers of used clothing did not share the concerns and superstitions of wearing used clothes that made this practice unacceptable to many of the older generation. In 1992, for instance, fashion design students returning from a visit to Europe, told me how they had bought hats and other second hand clothing in flea markets in Paris, but that they would not wear their purchases in Hong Kong for of fear of censure from parents and older relatives. As one journalist observed, 'In Hong Kong culture, wearing used clothing traditionally carries a ghostly taboo, but much of the younger generation couldn't care less. It's all about looking cool' (Leung, 2001). A substantial cultural shift occurred therefore during the 1990s when second hand clothes became not just acceptable, but fashionable and 'cool' in Hong Kong.

In 1999 an exhibition staged by the Hong Kong Arts Centre entitled *My Poor Dear Hong Kong – Poor but Cool* served as a marker of cultural change. In the wake of the Asian economic crisis the show lauded the creative and ethical value of recycling. Exhibition Director, Oscar Ho, stated that,

> Being poor does not necessarily mean being miserable. With limited resources, one could still create beautiful results. With an ordinary matchbox, I remember, I could make a tank and a basket out of it… In our rich, modern society, increasingly we let the big companies that employ all these creative professionals do the creative works. We are consumers just going to the shops and buying all the fantastic creative products. Creativity and resourcefulness is no longer needed for children, for the parents can take them to toy shops and they can purchase all these wonderful products creatively designed for them… Let's not romanticize poverty. Being poor is tough… But poverty could force one to be resourceful, and make one be sensitive about alternative solutions (Ho, 1999).

The exhibition responded to the wake of the Asian economic crisis of 1997 that had served to stimulate more active and creative consumption. The loyal following of 'stylists, students, and housewives' who typically patronized the boutiques mentioned above, were making more individual choices in looking for what they liked, not just passively consuming brands. '"We don't care about brands, but sometimes I'll write down the names to look out for," says Me & George owner Lau, wearing a striped shirt purchased at the shop. "But the shop assistants don't have a clue. They only remember Giordano"' (Leung, 2001). Some younger consumers were becoming more confident in their choices and beginning to play with the construction of their own appearance. Dick Hebdige has referred to the way that subcultural groups repositioned and recontextualized commodities as the visible politics of their subversive self-definition. In this sense younger people in Hong Kong began to attempt to express their own style by wearing second hand clothes in the 1990s (Hebdige, 1979: 102). A similar interest also emerged amongst their peers, the more mature and higher salaried people who became involved in buying and selling used clothes.

The Higher-Income Shopper

In November 1996, the second celebrity used clothes sale organized to raise funds for the Tung Wah Group of hospitals was reported in the local press. The auction featured items donated by stars from the local television station TVB. A leather jacket owned by Kelly Chan and Aaron Kwok's leather vest received the most bids. (*Oriental Daily,* Sunday November 10, 1996). Miss Hong Kong, Pauline Yeung Yuen-yee had donated a virtually unworn diamond and jade brooch valued at over $HK160,000.00 ($20,600.00$ (US)). But she did not choose to donate *cheongsam* or jeans to the sales, considering them too ordinary and therefore uncharacteristic of her personal style. Celebrity cast-offs did not rely only on their known association with the original owner their appearance had also to represent the image of the star.

The occasional sales of celebrity clothes that began in Hong Kong in the early 1990s paralleled similar charity sales in Britain and the United States selling the cast-offs of the internationally known celebrities like pop star Elton John, or Princess Diana (Clark, 1997). The items sold in Hong Kong represented local media stars and many pieces would have been purchased as investments, to keep not to wear, in the hope that they would increase in monetary value. For the celebrities the sales provided publicity as well as a means to clear out their closets and to raise some money either for themselves or for charity. Typically the sales lasted four or five days and were held in large venues such as hotel ballrooms, exhibition halls, or vacant retail spaces, and some were actually organized by the stars.

Perhaps the best-known sale organizer was Teresa Cheung, a prominent socialite, one of the ten best dressed women in Hong Kong and the former spouse of the locally popular music star Kenny Bee. Cheung relied on her circle of friends and contacts to supply the merchandise and used her reputation to gain publicity for the sales. Likewise, professional fundraiser Margery Au, well known for promoting prestigious events in Hong Kong, staged her first charity used clothing sale in November 1996, to raise money for a children's ballet and drawing school. The unexpected sale of over a thousand items donated by female friends led to Au running sales on a regular basis for the rest of the decade.

When I interviewed her in June 2000 Au had staged nine sales, the most recent in May of that year and she was preparing for the next in December. Although she described the events as 'high class jumble sales', they had little in common with their humbler predecessors. The merchandise was provided by well-off women who were usually 'cleaning up the closet' of items either no longer in fashion or simply unworn. The quantities provided per individual meant that it did not take many suppliers to produce enough pieces for a sale, as few as fifteen could be sufficient. One married couple regularly provided 170 to 180 pieces each sale and gave 300 items for the May 2000 event. Typically, some items were only a season out of date while others, especially designer brands, could be much older. A seven-year-old Chanel item in good condition, for example, would still have resale value. The prices were kept relatively low, certainly in relation to original retail prices and profits were split 50:50 between Au and the supplier. Comparatively these were real bargains. A piece that cost around $HK6,000 ($772 (US)) new, would typically sell for $HK300 ($38.00 (US)). Au set the prices based on what the supplier suggested and what she considered the market would meet.

The consumers were typically middle- and upper-income local residents and foreigners; the majority were Chinese women, but they included men, expatriates and well-known local professionals and celebrities, as well as secretaries, lawyers and doctors. Male customers would buy for themselves and 'for their wives'. Some people came to look for specific items and others just out of curiosity. The venues ranged from vacant retail spaces to the more prestigious ballrooms of five star hotels, like the Ritz Carlton, or as the sales grew in popularity the Hong Kong Convention Centre. Au described the first day of any sale as being 'like a market' with some items being offered at very low prices as an attraction. The social aspect was appealing as well as the desire for a bargain. Some clients came on more than one day; others chose to wait until the last day for bargains. At the May 2000 sale one woman bought fifty-six pieces on the final day, when everything was marked down by 30 percent, spending a total of $HK12,000 ($1500 (US)). She was one of around 120 to 200 visitors over the five days of this sale.

Au's sales typically comprised 75 percent clothing, 20 percent handbags, and only 5 percent shoes, as they were less likely to sell. Approximately 30 percent was brand new menswear. They included popular styles and familiar American or Japanese brands, not necessarily designer brand labels, but certainly pieces that were considered stylish or had been recently fashionable. Prices ranged from around $HK180 ($23.00 (US)) for a casual top or jacket to $HK5,000 ($640.00 (US)) for a Chanel suit. Brands that were currently in highest demand in the retail market would command the top prices, such as $HK11,000–12,000 (approximately $1,500.00 (US)) for a Hermes garment, or even $HK20,000 ($2500.00 (US)) for a 'Kelly bag', if one ever became available. The suppliers varied in their motivation. Some supported the ecological benefits of recycling, others welcomed the chance to earn some money, but for the majority the greatest incentive was the opportunity to clear out the closet to make room for newer and more fashionable clothes. For the consumers the sales provided an opportunity for leisure shopping in an unfamiliar retail environment and the lure of a 'find', that is something recently fashionable, in good condition, on sale much lower than its original retail price. With the economic downturn in the late 1990s even the better-off needed to spend more carefully. Also none of Au's clients seemed to object to the fact that the merchandise was used, as long as it was clean. These sales had parallels in the United States, but in Hong Kong they provided, in addition to the actual merchandise, an entirely new form of shopping experience.

The Well-off and Fashion Conscious

Another variant on this trend was the well-off Hong Kong women who bought second hand fashion outside of the territory, particularly 'vintage couture' purchased on the west coast of the United States. One journalist attributes this as a trend amongst the upper strata of Hong Kong society that started in New York and then moved to Los Angeles (Daswani, 2000). On the west coast the beginning of the popularity of vintage clothes with movie stars and celebrities was marked by the media attention given to a 1940s studio-designed dress worn by actress Demi Moore to the 1992 Oscar awards. Rita Watnick, owner of the 'ultra-exclusive vintage store' Lily et Cie in Los Angeles has attributed this fashion trend towards a quest for individuality and exclusivity, 'There is just a simple thing that motivates people: when you don't have money, you want the things that people with money have. When you have money, you want things that people don't have. That's my customer in a nutshell, from Hong Kong, from anywhere' (Daswani, 2000).

Shopping for used clothes had become a new form of leisure activity for the well off. Actress Anita Pallenberg's description was that:

> It's a bit like taking drugs or drinking. I roam around and get off on the fact that I can find something cheap. Whenever I get that compulsion to make myself feel better, I go to the second-hand shop. The other day I went out at 2pm and at 5pm I was still in that shop, rummaging and talking. It's part of my thing (Frost, 1997).

In the 1990s in Hong Kong some women had started to go on one day shopping excursions across the border into Shenzhen to buy copies of designer label fashion merchandise. Others, mentioned above, went to California to purchase vintage clothes. Not only were the local and the global coinciding to create fashion trends, the dual influences also affected where and how people shopped, as much as what they bought.

Conclusion

Returning to Hong Kong, the fashionable recognition of second hand clothes in the 1990s marked a major cultural shift. Used clothes had gained a new status. A significant transformation had taken place since the 1950s and 1960s when second hand clothes were worn for need, to being generally despised as being socially inappropriate in the 1970s and 1980s, to becoming not just acceptable but fashionable to a variety of consumers in the 1990s. The young and quasi avant-garde, the higher-income group and the well-off and self-appointed local fashion leaders all consumed used clothes. Validated by the global fashion system's obsession with nostalgia Hong Kong consumers put aside cultural taboos and began to buy, sell and wear used clothing in the 1990s. For some shopping for second hand introduced a more active and informed consumption, concerned with selection and choice, as opposed to the more passive obsession with brands.

This international fashion trend arrived at the time that Hong Kong was seeking to establish its own post-colonial identity. Second hand items offered some sense of authenticity and link with the past and with other places whose cultural identity appeared more defined. In their consuming practices, the young and avant-garde who wanted to 'look American' or 'Japanese', the higher-income shoppers who purchased the cast-offs of local celebrities or of their peers, and the well-off and fashion conscious who shopped overseas for vintage, all challenged longstanding cultural taboos associated with used clothes. 'Glocalization' had occurred as the global fashion trend for second hand and its associated practices of consumption had taken on a local dimension. Just as the international fashion system influenced the acceptability of second hand clothes in Hong Kong, the territory in its turn, developed a local response to this global phenomenon, which also served as part of its own project of establishing and representing a post-colonial identity.

Notes

1. 'Glocal' is a term that came into use in the early 1990s to express the global production of the local and the localization of the global.

2. The survey, conducted by the Social Sciences Research Centre of the University of Hong Kong in collaboration with RTHK (Radio Television Hong Kong), covered students in forms three to five (14–16 year olds), related their pocket money amounted to the basic salary of a Beijing university professor, which was typically half as much, at around 400 yuan ($372 (HK) or $47.00 (US)) a month.

3. Grunge originated in Seattle in the late 1980s and drew upon hippy and Punk styles and items. Associated with the loud rock music of bands such as Nirvana and Pearl Jam, it formed a point of identification for 'lost generation Xers', that is the young white middle-class kids who could not or did not want to maintain the economic and material achievements of their parents. The style combined second hand items such as flimsy 1930s frocks, jumpers, jackets, worn, ripped and faded denim jeans and heavy boots, as well as lumber jack shirts, well-worn leather jackets, worn with long, tangled hair and a generally unkempt appearance. It has been described as a thrift shop inspired style, a form of dressing contrived to suggest poverty (de la Haye & Dingwall, 1996).

4. I am indebted to Teresa Ho for drawing my attention to *Man and Earth*, which she visited and photographed in the mid 1990s. Unfortunately it has not been possible to establish the exact dates that the shop opened and closed.

5. In 1993 fashion design students at the Swire School of Design, Hong Kong Polytechnic, described to me how more boutiques in the Beverley Centre were stocking second hand items (despite, they observed, the fact that many Hong Kong people did not like second hand clothes for reasons of hygiene). More of these young, and more avant-garde consumers were willing to pay, for example, $500 (HK) ($64 (US)) for a pair of used jeans with a US brand label. The students described these consumers typically as being interested in status dressing and as people who would buy clothes to keep as well as to wear.

Part 3

Contemporary Refashioning

Introduction

Alexandra Palmer and Hazel Clark

Arnold has described contemporary fashion as 'display[ing] the promise and the threat of the future, tempting the consumer with new identities that shift with the season and expressing the fragmented moralities of cultural diversity and social uncertainty' (2002: xiv). This section, Contemporary Refashioning, provides three diverse examples of new identities that are constructed from the contemporary second hand fashion system. The theme of traversing time in an attempt to create new and unique identities with vintage or reworked second hand clothes runs throughout this section, though each chapter addresses this from a new viewpoint. Second hand dress becomes the material whereby consumers can play with the past to create modern identities.

Wearing clothes that are obviously out of fashion has historically often been associated with artistic taste that positions the wearer as eccentric, because their dress operates apart from mass sanctioned taste. The 'poor look' associated with a bohemian lifestyle set out to 'turn the banality of everyday life into an ongoing work of art with oneself at the centre', which women of the New York Beat generation in the 1950s achieved in 'limp, thrift shop dresses made interesting with beads', as described by Elizabeth Wilson (1998: 230–4). Wealthy Europeans have a long history of wearing non-Western dress as a form of exoticism. For instance Manchu embroidered court robes operated outside of the pejorative connotations of the second hand clothing market and were signals of elitism and connoisseurship in the late nineteenth and the twentieth centuries ('Veilles Robes de Chine,' Femina 1921 (10)np; V. Wilson, 1999, 2002). In the late 1960s and early 1970s hippie fashion promoted the beauty and authenticity of non-Western and vintage clothing discovered in flea markets, antique stalls and charity shops. Galanos, a designer whose work upheld a traditional, mature couture style remarked at the time, 'It's ridiculous to say they [hippies] are making fashion. Most of them wouldn't be allowed in the best restaurants in town

... a woman in her '40s or '50s – even '20s or '30s – going out and buying a smelly old thing that someone else has worn' (quoted in Loebenthal, 1990: 135). Nonetheless, such 'smelly old thing[s]' have become highly desirable and fashionable. Now, celebrities and socialites are noted in press reports wearing vintage, and it is often believed that 'the next best thing to a new dress is an old one ... [because] Kate Moss, Cameron Diaz and Jade Jagger ... have a passion and flare for vintage' (Chong, 2000: W13).

Today wearing second hand clothes has become a mainstream phenomenon that is highly commodified within the global fashion system of production, marketing and consumption. The term 'vintage' is used to cover a huge spectrum of clothes that are not newly designed. Second hand 'vintage' designs are worn internationally by the avant garde be they young or mature. Middle-income to wealthy consumers obtain their 'new' used clothes from global and local sources as they seek to establish individuality through these garments that cannot be replicated. The quest for originality and the one-off is, in part, a reaction to the globalization of enormous fashion chains at all price levels. In the Diesel Denim Gallery in Soho, New York, jeans, formerly a vernacular, working-class and egalitarian garment, are positioned as works of art. They are 'hung' on the walls in 'various washes of jean, atrophied like filthy, wrung-out rags, with discreet price cards on the wall' (Kastner, 2002: L1). As Palmer and Rovine discuss, by the late 1990s even upmarket fashion and style stores, like Barneys, and Henri Bendel in Manhattan, were offering new, vintage and hybrid recycled garments along side one another.

The current nostalgia for second hand dress from all periods is yet another interpretation of fashion as a form of *bricolage* that reconfigures used clothes. These same clothes are also trophies with complex cultural and economic histories and are signifiers today of unique fashion. Nostalgia and a search for authenticity have been identified by scholars as characteristics of the late or post-modern period that preceded the millennium (Jameson, 1984). Second hand clothes fit both categories being able to serve nostalgically as 'authentic' representations of another time or place. But of course the availability of second hand items is not predictable. As Jenß notes, in the desire to create a neo-mod self-image, home sewing retro designs is a viable option in the face of dwindling authentic stock. Just as being able to sew for oneself is a symbol of fashion independence, so too is being able to find and wear vintage clothing. Each displays an individuals' ability to operate outside of the fashion industry's seasons and dictums by being one's own designer. Jenß's fieldwork in Germany examines how young people in the 1990s looked back to the 1960s to construct their own image of a decade where dress was a leading signifier of lifestyle for younger people. She shows that this refashioning is not restricted only to certain income groups and social classes, it is a global style. While 1960s fashions are used as historical artifacts of the past this is not a simple nostalgia, but is repeatedly made relevant for current time, as 'their perception of history corresponds to their contemporary demands and is thus not only fragmentary, but also subjectively shaped and consciously selective.' Thus the original 1960s fashion is utilized as a cinematic trope, like the flashback, to achieve the desired style where originals, modifications and copies, all merge to construct the present.

The range of vintage fashion marketing and consumption is discussed by Palmer, who sets the wearing of vintage fashion into mainstream fashion. Vintage fashion is clearly identified as a symbol of individuality that defies exact reproduction. Vintage is an alternative style to the latest designer look that is produced in multiples and available internationally. It is the uniqueness of vintage that appeals to consumers who now consider themselves connoisseurs and collectors, and that makes buying an old garment complex in terms of style and price.

As the masses take to sourcing vintage so too do fashion designers as both Palmer and Rovine show. Some, such as New York-based Norma Kamali, have made new fashion lines from their own remaindered garments, while boutiques and department stores also stock authentic vintage fashions. Large-scale manufacturers sell retro styles in chain stores globally as Jenß points out, while other fashion designers choose to deconstruct and reconstruct previously worn garments and to re-use them in part or in full. Rovine, reveals how XULY.Bët is one of a number of contemporary fashion designers who are utilizing second hand clothes as a cross-global and intellectual means to challenge fashion stereotypes. When placed in this perspective, the entire development of deconstruction in fashion that emerged in the late 1980s is perhaps not so radical and can be seen to have a long history in traditions of remaking, as noted earlier, which are clearly still evolving.

Rovine discusses how the fascinating reworking of old clothes appropriated, recycled and reconfigured by Paris-based designer Lamine Kouyaté, under the XULY.Bët label, parades the less than pristine origins. She sets these designs not only within the Western fashion system but also within the designer's Mali heritage, something that is constantly referred to in the fashion press but not at all well understood at any level of complexity. Rovine offers a sophisticated interweaving of West African and Paris fashions bringing together issues that run central to this book; the global and transcultural nature of using second hand dress that re-shapes fashion. XULY.Bët's used clothes and textiles become transformed as even the definition of garment type is reconfigured. The reconstructed designs recall the late nineteenth-century aesthetic of the Arts and Crafts movement, a Morrisian ideal that cherished the evidence of the hand of the maker left on an object during a similar time of concern over mass production destroying artistic individuality. XULY.Bët's designs rudely show signs of the original wearer and the physical labor of reworking the garment on his 'mutated' clothes that challenge traditional ideas of the craft of tailoring.

The varied themes in Contemporary Refashioning each demonstrate the significance of old clothes as signifying previous periods and owners. The second hand designs enable the reworking of history that is discarded in favor of a new, non-replicable individuality. Second hand fashion is seen to cross and blur identities of origin and time, creating both a historical past and a historicized future in the search for suitable fashions for the present.

10

Sixties Dress Only! The Consumption of the Past in a Retro Scene

Heike Jenß

> It is reasonably easy and affordable to recreate a nice 60s look 30 years later. A well stocked wardrobe should have a mix of current items and retro items that can be worn together. For a proper 60s look, vintage dresses are the best...
>
> 1960s Ladies' Style site

The 1960s Ladies' Style site on the Internet, the source of this quote, gives useful advice on how to create a style from the past today (www.geocities. com/SoHo/4473; accessed: March 13, 2003). The website is made by and targeted at a group of young stylists who belong to the contemporary mod or sixties scene. This is an internationally connected style tribe whose members practice a lifestyle marked by an affinity to 'everything sixties', which is expressed in their daily dress practice, domestic interior, lifestyle, dance and music preferences. Dressed in most cases either in original vintage clothes from the 1960s or in self-made garments remodeled from old patterns, their appearance is marked by a look which is striking in its 'authenticity' and detailed study of the historic model (Fig. 25). What motivates these young people to adopt a look from the past and wear old clothes? Where do they buy their items and what kind of consumption practices do they develop? How do their looks differ from retro-styles in contemporary fashion design? And how does the appropriation of the past relate to the perception of time and history?

By drawing on participant observation during sixties-events, on interviews with members of the German sixties scene and their material culture, this chapter will focus on the use and meaning of historic fashions and

Figure 25. A contemporary sixties-stylist in original dress and boots, sitting in Columbus Chair, photographed in the living room, Germany 2000. Photograph by Heike Jenß.

second hand dress in a particular youth culture. It will investigate one particular variant of a phenomenon that is regarded as characteristic of our contemporary culture: the consumption or re-performance of the past, frequently labelled as 'retro'.

Although the consumption of the past has been highly visible for several decades, and young people now appear to be the main cultural actors of retro-styles, they have been largely ignored by researchers on youth as well as by fashion scholars. There were until recently only a few studies dealing with historic revivals and retro in fashion design (Baines, 1981; Martin & Koda, 1991; Trosse, 1999). Postmodern theory (Jameson, 1984; Baudrilliard, 1982) and debates around *nostalgia*, (Fischer, 1981; Helmes-Conzett, 1995; Horx,

1995) show that *retro* has been applied as an all-encompassing catchword to cultural forms and practices, which in reality can have multiple facets and very ambiguous cultural meanings. These should be analyzed and placed in context. A more in-depth look at retro consumption has been provided only recently by Gregson, Brooks & Crewe (2001), who focus on seventies revivalism among British students, highlighting different modes of second hand consumption and the appropriation of the past, though excluding a closer look at specializing retro-groups like the sixties scene.

The term retro (Latin: *back, backwards*) goes back to the so-called 'nostalgia-wave' of the 1970s which was paralleled by a growth in second hand consumption (O'Hara, 1986: 213; Steele, 1997a: 285; Childs & Storry, 1999: 455). But even though it has mainly been used for old second hand clothing (Silverman, 1994; McRobbie, 1989), it is apparent that neither in German nor in English does a common understanding of the term *retro* seem to exist. The interviews I carried out show that people have a very individual understanding of the term. Some people apply the word precisely to the mix of old and new items of dress in one ensemble. Others use it for original second hand dress only, whereas a number of the people questioned apply it, like the fashion media, to new garments which copy old forms, as for example Adidas's *Originals* line. Many of the sixties stylists are also tired of the word. Because of its frequent use, retro is perceived as a trendy though quite meaningless term, that is used by the fashion industries to announce the diverse fashions from the past as new looks.

Perceived as an established and commonplace word now, and as a characterizing feature of postmodern fashion (Steele, 1997a: 286; Lehnert, 2000: 105), retro cannot clearly be restricted to reproduction or original. In order better to understand the effect and impact of retro in dress, a retro-look or retro-style can be defined as a visual or rather materialized recourse to objects and images of the past, stimulating memories or subtle associations with images and objects from other decades and centuries. Comparable to film technique, this quasi 'textile flashback' can be seen as a creative process. When considered in this sense, retro implies the construction of past images and historic looks which can be achieved with original objects as well as with new ones that look historic. It uses the potential of dress as a cultural signal of time and an important component of cultural memory, historic consciousness and imagery. In fashion, understood as body technique (Craik, 1994: 1), retro gains a very particular quality; because with the garment as the object closest to the body, time and history – even in a fake or synthetic form – are literally 'in touch'. This, it seems, is especially appealing to people, who have not themselves experienced the time they now consume through dress.

The Contemporary Sixties Scene

The majority of the people in the German sixties scene, and also of the ten men and ten women I interviewed, were born between 1968 and 1983. Most of those who are now in their early thirties got involved in the scene during the late 1980s and early 1990s, when they were in their late teens and early twenties, and a younger generation has started to take up the style more recently. This youth culture covers quite a wide age span, which can be observed in other contemporary youth scenes as well. The involvement of people around thirty is a sign of the extension of youth, caused by changing, less stable social conditions, such as longer educational periods, periods of unemployment and the changing attitudes towards family and getting settled. What we now call 'youth' is a transition process and orientation phase that can actually lead right up to the middle of the thirties and even beyond.

Newcomers usually become aware of the sixties scene via friends or by going to sixties parties and concerts. Through the interaction or observation of sixties stylists, they may feel attracted to the style and start to get into it. Nonetheless, due to the medialization[1] of youth cultural styles, it is possible to develop an admiration for the style without being actively involved in the scene. The sixties scene is particularly mobile and brings together youth, not only from all over Germany but from elsewhere in Europe as they meet at international events in Spain, England or Italy. In fact, the German scene can be seen as one branch of an internationally connected youth culture, which has members in all the industrialized countries in Europe and North America and also in Australia and Japan (Lentz, 2002). Even though I participated in international events, my ethnographic fieldwork is mainly restricted to the sixties scene in Germany and in particular in the industrial area of the Ruhr Valley and Cologne.

The term 'sixties scene', which is used by the people I interviewed, can be seen as a credit to a famous 1960s London-based nightclub, called The Scene (Barnes, 1991: 13). Contemporary mod fanzines and websites (www.thescene.de) also refer to this legendary club in their use of the word 'scene'. In the 1960s the club was frequented by a new youth culture that presents the historic reference model for the contemporary sixties stylists; namely, the British mods, who formed into a youth subculture by the end of the 1950s. The style of the mods turned into a mass phenomenon by the middle of the 1960s, becoming synonymous with the young and dynamic pop fashions offered by the boutiques in London's Carnaby Street. Eventually the popular catchword 'mod' covered everything that is now connected with the myth of Swinging London (Hebdige, 1974: 4). However, even though

Hebdige emphasizes that the definition of mod must be limited to 'working class teenagers who lived mainly in London and the new towns of the South and who could be readily identified by characteristic hairstyles, clothing, etc.' (1974: 4), for the contemporary sixties scene this strict definition has been blurred.

It was in the context of punk, particularly, that the style of the mods was for the first time rediscovered on a broader scale. The punks created a style that was in itself a bricolage made of youth cultural styles from the 1950s onwards and there were other youth cultures contemporary with them, who attempted to recreate one particular style, like the 1960s mod look. Disconnected from its original spatial and historic context, new generations transferred the mod/sixties style beyond England, and turned it into a process of continuous reproduction. There followed not only editions of the sixties style but also many alterations and further developments of it. Today the original style has split and fragmented into very diverse, though stylistically sometimes linked, scenes and styles, ranging from Psychedelic, Northern Soul, Casuals, Scooterboys up to Acid Jazz and Britpop (see also Polhemus, 1994, 1996; Hewitt, 2000; Muggleton, 2000).

The use of the term 'scene', however, must also be seen in its sociological connotation. Compared to 'subculture' the term 'scene' implies a more open and hybrid community or network of like-minded people (Hitzler, 1999). According to sociologist Roland Hitzler, scenes or tribes emerge today not because of collective living conditions or due to social class like the traditional working class subcultures of the 1950s and 1960s, i.e. the original mods. Rather, group consciousness and a feeling of belonging develop from the belief in a common theme or a shared affinity (Hitzler, 1999: 12). Getting into a scene is more a question of aesthetic preference than of class solidarity, even if the relevance of social background cannot be dismissed. The ability to travel to sixties events across Germany and Europe surely demands certain economic capacities and the people I interviewed have jobs or are students working on a part-time basis. In a broad sense, all those interviewed share a middle-class lifestyle that is the social frame of their cultural practices.

The shared interest or 'theme' that the members of the sixties scene collectively engage in obviously is *the sixties*, in particular the attachment to rare 1960s music and the consumption of the aesthetic and material culture of this decade. Most visibly, the affinity to the past is expressed in the performance of the sixties fashion style. Performance – in German *Inszenierung* – implies the conscious selection, organizing and structuring of the media of (bodily) performance which is strategically calculated to have an effect on an audience, to 'the others' (Ontrup & Schicha, 1999: 7).

The performance aims at the creative and transformative engagement with the self (Fischer-Lichte, 1998: 88), because body and identity are not fixed or naturally given, but can be created and changed in endless performances (Lehnert, 1997: 47). Dress is, in that process, the decisive means 'with which we write or draw a representation of the body into our cultural context' (E. Wilson, 1992: 6), thereby linking performance with consumption practices. Sociologist Steven Miles emphasizes the particular importance of consumption for the construction of young people's identities. According to him, consumer goods are the last and only way to localize oneself socially in a time when traditional structures like family and work are more and more unstable (Miles, 1998). However, consumption practices serve not only in the construction of personal identity but also generate social relations and a feeling of stability and belonging (Mentges 2000). Thus it is a constitutive cultural practice, especially in youth cultures that share the affinity for a particular product or consumer activity.

Sixties-Consumption: Sources, Knowledge and Practices

'I always loved to watch old movies,' says Christina (21) who records sixties movies on video to use the costumes as models for her own dress creations. When she sees a nice dress, she stops the video and draws it in her fashion book. Whenever she wants to have a new or special dress, she consults the book as a source of inspiration. The plot of the movies is outside her main interest, but the focus of attention is the represented aesthetic, stimulating the refashioning of the sixties.

Movies and photos, particularly on record covers, are quoted as the most important sources for getting ideas and information about sixties fashion. Further knowledge about the time and its costume history is gained from costume books, literature, advertisements, old fashion magazines and material survivals. Sandra (29) says that after an increasing engagement with original dresses in second hand shops she got more and more an eye for details, developing discernment and specialist knowledge. She also teaches her eye by dating the dresses of others. The direct contact with sixties objects forms the constitutive step into the style. All of the people I interviewed can remember the point when they felt 'truly sixties', achieved by a complete sixties attire, which was at the same time perceived as an initiation into the scene. Hence, the knowledge of the relevant fashion history as well as the knowledge of good sources for obtaining original artifacts is essential for their retro-performances and in the sense of Pierre Bourdieu, an important component of their (sub)cultural capital (Bourdieu, 1998; Thornton, 1995).

Purchasing second hand clothing and reproductions, either homemade or offered by the fashion industry, can be seen as the main ways of getting access to sixties clothing. Original sixties clothing is purchased in the common places offering used clothing, such as second hand fairs, jumble sales, second hand shops or from dealers and boutiques specializing in sixties or seventies design. Because the sixties-stylists find it more and more difficult to get good pieces at the usual second hand stores, specialized dealers are often a better source, though also a lot more expensive due to the limited selection of items of clothing they have on offer.

Some of these dealers go directly to their customers by selling at sixties events. The structure or time-schedule of a usual mod-weekend for instance consists of a club at night and a more casual get-together the following day during lunchtime sessions. Here people can purchase records and clothes at stalls that have been set up either by professional dealers who offer a special selection of sixties items, or by people who want to earn a bit of extra money. Actually, to a certain degree it is apparent that retail here is being divided into men's and women's business. This is particularly true for record stalls, which, nearly exclusively, are run by men, while clothes stalls are mainly, though not exclusively, set up by women. Some of the interviewees even suggested that the girls tend to define themselves more through dress and the associated knowledge, while the guys prove their subcultural capital through the acquisition of rare records and musical knowledge. There are in fact numerous girls in the scene who have good record collections and an equally specific knowledge concerning rare original records and obscure 1960s artists, though the line up of sixties events is still dominated by male DJs, reflecting very much the general gender order in the music business (Grimm, 1998). Therefore we still find the same inequalities Angela McRobbie noted in 1989 that it is easier for girls 'to develop skills in those fields which are less contested by men than it is in those already occupied by them' (1989: 37). The fact that there are more girls dealing in sixties clothing may also be due to the practice of selling clothes they initially bought for themselves, and reselling them because they do not fit or they got bored with them. Second hand clothing for women is more available than for men, a problem well known in museum collections. The men mentioned that one is likely to get a shirt, but to find original trousers or even a suit that fits is nearly impossible. To alter these garments is more difficult than to alter women's dresses, so men tend to get them made to measure and are likely to wear them for a longer time, hence do not deal in them.

Regarding shopping, it is important to keep the eyes open all the time. The hunt for everything sixties that survives, in markets and in unknown places, and specialized stores, turns into a popular leisure activity and becomes part of everyday shopping practice, which is very different from purchasing in high street chain stores. Sandra refers to sixties consumption also as collecting or treasuring and as a process of searching and finding. Thus the shopping and the searching out is an important component in the practice of the 'authentic' style as a means to perform identity and construct difference, in contrast to the consumers of mass-fashion (Gregson et al., 2001: 17).

Even though virtual auction houses like www.ebay.com do not replace the popular weekend and outdoor activity of shopping at jumble sales, the Internet has become a very important market for the purchase of sixties clothing. 'Manual' shopping at markets is somehow determined by the 'surprise' of a good find in thousands of often quite 'trashy' objects. But one can still be lucky and get a gorgeous piece for very little money. In contrast, digitalized shopping offers the more systematic search for specific objects in the most diverse range of products, offered worldwide in one single market, though usually the prices are then higher. While many people regard original sixties clothing today as collectors' items, some people still react with dislike and are even disgusted by the reuse of old garments. Due to the fact that they have been worn by 'other people' and show traces of wear like sweat or holes, used clothes are often perceived as unhygienic. They are referred to as trash and rags, which others no longer want (Ginsburg, 1980). Second hand clothing has for some people an association with poverty and need. These clothes are often not seen as *fashion*, and therefore are seen to be without value. But for the sixties stylists it is precisely the time preserved in the old dress that turns it into an unique object that is worn by nobody else. So in the context of the scene, the used clothing is given a particular value, as it is highly estimated as an artifact of the past. Adherents appreciate the history which is carried by such a piece: 'It is interesting to speculate about what a garment has been through, it is a witness of an other time,' says Chris (23). The material object has its own history that becomes a quality or attribute of the garment. However, time also makes the clothes transitory and susceptible to decay:

> Sometimes you wash the garment only once and you realize how fragile the seams are and that there is no point in wearing it. Or shoes, authentic shoes are really a problem. It's hard to get them in good condition. You wear them once or twice and then you lose the sole. Well, what can you expect, when they lie about without any care for ages in some rotten place. So you have to head to the shoemaker a couple of times, who faces you with shaking heads, because you love these old things. You really take great pains sometimes (Jochen, 33).

Handling the garments with care, for example by hand-washing or by repairing them again and again, shows a certain respect for the material culture of the past, which is, nonetheless, appropriated and used. But the efforts and difficulties associated with historic survivals are easily accepted, because the consumption and appreciation of the authentic and unique guarantees a feeling of individuality and distinction from others. The wearer's sense of the garment's value is that it defines the wearer and marks her/him as singular. This perception is what makes this scene appear rather elitist. Their practices resemble very much what Elizabeth Wilson already stated for the 1960s hippies' second hand consumption, that 'did involve the expenditure of much time if not money, and reintroduced the snobbery of uniqueness, since there was, necessarily, only *one* of the "frock" you had found – just as much as if you'd bought a Dior original' (1985: 193).

Original Copies: Sixties Customizing

As the introductory quote from *The 1960s ladies style site* indicates, in order to achieve a 'proper sixties look, vintage clothes are the best' (www.geocities. com/SoHo/4473; accessed: March 13, 2003). Wearing the original is a way to distinguish oneself from the mass market retro copies, and the better the copies are, the more the original is valued. According to Hillel Schwartz it is only within a 'culture of the copy' that uniqueness and originality can be perceived this way (2000: 219).

> You just see it. I simply see the difference. The original is more aesthetic in design, material and cut. The sixties fashion was very playful, more elaborate in detail. I like the zippers and the buttons which are decoratively displayed on the garments. I bought a jacket from *Hennes & Mauritz*, it is horribly sewn. The fabric is a disaster. The cut is nice though and the fit is good, similar to an original one. But let's wait until it's been in the washing machine (Sandra, 29).

But although quality and the love of detail is said to be missing in contemporary chain store fashions, there is apparently not an absolute resistance to new retro-clothes and to the mixing of old and new items. Limiting oneself only to originals would obviously result in a very reduced wardrobe, especially as second hand garments are sometimes not in good condition and do not last very long when worn regularly. The contemporary market is especially useful for basic clothing with a sixties touch like tight shirts and hipster trousers, which are currently also fashionable among consumers who do not belong to the sixties scene. Often these clothes are only used as part of everyday wear, instead of wearing out the rare originals, which are saved for sixties events that are the prime stage for displaying the authentic.

The sixties stylists tend to personalize new retro garments by altering or combining the new garments in a way that gives them an original appearance, thus creating a hybrid sampling of old and new garments, which is not particularly evident as such. They alter seams to make trousers shorter or tighter, add wide loops for hipster belts with original buckles, exchange new buttons for original more decorative ones, or transform plain contemporary garments with Op Art applications into groovy sixties items. Because of the need for authenticity these alterations and details turn into subtle means of distinction 'It's the accessories that make the difference. You see immediately if somebody belongs to the scene or not. Most people don't practice the style so consistently' says Sean (33) referring to current retro fashion design.

The production of self-made clothing is gaining in importance, as the originals are getting scarcer or cannot be found in the right size. As could be observed in retail, here as well, gender differences are clearly visible. Even though today girls are no longer automatically trained in traditional domestic practices like sewing, they are still the ones who have more skills in sewing than the men in the scene. Moreover, none of the males interviewed even considered making their own clothes. Instead they consult a professional tailor or get their clothes made by female scene members, some of whom are training in fashion design. However, compared to men's sixties clothing, women's sixties dresses are easier to sew as the cut is often quite simple, and many girls alter their garments even though they have limited sewing skills.

Homemade clothes are generally created from original patterns. Also domestic textiles or old clothes that do not fit are bought and reused to make new 'old' garments. The texture of fabrics should look original. Fabrics from the 1960s are preferred because they tend to have a different texture from new fabrics, which influences the shape of the garment and thus affects the retro-appearance. If old fabrics are too expensive or unavailable, new synthetic fabrics that have some resemblance to the originals are used. Available in a range of bright colors, fabrics can be combined to create dresses with geometric patterns, in the style of Yves Saint Laurent's famous Mondrian dress from 1965 (Fig. 26). These fabrics are cheap and are made of polyfibers so that they do not shrink or wash out.

As there is quite a demand for fitted sixties dress, professional custom-made clothing is another opportunity for obtaining garments in the right style. Some scene members have specialized in the production of sixties clothing, thereby contributing to a subcultural entrepreneurial infrastructure. The introductory text on the website www.dadadress.com, which offers custom-made sixties dress, declares: 'Vintage clothing is becoming scarcer

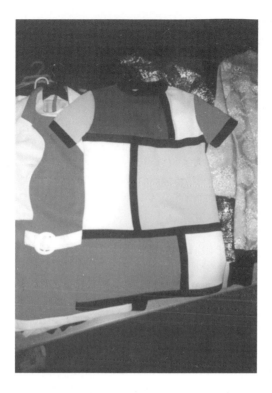

Figure 26. Mondrian/YSL inspired mini-dress, custom-made in 1999. Altered with short sleeves, different combinations in the squares and shorter than the original from 1965.
Photograph by Heike Jenß.

and scarcer to come by. And unlike what's to be found in vintage shops and thrift stores, the clothing we offer is new and available in your size.' Jessika Madison and Estelle Thielen the designers who make '1960s style clothing available world-wide' react to the lack of original and eccentric sixties clothing, saying, 'You will find these clothes to be similar to vintage clothing in the attention to detail, unique fabrics and quality' (www.dadadress.com; accessed: March 8, 2002). The new clothes are made from new as well as from 'deadstock sixties fabrics' with typical sixties patterns, like flowers and geometric prints. However, depending on the cut, rather than on the fabric, prices for these custom-made dresses range between $90 and $110 (US). A number of the clothes offered on the website are copies and interpretations of sixties designer dresses. The recreations of the iconic looks from famous sixties designers such as Pierre Cardin, André Courrèges, Mary Quant and Rudi Gernreich, provide key historic prototypes. The website offers variants of sixties clothing for men and women, and customers can choose garments from a wide selection. However, according to the designers, all garments are produced in a limited number, 'steering away from mass-productivity and remaining truer to the one-of-a kind nature of vintage clothing'. The website presents the designs through fashion drawings with brief descriptions and close-up views of the fabrics. Following closely the original look, many of the designs are also displayed in photographs, showing the dress worn by models with an 'authentic' styling and equipped with original shoes or boots, hairstyle, make-up and matching accessories.

In the accuracy of combinations the sixties stylists separate not only from mass-market sixties variants but also from other retro-consumers. Examining the seventies revival, Gregson et al. (2001) found two main modes of appropriately appreciating seventies clothing. In the carnivalesque mode, seventies clothing is not worn on a daily basis but only for special occasions such as seventies nights. 'Dressing up' in seventies clothes, these producers of retro-looks tend to 'overdo' or caricature the style for fun, using particularly 'trashy' or glamorous clothing like the disco style. In contrast, in the knowing mode of appropriate appreciation, retro-clothes are part of the daily, ordinary wear. The authors refer to the latter as 'clever dressing for knowing audiences' (2001: 12). The preferred seventies clothes belong rather to the category of everyday casual clothing, like T-shirts, flared jeans and corduroys, which are combined with modern garments (Gregson et al. 2001: 8–18). In this mode the historic style may become blurred and modified in new combinations. While both of these modes create a certain distance to the historic style, the practices in the sixties scene are aimed at the construction of a 'historically correct' style, achieved with original or original-like clothing, and corresponding combinations. This marks not an 'ironic distance' (Silverman, 1994) from the past but in contrast their full identification with the aesthetic of the sixties that is not only evident in dress practices but in the entire lifestyle.

Doing the Timewarp: Sixties Settings and (Collective) Performance

The affinity to the sixties is not just limited to clothes, but includes also the design of the domestic setting. Here, too, the sixties stylists like to be surrounded by the design they appreciate. Nearly all of them give their homes a sixties flavor. This is achieved through pictures and movie posters, of *Barbarella* for instance, and by collecting original furniture and accessories. Searching out pieces of furniture from second hand furniture halls or jumble sales, can lead to special finds that are often cheaper than new items. In some apartments the genuine sixties setting is even enhanced by hiding contemporary design, for example when the 'ugly design' of the modern answering machine is kept in a box with original sixties decor. So, consuming the material culture of the sixties does not mean to go without the comfort of modern technology.

Dress and private space are merged into a self-created sixties world that can evoke a feeling of really living in the time. Gordon (32) who is a graphic designer and has specialized in dealing with sixties furniture indicates how the entirety of the setting affects his personal feeling and imaginary. 'You want to create your own kind of world, [*Erlebniswelt*]. When I listen to the music ... then I also want to have the right surroundings and like to sit in a matching living room, it feels different and better and you really feel a lot more sixties.' This immersion into a fictitious sixties world can be seen like a personal time travel into the past that looks very much like 'nostalgic escapism'. However, that 'it feels different and better' implies that this is less a 'yearning for yesterday' (F. Davis, 1979), than a longing for the unusual and exotic within the context of contemporary culture. Original furniture is regarded as a lot more 'cool' or beautiful than modern design. Consuming 'the authentic' enables a differentiation from products for 'the masses', that may integrate consumers into a monoculture produced by internationally popular brands like IKEA (Düllo, 2000). Furthermore, the original items are valued more highly because they transport history and offer the personal appropriation of things with 'life', which bear an important potential for fantasy. The timewarp is not only a product of individual creation and restricted to private space but also produced by collective rites and events. 'The best is when you are with a crowd of sixties people. Then you feel a lot more like time travelling,' (Christina, 21), and the collective performance at events, which resemble altogether the setting of a stylish sixties movie, appears in fact very different to outsiders, who are visibly excluded by dress boundaries.

> Don't we like to go to events like U.N.K.E.L., because we show up in sixties dress, because they are part of our identity? – Don't we like to see others, who also dress up in sixties style, with lots of love of detail, because nearly everybody makes a big effort style-wise so that we can 'truly' experience the sixties for three or four days? Therefore my request: Smart dress – not only – but mainly (www.thescene. de, June 14, 2001, translated by author).

This request was published in the guest book of a modzine on the Internet and is addressed to participants in the annual German mod weekender in

Unkel (a village at the Rhine incidentally referencing the sixties series *The Man/Girl from U.N.C.L.E*). The advice is targeted at people who break with the collective habits and interrupt with modern clothing the timewarp and self-created sixties flair of mod events. Compared to the usual contemporary setting the sixties environment is regarded as 'different and better', because it enables members to step out of the everyday routine into a self-created world, in which they can fully live the style they have consciously selected for themselves. The dress code 'sixties dress only', which can be found on many flyers announcing sixties events, guarantees a closed setting for this. However, these events achieve the effect of a virtual time travel not so much into a past or bygone time but rather into an exotic and simply different (present) time, that is based on how *they* see the sixties.

Despite all efforts towards historical accuracy, the prevailing style in the scene is the product of their actual perception and interpretation of the sixties, particularly of the 'mythic' British 'Swinging Sixties', transferred to them via music and fashion. Martin (30) remarks: 'What fascinates me is the picture that I have of this time. It consists only of fractions, you see, only what's spilled over into our time.' Naturally aware of the difference between real past and pictorially represented past, their perception of history corresponds to their contemporary demands and is therefore not only fragmentary, but also subjectively shaped and consciously selective. They can choose what they like most about the decade and may leave out or remove the things that they do not like. Due to the dominant popular images, which are the images of fashion, public figures and stars, choice, however, is in a way limited and determined by the rather iconic looks of the decade:

> What people in the mod scene wear today is not what they wore back in the sixties. These are now the clothes of rock stars. That's what people wore in London, around the rock- and music-scene. People on stage had these clothes. And now people mirror themselves against the photos of the hip and famous. Oh, you see, Ron Wood has this nice striped jacket. Oh look, Peggy Moffitt. Everything is copied (Sean, 33).

'Mirrored' against the popular images of the past, the performance of the authentic in the sixties scene appears nearly more original than the original, thus exaggerating and subverting history, rather than reconstructing it. This is also evident, as the sixties scene altogether is a melting of diverse styles from the sixties era, that include not only mod style, as Hebdige would define it, but also psychedelic or hippie, space age looks from French couture and even seventies looks. However, according to Christina (21) two main stylistic tendencies can be observed which are closely linked to music:

We prefer to listen to soul, and this means kind of early sixties. That's also visible in dress. That means that the men usually wear suits and have short hair and women are definitely in dresses, these gorgeous pop-art dresses, nothing with flowers, that's already late sixties. Then there are the psychedelics or psych-kids, and they wear hipsters of course and these wild and colored flower shirts and some of the guys have long hair and scarves.

Julia (20) characterizes her style in contrast as psychedelic and hippie-like: 'Nothing from the early sixties, no '63 costumes or so. It's late sixties and early seventies. Bell-bottoms, colored shirts, miniskirts, boots. But nothing later than 1972'. Dating or labeling their own style as 'early-sixties' or 'late-sixties' is a way to prove knowledge and discernment, even though it might not in all cases correspond necessarily with costume history. Furthermore, labeling one's style functions as a conscious self-localization and self-differentiation.

Body History in the Image: The Availability and Transformation of the Past

As Gabriele Mentges emphasizes, dress is especially encoded through its imagery (1998: 218). The pictorial world, generated through the multiplication of images like record covers, movies, television or fashion photographs that provide a pool of historic body appearances and bits of fashion-time, forms the constitutive basis for the consumption and bodily performance of history. Technical images, as Vilem Flusser describes so well, absorb history, making up the always spinning and turning memory of society (1983:17). Due to this reproducibility in images that make 'history' eternally present, historic styles get separated from their original context, 'the real' history behind them is blurred.

Fredric Jameson compares retro with pastiche or the simulacrum, a copy with no original, representing no more than stereotypical images. He sees retro as the 'cannibalistic plundering of the past', that is random and without meaning or content (Jameson, 1984: 65). For the sixties stylists, however, the consumption of the past is not at all random, but very focused and the history of the style not irrelevant. They perceive the sixties as a positive, dynamic and revolutionary decade, projecting into it an attitude and enthusiasm that they sometimes miss in today's world. If we look at costume books the sixties are one of the most positively *represented* decades. The typical labels, homogeneously applied to the ten years of this decade are: Youthquake, cult of youth, revolutionary sixties, futuristic fashion, swinging London, youth revolt, or even 'sex, drugs and revolt for a better world' (Seeling, 1999). So obviously, and in the eyes of young people who did not experience the time, 'the sixties' appears as a very attractive decade. Youth became emancipated and an entire market was exclusively targeted at them. There were young designers like Mary Quant, who designed miniskirts, ensuring that girls no longer looked like their mothers (Whitley, 1987: 95). It is the myth created around the sixties and of Swinging London, to which Dick Hebdige refers, that makes it so appealing. But, as Roland Barthes notes, a myth is always determined by the loss of the historical qualities or characteristics of things (1996: 130). One lost quality today is the social dimension of the mod style, like the visible blurring of class and social hierarchies in England during the 1960s and the subculture's subversion of bourgeois conventions, which will not necessarily work with sixties attire today.

A further aspect is the construction of gender difference through dress, which was partly confused by the mods' subversion of traditional images of 'manliness' and the play with androgyny. Although Barnes sees the mods as a male-dominated youth culture (Barnes, 1991: 8), Garber and McRobbie argue, that the mods were the first 'softer' working-class subculture, in which girls could participate more open and directly (Garber & McRobbie, 1979: 226). Obvious similarities between male and female appearances were in fact a characterizing feature of this subcultural style (Garber & McRobbie, 1979; Benn De Libero, 1994). The girls adopted many garments from the boy's clothing repertoire, such as hipster pants with the fly in the front, men's shirts and cravats. The boys, on the contrary, appeared more 'feminine', because of their style, which included long hair, and their interest in shopping and clothing that often appropriated traditional feminine designs such as florals and overt pattern, and colors such as pink and turquoise, which were at that time still clearly defined as 'female' (see also Benn De Libero, 1994). As Nigel Whitley remarks, referring to the unisex style of the 1960s, 'mod' became a blanket term for both male and female pop fashions (Whitley, 1987: 101). Considering Christina's remark then, that 'the men usually wear suits and have short hair and women are definitely in dresses', it seems in our contemporary view, that gender boundaries are rather re-emphasized than blurred.

The play with gender appearances as practiced by the mods in the 1960s has partly lost its impact in today's context, where androgynous looks seem to have become more normal among youth. Thus, the reconstruction of gender boundaries through traditional gender uniforms, was mentioned by some as a motivation to separate especially from 'baggy' unisex fashions. But replaying former gender images, does not mean to reproduce them in substance. Sandra (29) emphasized that she would not like to exchange her twenty-first-century lifestyle for being back in the sixties: 'I don't think that anything was great at that time. Definitely not the political situation or the state of emancipation.' However, 'it is hard to conceive an unproblematic image of masculinity, femininity or, indeed, androgyny' (Arnold, 2001: 124). Looking at recent fashion and advertising, Angela McRobbie observes in fact a general retraditionalizing of gender (though often hidden in the name of 'irony') that can be linked to the less stable and highly individualized conditions in society (McRobbie, 2002; see also Gaugele, 2003; Reiss, 2003).

Nonetheless, the anachronistic appearance provides young people with a space in which to separate from their parents, who probably feel uncomfortable, seeing the clothes of their past in such a different context (Richard, 1998: 55). Many of the interviewees confirmed this, saying that their parents cannot understand their attachment to all these 'old rags', and ask why they cannot dress in nice modern clothes. The aesthetic restoration of traditional gender images might also function as a way to provoke the generation who regards the interrelated gender images as obsolete and anti-feminist.

In her thesis on second hand retailing Alice Cicolini links vintage dress with the youth's need to express difference from the parental generation and the maintenance of parental identifications:

> Since second-hand clothes are necessarily identified with the 'parents' (in that they 'belong' to a former time), but are also associated with a rejection of those times (in that they have been discarded), they do present themselves as an ideal site for the expression of autonomy in the re-adoption of what has been rejected, but without abandoning the 'parents' entirely (2001).

Comprehension of the sixties scene does not follow from the logic that Cicolini sees partly uncovered in the arguments around second hand fashion, '... when the judgment on whether an object is backward- or forward-looking turns on the aesthetic: "if it looks "old" it must be nostalgic (bad), if it looks "new" then it must be innovative (good)' (2001). As Gabriele Mentges notes, fashion is a complex cultural practice, in which the forms and meanings are not fixed but always newly negotiated by the historic actors (2001: 11). Thus, the reproduction of the historic style does not aim at a reconstruction of 'original' meanings, but serves new constructions of meaning instead, as they are relevant to the new historic actors in a new historic context.

'The Sixties' as Identity Wear

Within the multi-optional postmodern world sixties dress is consciously chosen out of an apparently endless range of possibilities. The consumption and use of old clothing styles enables the sixties-stylists to step at least partly outside the rhythm of fashion and to create an 'own time' niche, contrasting the always 'old' against the always 'new'. Selecting one particular style as identity wear, because this is what they 'like the very best', can therefore provide at least one constant within the context of constantly changing living conditions and the acceleration of time (Harvey, 1995).

But seeing the reuse of sixties dress as a symptom of nostalgia, infecting the younger generations because they cannot cope with the present condition, would be a too easy and quite superficial conclusion. Rather, history and time, appropriated through second hand dress and retro styles, are utilized and turned into means of self-performance and the construction of individuality, difference and at the same time integration into a tribe of like-minded people. Here, the sixties scene can be understood in terms of a fan culture that selects out of the multiple options of contemporary culture specific cultural products and practices (see Fiske, 1997; Winter, 1997). Within these processes of selection, specialization and search for differentiation that are part of an active identity formation of 'the sixties' are not just rediscovered and reimagined, but due to temporal and spatial decontextualization, they are newly interpreted and eventually newly invented.

Keeping up with this past style can be seen as a passion, at least for middle-class youth, as it depends of course on certain financial capacities. To the members of the sixties scene it functions as an avoidance of mass-produced and 'uniform' products offered by the fashion industry. Finding unique pieces provides fun and excitement. For my informants the clothes cannot be measured in money, instead they are regarded as items with a surplus value due to their time-value. Because of their value as material history, in contrast to modern mass-commodities, historic garments – even though formerly mass-fashion as well – rise into the rank of highly estimated acquisitions, original and rare. Original sixties clothes are felt to have a better quality and a better look, enabling the wearer to appear as original as the historic model. The 'authenticity' of the item is transferred to the self and to the performance of a unique and authentic identity (Jenß, 2004). The sixties stylists are in fact commuting between the past and the present time, navigating their dress practices between historical accuracy and its idealization of the original, and their personalization and customization of the sixties as it responds to their contemporary demands and preferences.

Longing to *wear* the sixties does not equal longing to *live* in the sixties. Despite their appearance, sixties stylists appreciate their twenty-first-century life, including easy global travelling and electronic forms of communication. Merging new technology and modern living conditions with historic looks, their cultural practices do not aim at a reconstruction of a past time, but at *their* construction of modern time. However, most admit that they would love to go back for a weekend for clubbing and shopping, but as Christina (21) remarks, 'on the other hand, there you would belong to the mass. When everybody wears sixties dress, it would be nothing special.'

Notes

This chapter is drawn from my MA thesis (Jenß, 2001) and from ethnographic fieldwork on dress practices in the German sixties scene that I have been carrying out in the 'Uniform in Motion: The Process of Uniformity in Body and Dress' research project, funded by Volkswagen-Stiftung (www.uni-frankfurt.de/uniform; see also Jenß, 2002, 2004). The group I interviewed consisted of ten women and ten men between the ages of 16 and 35 who are either students or working in a range of diverse professions such as lawyer's assistants, designers, nurses, architects, craftsmen, etc. I mainly contacted them at sixties events. Their names have been changed and ages added, when they are mentioned for the first time. I want to express my special thanks to all of them for allowing me to gain insights into their attitudes and lifestyle. Thanks also to Hazel Clark and Alexandra Palmer, who provided a very helpful set of questions and suggestions for this article.

1. 'Medialization' means the entire universe of imagery and communication – record covers, flyers, Internet sites – as well as media produced by youth culturalists themselves.

Copied Vintage

ebay

-buying vintage - as not needed to much
it may come back into Style / individual

Buyer - for clothing / - Job

Decades shop LA

Large fashion houses - Chanel look to
old Stock / Styles to resell

11

Vintage Whores and Vintage Virgins: Second Hand Fashion in the Twenty-first Century

Alexandra Palmer

> Why would you wear a new Dior dress that six other women are wearing at the same party when you can buy a dead-designer dress and nobody will have it?
>
> Keni Valenti, vintage collector and dealer, quoted in
> Karen von Hahn (2001)

Contemporary Western fashionable dress offers numerous style options that cross traditional ideas of age appropriateness, race, class and gender. Today vintage fashion has moved away from its historical outré and shabby associations, and has become a mainstream and highly commodified fashion alternative to wearing new designs. As recently as the 1980s wearing vintage was identified 'as part of the current vogue for nostalgia ... [and] as a way of bringing history into an otherwise ahistorical present ... and part of post war subcultural history' (McRobbie, 1989: 23–4). Vintage has now shifted from subculture to mass culture because of the disappointing fact that, regardless of price, fashion today is rarely exclusive. The popularity of vintage has even 'outed' second hand wearers such as *New Yorker* fashion correspondent Judith Thurman who can write about the activity of 'thrifting' in New York charity and resale shops and who employs the language of art museums when describing getting rid of her 1980s handbags – 'de-accessioning' – thereby raising the profile of the 'feral thrill of foraging in the wild' (2003: 88–9).

Vintage is regularly featured within the pages of the leading fashion and lifestyle magazines and is promoted as a sign of individuality and connoisseurship. Los Angeles vintage clothing dealer, Rita Watnick, markets the trend as 'a magic about wearing something that nobody else has' (Vintage Diva, 2001). Today vintage dressing encompasses choosing accessories, mixing vintage garments with new, as well as creating an ensemble of various styles and periods. As with other style choices journalists and fashion editors demonstrate and discuss how to adopt this fashion into one's wardrobe. One repeated technique is to feature 'real women' who serve as lifestyle models; no longer the unapproachable supermodel of the 1980s and early 1990s. For instance, *Harper's Bazaar* selected Katy Rodriguez, co-owner of the New York City vintage store Resurrection, to epitomize 'individual creativity' in dress, explaining that her 'Style Rules' are to 'mix vintage with new'. Her ideas were corroborated and validated by sociologist, Ruth P. Rubinstein, and fashion historian, Valerie Steele, who noted that the 'Vintage Cool' person sees herself as 'an individualist ... who likes to try to create different personae through ... clothes' (Jackson, 2001: 134).

For a generation too young to have worn clothing from the 1950s, 1960s or 1970s, there are numerous new guides aimed at assuaging anxieties of how to achieve vintage modernity (Bardey, 2002; Dubin & Berman, 2000; Tolkien, 2000; Mason, 2002). Lees-Maffei has pointed out that using historical advice guides as an academic research tool is often considered suspect as these guides have 'had to contend with a lowly position in the academic pecking order based on a patriarchal sense of what occurs in the home is of less import than what occurs in the extra-domestic sphere of work...' (2003: 10). Nonetheless, the amount of new etiquette guides related to vintage shopping clearly highlight the phenomena, and these sources are an obvious and suitable method for understanding the mass interest in vintage today. In one of these guides Catherine Bardey explains to her vintage virgin readers that:

> It's no longer about one style or one designer's signature; its about hundreds of styles and thousands of designers. It's about a subtle blend of elegance and ease, a juxtaposition of the old with the new, a little tradition mixed in with the avant-garde... It's about vintage (2002: 8).

Another guide, *Vintage Style* is lavishly illustrated with photographs of socialites and the authors' friends demonstrating in a very literal way 'how to' mix old and new styles (Dubin & Berman, 2000).

Another category of books assumes that readers are already vintage whores, or are on the verge of becoming dedicated second hand clothes consumers, who are prepared to get their hands dirty and sift through consignment stores and charity shops. Importantly, these vintage consumers must buy without being too rigid regarding their needs, as time spent shopping does not necessarily result in immediate gratification. Buying items out of season, or acquiring a dress without a particular event in mind provisions for the future. These vintage shoppers are positioned as experts who are prescient with a 'buy-it-when-you-see-it philosophy' (Jackson, 2001: 130). *Secondhand Chic* explains that 'for shoppers who know how to spot value, this translates into incredible deals' that charges the act of second hand shopping with dynamism and victory over a fashion system that 'dupes' consumers into overpaying for new merchandise. The author clearly describes a game in which second hand buyers can hone their skills and successfully hunt and bag vintage attire (Weill, 1999: 1).

One antecedent to the popularization of vintage shopping occurred during the 1980s with the increased formality and acceptance of discount shopping for high-end brands, particularly in North America. Specialty discount shops and large outlet malls have led to an entire school of consumption that prides itself on buying and wearing high status designer labels at discount prices. The cachet of the designer label, coupled with limitless potential for discount consumption has produced innovative rogue dealing. One woman picks (a 'picker' is a term for a person who finds vintage clothes or textiles for a dealer) clothing from outlet stores and then sells them on eBay for around $100 (US) more than she paid. She then turns her profits into new clothes for herself, often purchasing them on line. If the item does not sell, she will return it to the outlet store and get her money back. But, as she says, most things sell because, 'Frankly, there's a lot of label whores out there.' She explains that each time she clicks the eBay icon, she feels as if she's somehow undermining the fashion system. This scenario creates a virtual street market for hawking worn and unworn clothing. Another discount fashion junkie remarked: 'Who wants to pay full price for anything? I don't. You're definitely beating the system' (Sullivan, 2000: 301). Vintage shopping can be viewed as a continuation of discount culture, while simultaneously achieving an individual identity and exclusivity that the brand names have lost.

Experience in acquiring second hand clothes can also lead to connoisseurship that is explained as important because:

> Every experienced consignment, vintage or thrift-store shopper has the same gripe: resale shopping takes an awful lot of time... *Here is where connoisseurship comes in*. Once you have strengthened your expertise, you will be able to move down a rack at speed. Your fingertips will be sensitized to top-quality materials. Your eyes will latch onto the properly set-in shoulder, the expensive button, the extraordinary tweed. In this way you will go straight to the best goods, leaving the other stuff behind for less choosy shoppers (Weill, 1999: 3).

Though this description discusses second hand, it could as well apply to the consumption of new fashion where there is also a dazzling array of styles, designer labels and prices. Clarke and Miller have noted, 'Individuals are frequently too anxious about the choices to be made [when shopping] to proceed without various forms of support and reassurance' (2002: 209). Weill describes expertise and connoisseurship as skills that can be acquired and employed to counteract the emotions of bewilderment and anxiety that shopping arouses in many consumers.

This anxiety may be amplified for those who want to wear vintage but are not confident about how to successfully select it. Part of the anxiety rests in the subtle nuances of when an item is suitably vintage. The danger exists of making a faux pas and being merely out of date; a situation that is avoidable by purchasing the latest designer styles. Vintage highlights the complex requirements of proper timing that signals being 'in' or 'out' of fashion. Vintage dealer, Cameron Silver, notes that 'There's a visceral reaction if you carry an item past its prime' (Zimbalist, 2002a: 125–6), and he clarifies what is merely second hand stock from his vintage stock by selling new or very recent designs in his consignment shop Decadestwo, that is distinct from his higher-end vintage premises, Decades. Yet, 'vintage' is used to identify an enormous range of clothes, from a couture dress of the 1920s to last year's 'must have' Fendi baguette handbag. On eBay this is resolved by placing clothing pre-1980 in the category, 'Vintage Clothing and Accessories'. Still, the possibility exists that any fashion that was recently démodé has potential future value and meaning. The transformation of old clothes into 'vintage' and 'collectable', refutes Veblen's theory of conspicuous consumption and validates new and second hand fashion by placing it within the economic and status-giving arena of the art and decorative arts market (Veblen, 1979). Thus fashion, that is commonly trivialized and considered disposable, has the potential for becoming a valuable commodity. The smart consumer can attain the status of a connoisseur, an achievement that mitigates against established associations of fashion consumption with irrational and hysterical feminine traits.

The interpretation of vintage as a means of provisioning for future fashion potential makes selection even more complicated. Tiffany Dubin-Celine, 'the doyenne of vintage', discusses a 'have to have' Fendi dress that was advertised and modeled by Kate Moss. She notes, 'I'm only going to wear it once and then stash it in the back of my closet... Wearing it now is so, 'She went out and bought the dress of the season.' And next year, it will be just last year's Fendi dress. But in five years, it will be a beautiful dress that really represents a moment in fashion' (Talking Fashion, 2002; Zimbalist, 2002a: 125). Thus, a cult designer label and a design that is marketed complete with supermodel, results in a future fashion icon according to Dubin's calculations. Accordingly, investing now and storing clothes to age, as one does wine, is advised as a form of future vintage consumption that validates buying contemporary fashion (Morra, 2003). This complex thinking charges shopping with a new – and potentially overwhelming – component that goes beyond the responsibility of being fashionable in the present. In this scenario the consumer buys with an investor's requirement for fashionability, recognizing that that exclusivity does not exist in the present fashion market. Success in this manner, as the psychoanalyst, Muensterberger, has observed, is clearly linked to the collector's sense of identity and the collected objects 'function as a source of self-definition ... [proving] ... to the collector and to the world, that he or she is special and worthy of them' (1994: 4, 256). This implies that the connoisseur recognizes new designs as already clichéd.

Interest in vintage has also raised the profile of an older generation of socialites who are able to reach into their wardrobes for their own personal, now vintage, clothes. Wearing a design that is five, ten or twenty years old is touted as the height of fashion, marking the wearer as prescient, since she did not dispose of her wardrobe. The fact that she can still physically fit into her older garments establishes her as an enviable role model with irrefutable good taste (Unseen C.Z., 2003). Worn and formerly out-of-date items in the wardrobe are now transformed and elevated to a 'vintage' status. Commonplace are comments such as those by executive Emilia Fanjul Pfeifler, who proudly remarked, 'I have one black Valentino gown I bought in London three years ago, and I've worn it, I'm serious, about 10 times.' Journalists too remind readers that 'rewearing evening clothes is a time-honoured tradition observed by the world's most fashionable: Style icons ... have always shown up at the most lavish affairs in beautiful creations they've had for decades ... that's the way it has always been in chic circles' (Zimbalist, 2002b: 129). Such remarks underscore old concepts of 'good' taste associated with class and birthright, rather than late twentieth-century hierarchies based upon youth, celebrity status and capital.

Philosopher Agnes Heller suggests that our idea of happiness has shifted from an objective archaic conception of wealth and power to a subjective idea about feelings that is emotional. She describes two kinds of happy moments in modern life. One is 'an exceptional occurrence of need, satisfaction and delight, mostly when it happens for the first time,' and can be likened to buying and wearing a new item. The other, 'felicity', she suggests is a feeling that 'is not diminished if the same or a similar thing happens to us, or if we repeat the experience' (1999: 223–6). Re-wearing clothes from a personal wardrobe and wearing newly acquired vintage and retro clothing, can be understood as a desire to recreate familiarity, or felicity, in a world that is rapidly changing and increasingly impersonal. Heller suggests that authenticity is 'the single most sublime virtue of modernity, for authentic people are the people who remain true to the their existential choice, who are pulled and not pushed, who are personalities. This also means that they get as close to perfection as a modern person can' (227). In this light wearing vintage clothing can be interpreted as a clear sign of individuality and authenticity, an ideal that is constantly held up as the pinnacle of fashionable modernity.

The fashion for vintage has expanded the sale of second hand clothing into innovative diversified markets that have created new hierarchies of vintage consumption. It has directly influenced the traditional charity industries that have, until recently, been an insignificant part of the high fashion system. Charity shops now market their products as fashionable, and indeed have to do so in order to compete with quasi-charitable shops, such as Value Village/Savers, that are infringing on their domain. In 1996 the *Wall Street Journal* reported that the vintage clothing rage had prompted the Salvation Army and Goodwill to revamp their stores and to market better quality pieces separately from the rest of the clothing (Thrift Shops ... 1996). In Toronto, Salvation Army launched designer boutiques located at the front of their stores, where men's, women's and children's wear from well-known brand names such as The Gap, Ralph Lauren and Giorgio Armani were sorted out from 'regular' merchandise. Regional director, Bob Moorthie, noted that the high-end stock was priced at about one-tenth of the original value, and explained the new policy saying: 'We get many Hugo Boss suits, many Chanel jackets and Armani suits and lots of Tommy Hilfiger ... people don't want to have to sort through lots of merchandise looking for special items. This way the discerning customer can go straight to the boutique' (Medicoff, 1999).

New trendy vintage boutiques reinforce the history of their goods by establishing premises near or in traditional second hand markets. For instance Yu, Shine Vintage and Cherry in New York, are located off Orchard Street, the traditional Jewish market for cheap, new and second hand clothing on the Lower East Side, while the Portobello Road in London has numerous vintage stores, and is expanding its margins by such stores as Relik. These locations serve to reinforce the vintage stock as authentic. The market site implies a bargain and a knowledgeable consumer who can negotiate smartly within a disordered and informal ambience. In this same spirit the youth-oriented British chain store, Top Shop, at Oxford Circus, London, has invited dealers to create a vintage market that has all the convenience of a high street location including preselected goods and large, well-lit changing rooms. Here, the boundaries of old and new styles, colours and stock are irrelevant and the shopper can freely mix and match a wide array of goods in order to create the appropriate melange of contemporary and vintage in an already mediated environment. Margins for taste errors are now narrowed within a familiar and 'normal' setting.

Up-scale market settings are also recreated for consumers who have neither the time nor the inclination to visit authentic sites. In New York the three day Vintage Fashion and Antique Textile Show takes place four times a year (Stevens, 1998). This second hand convention occurs in major cities across North America, and is usually set up as at an outdoor antique market with individual dealers' booths and tables, but is indoors at downtown hotels or trade centers (Turudich et al., 2002: 295). The consumer is virtually guaranteed to find a suitable purchase, given the range and amount of stock. These shows are also centres for contemporary fashion designers 'like Donna Karan, Adrienne Vittadini, Vivienne Tam and Jill Stuart and design crews ranging from J. Peterman to Burton Snowboards. Members of Giorgio Armani's design staff even flew in from Italy for the second day of the show.' In fact the importance of sourcing and acquiring vintage for design houses was legitimized when this show was added to the New York Fashion Calendar, 'the industry's date book' (Stevens, 1998).

Domesticating the chaotic market is a common strategy that is clearly seen in numerous small boutiques that sell vintage, often interspersed with new clothes, in new chic areas such as NoLita, NYC. In Montreal's hip St. Laurent area is Buddy Lee's vintage store. In 2000, on its plate glass window enormous lettering advertised, '$10 et plus'. Inside were second hand jeans, T-shirts and Hawaiian style shirts hung neatly around its perimeter, while the concrete floor was left empty except for an old gray army surplus blanket loaded with a mound of T-shirts (Fig. 27). This strategic merchandising of second hand clothes in both ordered, and seemingly, disordered manner recreates the experience of searching for treasures in a city market. Steiner points out in his study of the African art trade that such a strategy aims to heighten the consumer's sense of achievement in the selection process. He writes:

> If an object is uncovered by a buyer in what is thought to be its original or 'natural' setting it is presumed to be closer to the context of its creation or use and therefore less likely to be inauthentic or fake... The very process and act of discovery generally confirms the collector's sense of good taste... – the more difficult the search the more authentic the find (1995: 152).

Buddy Lee's highly controlled 'drycleaned view of the flea market' (Blau, 1999: 175) serves to mitigate the inherent anxiety of second hand shopping

Figure 27. Buddy Lee vintage store, in Montreal, summer 2000. Second hand jeans, T-shirts and Hawaiian style shirts are neatly hung, while the mound of T-shirts on the floor creates a market setting that contributes to the 'authentic' find.
Photograph by Alexandra Palmer.

that is an unreliable and unpredictable activity. It provides the random conditions that authenticate the experience though the 'random' goods are in fact sorted and pre-packaged. As Steiner suggests, 'the manipulation of context through the calculated emplacement of objects is a widespread practice among art dealers around the world, ... part of the collectors quest is to discover what has previously gone unremarked' (154). The second hand clothing market effectively emulates this, as is seen in the blanket presentation of T-shirts at Buddy Lee's.

Shopping vintage on-line completely removes consumers from the unsavory and conventional elements of second hand markets. In 1996 a site called Rusty Zipper boasted that it was the 'world's only virtual vintage clothing store' (Shapiro, 1996). Today's prime site is eBay, which lists over 1,600,000 fashion items. One regular buyer explained shopping on line as an alternative to purchasing designs that would normally be too expensive, and commented that 'Ebay has sort of democratized the fashion industry' (Johnson, 2003). In fact interest in vintage Internet shopping has been formalized with a handbook, *Virtual Vintage. The Insider's Guide to*

Buying and Selling Online (Lindroth & Tornello, 2002). High-end vintage clothing website, vintagecouture.com, begun by Lynda Latner in 1999, is a specialist vintage clothing site, 'not a catch-all like eBay ... It has no shopping cart.' Originally Latner sold her mother's 1950s and 1960s clothes that she priced in the 'semi-expensive' realm. She received interested buyers and also attracted private clients who wanted her to sell their clothes. She realized that she needed to have a few special pieces on a regular basis, so began to buy couture wardrobes and high-end garments from local socialites who wanted to clear out their closets. Now she sells internationally to individuals, collectors and designers (Latner, 2003).

Other vintage retailers also strive to disassociate themselves from the bustle, chance and foraging aspects of used clothing markets. Refined boutiques or department stores authenticate the merchandise as rare, which helps to sanitize the 'used' aspects of these designs. Here, high-end and vintage couture designer labels are inferred to be removed from the negative, tainted aspects of used garments as these designs were made for and worn by the elite. But, as museum collections testify, clothes of the wealthy may also show signs of wear (Palmer, 2001). The exclusive LA vintage store Lily et Cie, is modeled on a luxury French couture salon. In business for over twenty years, owner Rita Watnick has a huge inventory of over 500,000 pieces many of which are couture, and claims her store is 'another jump up altogether from what people call vintage' (Witchel, 1999). Watnick attracts an elite clientele and Hollywood celebrities note her as a key fashion source. Her prices are so high that fashion consultant Ellen Carey writes that 'Vintage used to be a clever way of being unique looking on budget ... but now it's more expensive than clothes that are new' (Agins, 2001). Modernity too sells vintage. Ex-cabaret singer and now vintage dealer, Cameron Silver, owner of Decades Inc, LA, runs a clean, sleek and contemporary establishment devoid of the fusty connotations of old clothing shops. Silver remarked that, 'When I opened, no one was doing a store with the philosophy of vintage looking modern... That's why celebs like Gina Gershorn, Courtney Love and Renée Zellweger can outfit themselves there without looking like they raided a thrift store' (Pike, 2002: 24). He believes that vintage is more contemporary than the latest designer offerings (Silver, 2002, 2003).

Some vintage dealers are sought after by high-end department stores that want to sell the latest fashions, including vintage. Didier Ludot whose Paris shop is located in the historic Palais Royale, also runs boutiques at department stores, Au Printemps, Paris and Saks, NYC. At Barney's, New York, Cameron Silver stocked an area for Decades (2000–2003), and Holt Renfrew in Toronto opened its vintage couture boutique in 2003 (Capelaci,

2003; Chetty, 2003; Johnson, 2003; Silver, 2003) (Fig. 28). Some dealers are even branding their merchandise or designing more. Decades has its own label that is sewn into its clothes that are sold outside the LA store, and Didier Ludot's, La Petite Robe Noire, sells vintage little black dresses alongside his own line of new retro-inspired ones. He also has his own perfume (Silver, 2002, 2003; www.didierludot.com). Resurrection owner,

Figure 28. 1960s–1980s fashions in vintagecouture.com boutique, Holt Renfrew, Toronto, spring 2003.
Left to right: Mannequin with lampshade over head in Halston crepe halter evening gown; (seated) red print gown by Giorgio Sant Angelo; jeans with white coat by Sylvia Myles, a British designer popular at the Ensemble Shop, Eatons, Canada; red fishtail gown by Claude Montana. Photograph by Edward Pond.

Rodriguez, acknowledges that 'People expect us to knock off our best-selling vintage clothes,' but also notes that she would be creating fashion that would not be 'special'. Instead, she produces an original line designed by artists, as well as a collection called 'Skate or Die', dedicated to skateboard apparel and accessories from the 1980s (Shea, 2001: 312, 316; Feitelberg, 2002). All these old and new products stand as a testament to the veracity of the vintage dealers' taste, the importance of their vintage stock and their influence as style leaders.

Today's fusion of the fashionable past and the present can be interpreted in terms of cultural critic Paul Virilio's discussions of dromology, the science or logic of speed. Virilio contends that our society is so inundated with high-tech systems and data, that we can no longer absorb information by going directly forward into the future, and thinks that, 'We are regressing because we have reached the limit of acceleration' (Sterckx, 2001: 146). He says that, 'whenever you come to a wall you bounce back. Before we can develop an intelligent idea of future societies, we need to note the current backwards movement.' According to Virilio's ideas, the speed with which we learn of the latest fashions makes it impossible for the average person to incorporate the new array of designs into a wardrobe, either for financial reasons, and/or because we do not have the time to constantly shop for the latest styles. But, more importantly, we are not able to transform our mental image of ourselves so rapidly. We struggle intellectually to consume at the same rate we produce. Virilio suggests that to cope, we should adopt the 'angle of divergence', that is a way of riding at an angle when negotiating a turn at speed (Sterckx, 2001: 148). The contemporary pursuit of vintage that re-assimilates the recognizable past can be seen as such a strategy – an angle of fashion divergence.

This is seen in an integrated manner in the fashions of New York designer, Norma Kamali, whose designs have always been influenced by her personal interest in vintage. She said,

> I collected vintage clothing nearly every day of my life when I was young, which is how I learned the craft of making clothes... I simply studied the techniques of good vintage clothing. In those days a dress could be $5 from a stall in Portobello Road. I used to go up to Harlem, in my high platform shoes and hot pants, and go to warehouses, dragging huge plastic bags full of vintage back on the subway. I built up my collection. Later, vintage dealers would come with bags and bags to the store (Talley, 2002).

In the fall of 2000 Kamali began to sell her own personal collection of twentieth-century antique clothing in her store (Fig. 29). She told reporter Ginia Bellafante that she 'just wanted to get rid of things... We've consumed

Figure 29. Norma Kamali Vintage and Very Vintage collections at OMO, West 56th Street, New York City, February 2003. Ms Kamali sells a fusion of her old stock she designed over the past twenty five years, mixed in with her personal collection of vintage clothes that have inspired and intrigued her.
Photograph by Alexandra Palmer, courtesy of Norma Kamali.

ourselves into oblivion.' Kamali distinguishes the vintage collection from her own designs, by a hang tag that reads 'Very Vintage'. The vintage clothes are interspersed with old Kamali-designed stock dating from 1968 to the 1990s, that she has stored in a warehouse. These pieces are tagged as 'Vintage Kamali'. She also offers some new Kamali designs, thereby presenting her shopper with a rich spectrum of the history of Kamali-approved clothes (Agins, 2001; Bellafante, 2000; Wolff, 2002). Kamali said, 'I like mixing the vintage with the new, the way young fashion editors do it today' (Talley, 2002). The Vintage Kamali designs reveal their roots in the prints and cuts seen in the archival Very Vintage pieces, that look less 'museumy' and re-emerge as contemporary within the setting of her 1980s polished concrete shop. For her loyal customers who may have been shopping at Kamali for the past thirty or so years, this selection serves to reinforce the correctness of their past and present taste.

Kamali designs, which have always traded on vintage imagery and cut, are set within a lineage that is actually possible to acquire. Interestingly, a customer's selection is guided by style, color and time of day, length of hem, day or evening, a marketing strategy that foregrounds the contemporary relevance of the fashions – not its historical value or date. Kamali's large vintage collection and her old stock have been personally selected and once a piece is sold, it is not replaceable. Kamali offers real designer exclusivity that high prices alone no longer guarantee. Her shop creates a sophisticated and harmonious fusion of twentieth-century fashion history that elevates fashionable clothes, whether old or new, in an avant-garde retail environment creating a new understanding of twenty-first century fashion.[1]

In contrast to Kamali's large vintage collections, the use of a few token or 'concept' vintage designs are employed by other designers, such as Ralph Lauren in his RRL store, in NoLita, NYC. Here vintage is minimally interspersed between large numbers of Lauren's new derivatives. In order to distinguish the samples of authentically old from the new retro products of plaid shirts and Western-influenced cuts and fabrics, the second hand clothes carry a hang tag that reads, 'This vintage product has been hand-picked for its unique accompaniment to the Ralph Lauren collections,' complete with a date and description of the item. Thus, like a museum's object label or catalogue record, the hang tag authenticates and interprets the vintage merchandise that is, in effect, curated. Lauren's designs are verified by the original source or 'accompaniment' that gives his new retro designs bona fide ancestry. Yet, the archival value of the source is undermined; its function having been served, the vintage design is now disposable and resold, focusing the attention squarely back onto the new Lauren products. Ralph Lauren's store perfectly embodies what one New York reporter explained as the trick for today's fashion, 'to look retro, and you're getting clean clothes' (Agins, 2001).

Of course, using historical styles as sources for new designs has been to a large extent the history of design (Martin & Koda, 1991). Curator, Susan North, remarked that 'Revivalism has been going on as far as we can document, from 1600 onward and possibly before that' (Erdem, 2002: 48), and vintage dealer, Tracy Tolkien remarked that ' Every designer I've ever heard of has come in [to Steinberg & Tolkein]. Galliano, McQueen, Lagerfeld, Ford, all of them' (Gunn, 2000: 8). What is different today is the overt usage and the exposure of this practice. The fashion world is predicated on creating 'new' designs seasonally, yet consumer interest in 'original' vintage designs has challenged designers who are themselves competing for vintage pieces in order to create 'new' designs.

The apogee of this is perhaps the recent debacle with Nicholas Ghesquière, designer for the Paris-based house Balenciaga, who 'didn't sound embarrassed', when he admitted plagiarizing 1970s wearable artist, Kasiak Wong (Horyn, 2002). The Wong/Ghesquière debacle clearly called into question the originality of the designer as creator/artist, an issue that is pivotal to the fashion industry today (Breward, 2003; Taylor, 2000: 121–42). Yet, Guy Trebay noted that, 'What was unusual about Mr Ghesquière's borrowing was not that it occurred but that it caused a brouhaha in the press. And what was edifying about Mr Ghesquière's reaction was his honesty.' Yet, he points out that this is nothing new as, 'Saint Laurent sues Ralph Lauren for copying ... [his] tuxedo ... Adolfo builds a wildly successful business on an interpretation of a boxy suit by Coco Chanel ... Tom Ford becomes famous for copying Halston, Alexander McQueen for aping Vivienne Westwood' (Trebay, 2002). The fashion trade newspaper WWD regularly reports on which designers and stylists are seen entering which vintage shops. For instance John Galliano was sighted visiting Decades and Resurrection stores in LA and it was noted that 'Decades has been a favourite of Tom Ford and Nicolas Ghesquière in recent seasons' (Fashion Scoops, 2002). Now fashion designers' creativity is rivaled by vintage dealers' connoisseurship. In fact, one journalist acknowledged, 'Vintage dealers not only spot the knock-offs but also control the inspiration supply' (Larocca, 2002).

Just as with contemporary fashion, vintage sales rely upon consumer recognition; either an obviously old garment or an identifiable designer. Marketing forgotten designer labels requires educating clients in order to cultivate connoisseurship and value. In 1997, one year after opening Decades, Cameron Silver launched a gallery and exhibits programme. Because Silver operates outside the bureaucracy of formal art institutions, he can respond smartly to upcoming fashion trends and clearly creates a market for vintage fashions that he understands to be suitable for contemporary wear. New discoveries are then collected by clients such as Imitation of Christ's designer, Tara Subkoff, or Chloë Sevigny, both of whom wore Harp designs to the opening of Silver's Holly Harp exhibit (Jones, 2002). Along with Harp, Silver has also revitalized and recontextualized Koos van den Akker and Leonard. In the case of van den Akker, the designer was able to sell his new original pieces at Henri Bendel, while Silver sold his vintage pieces in the Decades boutique at Barney's New York (www.decadesinc.com; Jones, 2002: 16). One of Silver's most timely exhibits focused on wearable artist Kasiak Wong, and even featured the notorious vest that Nicolas Ghesquière knocked-off for the house of Balenciaga (Silver, 2002, 2003; www.decadesinc.com; www.Hintmag.com). Each of Silver's exhibitions becomes a lesson in fashion history and adds to the fashion designer canon.

Selling vintage on the Internet relies heavily upon both the legacy and current marketing of the designer label, and not on the experience of touching fabric and inspecting cut. A little black dress may not read well on-line and languish, but if it is accompanied with the imprimatur of Yves Saint Laurent or Christian Dior, it is immediately understood and valued in a different light. The designer label conveys to the internet client information that speaks of good value in cloth, cut and design. The item has a pedigree. On vintagecouture.com, stock ranges from the 1950s to the 1970s, and includes high-end 1980s and 1990s newer 'vintage' clothes by leading designers who have the appropriate moniker, Galliano, Alaia, Beene, Prada, Montana and Chanel. Owner, Lynda Latner acknowledges that more recent 'recognizable' designs, colour and shape play an important part in her selection process, and that much of the black designs of the late 1980s and 1990s are hard to sell on-line even with a label. She notes that clients are familiar with designer brands and know their sizes, making purchase 'not a huge risk' (Latner, 2003).

The popularity of vintage also creates an interesting situation for large design houses whose business requires that they create and sell new merchandise to replace their previous designs that are now old. Simultaneously, the old designs are being re-evaluated, re-valued and re-worn forcing the design house to maintain a symbiotic relationship that validates both the old and the new. As fashion designers compete for vintage sourcing as an important means to retain exclusivity, they have also turned to archiving and re-making or re-issuing their older designs. Typically design house keep only sketches and press images of the products sold, and rarely the fashions themselves. Now companies are buying back their own clothes through dealers and auctions. Some design houses are even becoming specialist costume museums, such as Christian Dior, Paris, that has a large archive, a dedicated archivist and adds Galliano/Dior pieces seasonally to the collection.

Reaching into their own house archives is not only a means of securing exclusivity, but also reinforces the historical position of the house. In fall 2002 Yves Saint Laurent, Paris boutique sold a limited edition of re-makes of his 1996 smoking, and his safari ensemble of 1968 (Mower, 2000). Prada, one of the most widely copied houses in the 1990s, has created its own limited edition re-makes (O'Hagan, 2003: 136). In its SoHo, NYC, shop the re-issues are not identified by the original year or season; only the garment labels' design and color differentiates it from new stock. Prada assumes its client is well versed in Prada history, and as mentioned in the press, 'the chinoiserie-inspired vine-covered wedges that caused mass hysteria five years ago are sold along side this season's brocaded jackets'

(Zimbalist, 2002a: 125). Prada thus aims to sell not only its own latest fashion designs, but simultaneously creates a market for its own recently designed products, and implicates the latest contemporary design purchase as a future collectable, and not just a fashion item that will be 'out' next season. Such a strategy flies in the face of its own fashion system that deems new designs are required seasonally and the old is obsolete. Muiccia Prada remarked that, 'The proof that you did something good is the fact that you can use it again and again. So instead of going back and altering an important look – which I think I'd regret later – I consider what pieces make sense now, and I repropose them' (Comita, 2002: 197). Thus today's fashion designers are in a position to establish which of their own designs is iconic within their own self-referential market. In this vein, the Dolce & Gabbana Vintage red-label collection introduced 'historic pieces ... bring[s] back those classic ... items for young women who couldn't dress in them [when they first came out] because they were too young' (Colavita, 2003).

The escalation of vintage re-makes, from clothing to sneakers, derives significance from the archival process, but also competes with the actual vintage design. The re-make sanctions the vintage item as 'important' and 'collectable'. In the best case scenario, the re-make will retain a market value of its own and ultimately compete with the vintage, thus further blurring linear historic boundaries and questioning Benjamin's assertion that, 'The presence of the original is the prerequisite to the concept of authenticity' (1968b: 222).

If one considers the interest in vintage and retro fashions in terms of Virilio's angle of fashion divergence, these past fashions can be understood not only as a means of authenticating the present, but also as a route for future fashions. Silverman suggests that wearing retro and vintage, 'establishes a dialogue between present-day wearers ... and its original wearers, retro also provides a means of salvaging the images that have traditionally sustained female subjectivity, images that have been consigned to the wastebasket ... vintage clothing makes it possible for certain of those images to 'live on' in a different form' (Silverman, 1994: 195). Even though we carry multiple images of how vintage clothes were worn, whether it be from movies, paintings, magazines, TV reruns, or images of our relatives in photo albums, an important aspect of today's interest in vintage is that there is, in fact, little dialogue with the past. Modern vintage wearers seek authenticity in what is rare and cannot be duplicated, in what is old but does not look old or used. Ideally, wearing vintage positions the vintage virgin and vintage whore, not as historical, retrograde or subcultural, but as an informed, avant-garde fashion connoisseur.

Notes

This research was conducted over several years. At the time of going to press the vintage market and descriptions of retail environments have already changed. However, vintage as a design source, style and important fashion market is a well integrated strand within the contemporary fashion system. The term, 'vintage virgin', I first heard coined by Lynda Latner.

1. By January 2004 Kamali changed the marketing and interior of OMO as it has been described. It is now painted stark white and is brightly lit with her old and new designs hung on dress forms, not hangers. The minimalist interior is cleared in the evenings for 'wellness nights' featuring exercise instruction such as yoga or Pilates. She also sells beauty and health products.

12

Working the Edge: XULY.Bët's Recycled Clothing

Victoria L. Rovine

The Paris-based fashion designer Lamine Kouyaté celebrates edges, literally as well as figuratively. His work incorporates both the cutting edge of fashion and the frayed edges of the past. He uses recycled clothing to create high fashion, applying stitches on the outside of his garments to focus attention on the edges where threads hold garments together. He works at the edges of categories, creating work that embodies several seemingly irreconcilable dialectics, simultaneously mass produced and irreproducible, new and old, exclusive and accessible, African and European, emerging out of the extravagance of fashion runways and the gritty practicality of city streets. His designs lay bare the mechanics of fashion, exposing seams and loose threads. His work also turns the notion of *haute couture* inside out, creating garments that are one of a kind because they are made of used clothing that has been discarded. Kouyaté's recycled garments, created under his XULY. Bët brand, inspire rich analysis because they embody so many paradoxes. What follows is a meditation on the diverse cultures and histories evoked by Kouyaté's recycled clothing, and the contemporary, global markets in which they circulate. I will explore the layers of meaning contained by these garments, and their challenge to conventional fashion markets and design techniques. I will also offer a contextual background for the garments in African sartorial practices, concluding with a suggestion that XULY.Bët garments might also contain a broad cultural critique from the perspective of Africa and other non-Western locales.

100% Recyclé: Creating Salvaged Fashion

XULY.Bët's recycled clothing, one among several styles produced by the company, has consistently drawn the attention of the fashion and popular press in Europe and, less prominently, in the United States. Major periodicals including *Le Monde*, *The New York Times*, *Glamour*, *Essence*, *Elle* and *Vogue* have all featured articles on Kouyaté and his work (Renaux, 1994). The designer manages to balance the trendiness that generally draws the attention of the fashion press with a complex sense of his cultural and historical roots. The recycled clothes bring together diverse influences to create garments that retain the histories of their previous lives even as they suit the tastes of the moment. They also embody the struggle to define identities in an ever more globalized world. The XULY.Bët brand's recycled clothing and Kouyaté himself both offer points of departure for an exploration of the layering of meanings and movements in global fashion markets that has produced artifacts and identities that exist in the overlapping spaces between categories.

Kouyaté's line of recycled garments debuted in 1992, as part of the first major collection of the XULY.Bët brand. The garments were made of previously owned shirts, sweaters, dresses, pants and other clothing. Kouyaté treated each garment as an experiment, cutting, removing and restitching seams using bright red thread. The audacity and energy of his technique is preserved in the threads that he leaves hanging at the end of seams, like jagged remnants of the moment of fevered inspiration – the fashion equivalent of Jackson Pollock's drips of paint. The raw energy of these experiments with recycled clothing reflected, in part, Kouyaté's lack of inhibition concerning the techniques of fashion design, for he had no background and no training as a designer. In the recycled collections that have followed, he has continued to use these methods, as well as other means of modifying the clothing he purchases at flea markets, charity shops and low-end department stores.

As important as his use of salvaged garments as a medium for fashion, is Kouyaté's reclassification of his raw material as he transfers articles of clothing from one function to another. He frequently reassigns garments to new uses, transforming sweaters into scarves, several T-shirts into a dress, pants into a purse. One description of a XULY.Bët garment illustrates the designer's dramatic transformations, imagining new functions for even the most mundane garments: 'panty hose cut at the crotch, feet cut off and trimmed with contrasting knit ribbing to become a clever stretch top' (Jacobs, 1994: 144). Many of his recycled garments are further transformed by the addition of silkscreened motifs or slogans on backs, sleeves and fronts, including most notably the company's slogan: 'Funkin' Fashion' (Fig. 30). The company's line of recycled clothing, called '100% Recyclé', (Durry, 2003) challenged conventions and brought Kouyaté significant recognition, including the prestigious 1996 Trophée de la Mode. In addition to the brand's distinctive utilization of used clothing, Kouyaté's African identity has been

Figure 30. XULY.Bët, purchased in 2003. This T-shirt is adorned with the
company's slogan, 'Funkin' Fashion'. Though not a recycled garment,
this shirt was made using Kouyaté's signature red thread, boldly
stitched on exterior seams.
Private Collection. Photograph by Mike Breazeale.

the focus of much of the analysis and celebration of his work. This identity
has set him apart from the mainstream of French fashion design, which is
overwhelmingly populated by Western Europeans and North Americans.

Because Kouyaté's identity is an important aspect of the marketing
and reception of the XULY.Bët brand, a brief description of his personal
background sets the stage for the analysis that follows. Lamine Badian
Kouyaté was born in Bamako, Mali's capital, in 1962. His father was a
minister in the first post-independence government, his mother a doctor
from Senegal. Kouyaté's father was imprisoned during the turmoil of the
post-independence period, when President Modibo Keita was overthrown
in a 1968 coup d'état led by Moussa Traoré, who would lead a repressive
dictatorial government until 1992. The family left the country, moving to
Paris when Kouyaté was fourteen, then to Dakar when he was sixteen, where

his father worked for UNESCO (van der Plas and Willemsen, 1998; Revue Noire, 1997–8; Le Guilledoux, 1997). Both Dakar and Bamako were growing cosmopolitan centers where a young student might have found himself at the intersection of popular cultures from Africa and the West. Kouyaté succinctly described the global perspective of youth culture in the African cities: 'I knew more about rock and funk in the 70's than any of the kids in Paris when I got here' (Spindler, 1993: 1). He remained in Dakar until age 24, when he left to study architecture at the University of Strasbourg in France. In architecture as in fashion, Kouyaté was attracted to the notion of making do with little. He described his admiration for architect Jean Nouvel: 'With very few means, and many constraints, he succeeded in introducing new spaces.' Before completing his architecture degree, however, Kouyaté took up fashion design and moved to Paris, where he began work under his XULY.Bët label in 1989. Kouyaté's background in architecture may in part explain his tendency to reveal the structure of garments, often by disassembling them at the seams. The turn to fashion also emerged in part out of Kouyaté's interests in music and performance. He participated in the underground Parisian music and nightclub scene of the early 1980s and, as part of that involvement, began designing clothes for performances and for his friends in the clubs (Le Guilledoux, 1997: 15). His attention to the possibilities of multimedia expression continues to have an impact on his work, including most notably his presentation of designs at fashion shows.

On the Runway/On the Street

XULY.Bët's first major fashion show, held during the spring 1992 season in Paris, reveals his attention to performance in tandem with fashion design. The show also suggests one of several dialectics present in Kouyaté's work: its balance between the theatrical and the mundane. His debut fashion show's innovative staging emphasized the brand's raw, edgy aesthetic. Rather than introducing the designs at a major fashion venue, Kouyaté presented the show outside the conventional precincts of the fashion industry. The XULY. Bët show took place at a public park – the Jardin des Tuileries – without a runway or a sound system, elements that are customarily de rigeur at any fashion show. Instead, models emerged from a bus that pulled up at the site, each carrying a boombox that provided her own soundtrack to the event. No stage, no lights, no delineation of theatrical space separated the audience from the performers, just as the garments themselves were but subtly separated from their previous, mundane lives.

This dramatic entrée into the realm of Parisian fashion was immortalized, in fictional form, in the 1994 Robert Altman film *Ready to Wear* or *Prêt à Porter*. XULY.Bët clothing has an important role in the film, 'playing' the work of designer Cy Bianco (who was himself played by the actor Forrest Whittaker). Like Kouyaté, Bianco is clearly distinct from the many designers around him. He is black, though African-American rather than African, while all the film's other designers are white. His designs owe more to the street than to the rarified world of fashion: tight-fitting T-shirts with graffiti-like adornments, ripped and repaired skirts, bandage-like wrappings around arms and legs. Cy Bianco's runway show, one of many in the film, which takes place at the Paris Ready to Wear fashion shows, mimics Kouyaté's first major runway showing. The fictional Kouyaté held his show in the tunnel of a Paris metro, with models striding through a graffiti-covered subway car.

In 1998, Manthia Diawara described the effect produced by a XULY. Bët fashion show he had recently attended in New York City: 'During the show, Xuly-bet alternated between a Jimi Hendrix soundtrack and simply letting the models march by in silence, as if they were performing some world-transforming ritual' (Diawara, 1998: 87). While Diawara found an allusion to ritual in the silent models on the runway, one might also find ordinariness in the lack of a soundtrack, as if audience members were viewing real life rather than a performance. Kouyaté's presentation of his designs, like the designs themselves, transforms the relationship between fashion and the 'real' lives of clothing, creating a new space between the 'real' and the theatrical.

At other fashion shows, Kouyaté further emphasized the gritty reality his clothes inhabit and the previous lives they have led. In 1993, his models strode the runways wearing Band-Aids on their faces and bodies. Kouyaté explained the bandages as traces of the struggles these bodies have endured: 'People have gone through the jungle of life and these are to cover the scars where they need to be bandaged up' (Spindler, 1993: 13). In the reality embodied by XULY.Bët attire, neither garments nor the models who wear them are without previous experiences and past struggles. The garments incorporate visible seams, like healed wounds that have left their mark, the past lives of clothes that have been reshaped into new forms. Some of the garments Kouyaté selects offer extraordinarily vivid allusions to the stresses they and, by implication, their owners endured in previous lives. Torn pockets, discolored collars, frayed edges – these and other details mark this clothing as *used* rather than preserved. The bodice of one 1993 dress, now in the collection of the Metropolitan Museum of Art, is constructed out of a reshaped man's tuxedo shirt whose white collar is yellowed and frayed (Fig. 31). The shirt, which the designer has transformed into a woman's garment,

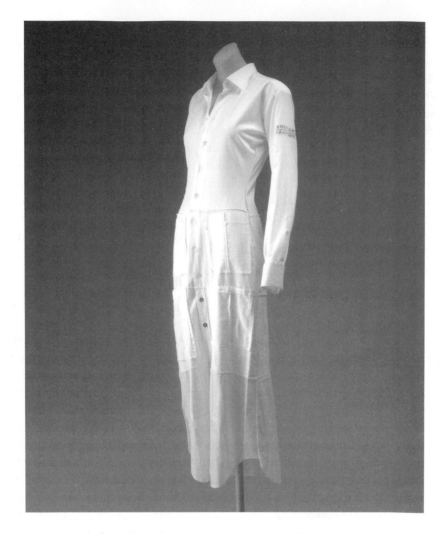

Figure 31. XULY.Bët, 1993. Assembled from portions of several different garments, this dress exemplifies the recycled style that has become the signature line for Lamine Kouyaté's XULY.Bët brand.
The Metropolitan Museum of Art, Gift of Amy M. Spindler, 1995 (1995.391.4). Photograph courtesy of the Metropolitan Museum of Art.

is suggestive of an irretrievable biography – was this shirt worn to formal events by a playboy, or was it the work shirt of a waiter? The recycled garments, and the designer's distinctive approach to presenting them, evoke the effort we make to become what we are; the history concealed beneath the surface.

Layered Biographies

An analysis of XULY.Bët's recycled clothing as expressions of the edges where categories blur and where identities may shift – between past and present, between the street and the rarified world of fashion, between the smoothness of exteriors and the strain to maintain that facade – is dramatically underscored by the literal doubling of identity indicated by the garments' labels. Kouyaté and his assistants leave the labels in the collars of used shirts and the waistbands of pants purchased at flea markets. These residual labels provide vivid evidence of the shifting fortunes of clothing that has been used, discarded and later revived via their selection by the designer. The garments' labels document the changing identities of these objects. The original label recounts the garment's first life; the bright red XULY.Bët label, usually placed on the outside of the garment, declares its current identity.

Kouyaté's methodology is illuminated by Kopytoff's influential essay on the 'cultural biographies' of commodities. Kopytoff addresses the life stories of commodities as they move in and out of varied categories and levels of status. He notes that the changing roles of objects can produce dramatic effects: 'an eventful biography of a thing becomes the story of the various singularizations of it, of classifications and reclassifications in an uncertain world of categories whose importance shifts with every minor change in context. As with persons, the drama here lies in the uncertainties of valuation and of identity' (Kopytoff, 1986: 90). By extending the fashionability and commodity status of clothing even after it has been relegated to the low status realm of the flea market, Kouyaté reverses the conventional life cycle of clothing. This resuscitation creates a sense of drama, as garments are transformed from refuse to fashion. Gregson and Crewe, in their recent ethnography of the trade in second hand goods in Great Britain, found the drama of resuscitation to be a compelling element of consumers' motivation:

> For many consumers both the attraction and the value of a second-hand good lies in the imaginative potential of its former life. Second-hand goods are imbued with a history and a geography and, theoretically, all the things of material culture have the potential to become meaningful, even when they have been effectively withdrawn and deactivated as commodities through, for example, disposal, damage, or decay (Gregson & Crewe, 2003: 145–6).

Thus, the power of an object's biography may adhere even as it changes hands via the anonymity of a garage sale or a thrift shop.

Kouyaté's work also brings together aspects of his own biography, which encompasses contemporary urban Africa and the fashion worlds of Paris and New York. His company's name – XULY.Bët – draws immediate attention to his personal origins, and, I will assert, his philosophical roots in Africa. In Oulouf (or Wolof), the predominant language of Senegal, *xuly bët* is a colloquial term that can be roughly translated as 'voyeur', or, in Kouyaté's own definition of the term, as 'someone who breaks through appearances' to see the reality beneath the surface (Kouyaté in Spindler, 1993). In other discussions of XULY.Bët fashions, the term is glossed as a slang play on the notion of a voyeur: 'wanna take my picture?' (Revue Noire). This notion, peeling back the exterior to reveal the often uneven surfaces layered beneath, is clearly dramatized by Kouyaté's recycled designs and his presentation style of exposing the seams and past histories of his garments. Kouyaté draws on Africa in a more literal sense, using African fabrics in several of his designs and, in recent years, working with dyers in Mali to create fabrics that he uses in his other clothing lines (Durry, 2003).

African Roots

An exploration of the XULY.Bët brand's recycled and reshaped clothing from the perspective of African art history, my own discipline, provides rich context and hints at possible influences on the designer's development. It is important to note, however, that Kouyaté's work is not defined or circumscribed by its Africanness, and Kouyaté does not market himself explicitly as an African designer. Yet, Africa is prominent in essentially every discussion of XULY.Bët and its founder. The titles of several articles on the designer from popular French and American publications, which include references to 'Mother Africa' and mistaken associations of Africa with jungles, indicate the degree to which Kouyaté is linked to his African identity. These titles include: 'Xuly Bët, styliste, entre Afrique, République et acrylique' (Le Guilledoux, 1997), 'Xuly Bet: An African on the Paris Fashion Show' (Vellard, 2000), 'Xuly Bet: A Brother from the "Mother" Turns Fashion Inside Out' (Jacobs, 1994), and 'La jungle fever de Xuly Bët' (Lewis, 1996).

While such titles refer to a generalized or, in some instances, erroneous conception of Africa, Kouyaté's work represents a particular Africa: urban, contemporary, sophisticated, and self-consciously global. Africa, long treated as a tradition-bound outpost on the frontiers of the West, produces its own modernity which Hanchard has described as 'Afro-Modernity':

a particular understanding of modernity and modern subjectivity among people of African descent. At its broadest parameters, it consists of the selective incorporation of technologies, discourses, and institutions of the modern West within the cultural and political practices of Africa-derived peoples to create a form of relatively autonomous modernity distinct from its counterparts of Western Europe and North America. It is no mere mimicry of Western modernity but an innovation on its precepts, forces, and features. (Hanchard, 2001: 272)

XULY.Bët recycled clothing is well suited to this model of modernity. These garments exemplify the creation of a new, distinctly modern cultural form that draws on a variety of practices and precedents, African and Western, without replicating any single model. Kouyaté described this selective incorporation of Western elements in the local fashion practices of his youth:

At home, all the products come from foreign places. They're imported from everywhere, made for a different world with another culture in mind. A sweater arrives in one of the hottest moments of the year. So you cut the sleeves off to make it cooler. Or a woman will get a magazine with a photo of a Chanel suit, and she'll ask a tailor to make it out of African fabric. It completely redirects the look (Spindler, 1993: 13).

While he has professionalized this practice, creating a brand and a distinctive style, Kouyaté acknowledges the proximity of his work to that of the tailors he saw at work in his youth.

That Kouyaté's medium of choice is fashion, rather than painting, sculpture, architecture or photography, makes his work a particularly powerful declaration of modernity. Fashion is defined by its location in a perpetual present-becoming-past, each season racing to distinguish itself from the season that has just passed. Definitions of fashion generally focus on its temporal quality: 'Fashion comes from Paris, and one of its greatest characteristics is that it changes. No sooner is something "in fashion" than it is "out of fashion" again' (Seeling, 1999: introduction). The shifts in hemlines or color combinations that mark fashion's changing seasons epitomize rejection of the past in an unending search for the new. Kouyaté's recycled clothing, in particular, exemplifies another prototypical attributes of fashion: its tendency to revive styles of the past in its perpetual quest for novelty. Walter Benjamin characterized this aspect of fashion in a poetic turn of phrase: 'Fashion has the scent of the modern wherever it stirs in the thicket of what has been. It is the tiger's leap into the past' (Benjamin, 1968a: 252–3).

The XULY.Bët approach to fashion takes this leap in a literal sense: rather than making reference to past fashion through a recreation or a reimagination of Classical Greek attire or by adapting the bustle, the corset or another sartorial element associated with past styles, Kouyaté literally bring the styles of the past into the present by reshaping old clothes. Used clothing, as any visitor to thrift shops and consignment stores has found, may encompass garments from the past season, the past decade or the past generation. The use of discarded clothing in contemporary fashion, thus, adds a fascinating layer of complexity to fashion's inherent temporality: 'As long as Mr. Kouyaté keeps drawing from the flea markets for inspiration, his designs will change because what is discarded or deemed undesirable will change' (Spindler, 1993: 13). Thus, XULY.Bët recycled fashions step outside the system of fashion chronology by reaching back to an ever-changing past. For Kouyaté, garments that have been discarded may still contain the kernel of fashion, which can be revealed by subtly reshaping seams or adding a stenciled slogan.

The designer himself, in numerous interviews, has cited his roots in Africa as an important source of inspiration for his recycled fashion. In one typical example, Kouyaté attributed his affinity for reusing clothing to Africa's ethos: 'It's an African – and any Third World nation's – philosophy to use things up. You don't waste anything, but create new from old' (Jacobs, 1994: 144). This ethic of investing creativity and energy in existing forms, reusing and modifying rather than acquiring new, was evident in my own experience in Mali and Senegal. In villages, towns and cities, markets of any size incorporate sections devoted to the reselling and reworking of bottles, cans, oil drums, magazines, tires and, most germane to the topic at hand, clothing. Though distant from Kouyaté's origins in West Africa, Hansen's work on the consumption of recycled clothing in Zambia offers valuable insight into the volume of this market and the many strategies by which local consumers make these garments their own (Hansen, 2000b). She describes the ways in which imported clothing is adapted to local practices, garments selected and combined to express cultural norms as well as individual preferences. Far from simple economic necessity, used clothing is part of Zambians' creative sartorial palette:

> The fact that we can identify Zambian terms for acceptable dress does not mean that everyone dresses alike. Nor does the desire to dress in 'the latest' produce passive imitation and homogeneity. It is precisely the opposite effect that consumers seek to achieve from salaula [a local Zambian term for used clothing] and that they find missing from much store-bought clothing: uniqueness (Hansen, 2000b: 199).

While Hansen's study offers the most thorough examination of used clothing in Africa, Zambians are certainly not alone in their transformation of discarded clothing into fashionable dress.

Baye Fall: **Recycled Garments in Senegal**

Closer to Kouyaté's own cultural background, a Senegalese religious movement that has important cultural resonance throughout Senegalese society,
the Mouride (or Murid) sect of Islam, offers a vivid example of the cultural
weight of recycled clothing. The Mouride practice of Islam was established
by Sufi mystic Sheikh Amadou Bamba, whose resistance to the French
colonial forces led to his exile to Gabon in 1895. Mouridism is based on
an ethic of prayer and hard work, transforming the practical struggle to
survive and thrive against all odds into a form of religious worship. The
religion might also be viewed as a form of resistance to dominant political
and economic forces. Certainly during the early colonial period, the great
wealth accumulated by Mouride communities, most notably through their
peanut farming, represented a counterbalance to the economic dominance of
the state. The visual arts associated with contemporary Mouridism illustrate
its practitioners' affiliation with resistance leaders from other religious and
cultural backgrounds, including Bob Marley, Martin Luther King, and
Patrice Lumumba (see Roberts & Roberts 2003).

Within the Mouride movement is a subgroup of adherents to Sheikh Ibra
Fall, Amadou Bamba's first disciple. Ibra Fall is mythologized as the embodiment of hard work and dedication to the prosperity of the Mouride society.
Amadou Bamba, recognizing the sacrifices of Ibra Fall and his followers,
excused them from some of the strictures imposed on other observant
Muslims to free them more fully to pursue work as prayer. Baye Fall, the
disciples of Ibra Fall, devote themselves to labor of all kinds, relying on their
communities to feed and clothe them and giving their earnings to communal
projects. Male followers of Baye Fall are often distinguished by their
distinctive robes, shirts and pants assembled of scraps of diverse fabrics.
Along with their work as farmers, traders, urban laborers, musicians and a
host of other occupations, some Baye Fall renounce all worldly comforts and
beg in the streets for offerings, including bits of cloth and used clothing.

The patchwork garments they construct from these scraps are a visual
symbol of their religious affiliation and may refer to specific local precedents,
such as the pants worn by warriors in the pre-colonial Wolof kingdom or
the magic square amulets created by religious leaders for healing and other
purposes (Roberts & Roberts, 2003: 115–18). The clothes may also be read
as symbols of the Baye Fall rejection of dominant systems of wealth and
status, for they wear rags despite the wealth that is held communally by their
religious leaders. Like Gandhi's adoption of an indigenous cotton garment
as a form of resistance to the dominance of British textile imports, the Baye
Fall wear clothing that is not controlled, stylistically or economically, by

non-local forces. The scraps of which their garments are made have been used and discarded, thus taken out of economic circulation.

Like the clothing of many sub-culture styles, Baye Fall patchwork clothing has been popularized among non-Mourides. Over the course of my ongoing research in Bamako, Mali (home to many Mourides, both Malian and Senegalese) I saw many young people who wore patchwork clothing as a statement of fashion rather than religious belief. Garments made of small squares of fabric sewn together are much more labor intensive to produce than clothing made of whole lengths of fabric, so that ironically the patchwork garments cost more. In yet another twist in the biography of Baye Fall clothing, during the early 1990s a Senegalese textile company mass-produced a patchwork-like pattern that imitated Baye Fall, transforming the cloth from the product of hand-labor and communal spirit to an industrial commodity. This fabric, printed by the Sotiba company, was available in several colors when I lived in Mali in 1993–4. Thus, necessity bred fashion in a process that calls to mind XULY.Bët's recycled chic. Kouyaté does not make a direct connection between his work and the Baye Fall patchwork tradition, yet the deep cultural roots of Baye Fall clothing offers a fascinating parallel to the designer's recycled fashions (Kouyaté, 2003).

In another similarity to the Baye Fall deployment of clothing, XULY. Bët's recycled garments might also be read as subversive, or at least as an astute testing of the limits and the logic of the fashion system. Kouyaté reshapes the detritus of Paris, a Western economic and political center and former seat of colonial power in Mali and Senegal, transforming discarded garments to sell them again as new. The garments might be interpreted as an ironic twist on the presumption that Paris fashion is always new, while Africa and other non-Western markets lag behind. Richard Wilk's work on consumption in Belize illuminates this aspect of XULY.Bët recycled clothing. He writes of fashion's role in the struggles against the flow of 'colonial time', a term that describes the temporal disjuncture between the West and the non-West in both colonial and post-colonial contexts: 'In colonial time the colony is described using metaphors that blend the connotative meanings of time, distance and cultural development. *Primitive, backward*, and *underdeveloped* are such blending terms' (Wilk, 1990: 84). Wilk describes how fashion has been used to mark this purported backwardness, for clothing styles far from the Western centers where contemporary fashion is 'made' are not expected to incorporate the latest styles. And yet, Wilk describes a means of countering the force of colonial time by stepping outside its system: 'Only when people obtain and consume objects outside the flow of colonial time, do they challenge and resist the social order of the colonial system' (Wilk, 1990: 89). Revivals of indigenous textiles and garments offer one example of such resistance, exemplified by Gandhi's return to indigenous cotton garments. My own work in Mali on the revival of an indigenous textile (*bogolan*) offers a comparable instance (Rovine, 2001). Yet, Kouyaté's work employs the products of the West itself to offer up an alternative to the flow of colonial time, creating garments that are global in their references and distinctly contemporary in style.

XULY.Bët and its founder, Lamine Kouyaté, exemplify the synthesis of influences and the evasion of neat categorization that is the hallmark of many African designers working in global fashion markets. Kouyaté is distinctive, however, for the edginess that he brings to his work, exposing the underside of fashion design and using his garments as allusions to the work of identity production in a globally oriented culture. He refuses the fashion industry's perpetual rush into the future, in which the past is rejected and discarded or, if it is to reappear at all, is remade in new materials or new styles. Kouyaté's recycled clothing demonstrates that the old and the new, the Western and the Africa, are in perpetual flux. He described this state as characteristic of Dakar and other urban areas: 'There, urban culture is in permanent mutation' (Le Guilledoux, 1997: 15). He uses that mutation, bending and reshaping the past to suit the tastes of the present, layering his creations with multiple lives to produce garments that speak to the experiences of diverse audiences.

Bibliography

Abbas, Ackbar. (1997). *Hong Kong Culture and the Politics of Disappearance*. Hong Kong: Hong Kong University Press.

Agins, Teri. (2001). Some Clothes of Questionable Vintage. In the Retro-Fashion Craze, Not All Oldies Are Goodies; Beware the Rot Factor. *Wall Street Journal*. 27 July: W12.

Allerston, Patricia. (1999). Reconstructing the Second-Hand Clothes Trade in Sixteenth- and Seventeenth-Century Venice. *Costume* 33: 46–56.

Appadurai, Arjun. (1986). Introduction: Commodities and the Politics of Value. In *The Social Life of Things: Commodities in Cultural Perspective*, edited by Arjun Appadurai, 3–63. Cambridge: Cambridge University Press.

——. (1996). *Modernity at Large: Cultural dimensions of globalization*. Minneapolis & London: University of Minnesota Press.

——. (1997). Consumption, Duration, and History. In *Streams of Cultural Capital: Transnational Cultural Studies,* edited by David Palumbo-Liu and Hans Ulrich Gumbrecht, 23–46. Stanford, CA: Stanford University Press.

Arago, Jacques. (1825). *Voyage autour du monde: fait par ordre du roi sur les corvettes de S. M. l'Uranie et la Physicienne, pendant les annees 1817, 1818, 1819 et 1820: Atlas Historique*. Paris: Chez Pillet Aine, Imprimeur-Libraire.

Arnold, Rebecca. (2001). *Fashion, Desire and Anxiety: Image and Morality in the 20th Century*. London, New York: I. B. Tauris.

Art Institute of Chicago. (1992). Five Centuries of Japanese Kimono: On this Sleeve of Fondest Dreams. *The Art Institute of Chicago Museum Studies* 18: 1.

Asakura, Haruhiko (annotator). (1990). *Jinrin kinmo zui*. Tokyo: Heibonsha.

Ashton, T. S. (1924). *Iron and Steel in the Industrial Revolution*. Manchester: University of Manchester Press.

Astbury, Leigh. (1985). *City Bushmen: the Heidelberg School and the Rural Mythology*. Melbourne: Oxford University Press.

Baines, Barbara Burman. (1981). *Fashion Revivals from the Elizabethan Age to the Present Day*. London: Batsford.

Baldwin, Francis E. (1926). *Sumptuary Legislation and Personal Regulation in England*. Baltimore: Johns Hopkins University Press.

Banim, Maura and Ali Guy. (2001). Discontinued Selves: Why Do Women Keep Clothes They No Longer Wear. In *Through the Wardrobe: Women's Relationships with Their Clothes*, edited by Ali Guy, Eileen Green and Maura Banim, 203–19. Oxford and New York: Berg Publishers.

Bardey, Catherine. (2002). *Wearing Vintage*. New York: Black Dog & Leventhal.

Barnes, Richard. (1991). *Mods!* London: Eel Pie.

Barnes, Ruth and Joanne B. Eicher (eds). (1992). *Dress and Gender: Making and Meaning*. Oxford and New York: Berg Publishers.

Barthes, Roland. (1996). *Mythen des Alltags*. Frankfurt: Main Publishing House.

Baudrillard, Jean. (1982). *Der symbolische Tausch und der Tod*. München: Matthes & Seitz.

Baumgarten, Linda. (2002). *What Clothes Reveal. The Language of Clothing in Colonial and Federal America*. New Haven and London: Colonial Williamsburg Foundation in association with Yale University Press.

Bellafante, Gina. (2000). Front Row. For Kamali, Its a Return to the Past, and her Vintage Clothes. *New York Times*. 14 November: B16.

Benjamin, Walter. (1968a, reprinted 1999). Theses on the Philosophy of History. In *Illuminations*, translated by Harry Zohn, 253–64. London: Pimlico.

——. (1968b, reprinted 1999). The Work of Art in the Age of Mechanical Reproduction. In *Illuminations*, translated by Harry Zohn, 219–53. London: Pimlico.

Benn De Libero, Linda. (1994). This Year's Girl: A Personal / Critical History of Twiggy. In *On Fashion*, edited by Shari Benstock and Suzanne Ferris, 41–58. New Brunswick, New Jersey: Rutgers University Press.

Benson, John. (1996). Working-Class Consumption, Saving, and Investment in England and Wales, 1851–1911. *Journal of Design History* 9: 87–99.

Berger, K. (1992). *Japonisme in Western Painting from Whistler to Matisse*, translated by D. Britt. Cambridge: Cambridge University Press.

Bigge, John Thomas. (1822). *Report of the Commissioner of Inquiry into the State of the Colony of New South Wales*. London: House of Commons.

Blainey, Geoffrey. (1963). *The Rush that Never Ended: a History of Australian Mining*. London: Cambridge University Press.

Blau, Harold. (1999). *Nothing in Itself: Complexions of Fashion*. Bloomington and Indianapolis: Indiana University Press.

Bogucka, Maria. (1998). Women and Credit Operations in Polish Towns in the Early Modern Period. Unpublished papers presented at Session C59, Women and credit in European Societies: 16th to 19th Centuries, 12th *International Economic History Congress*, Madrid.

Bond, Michael Harris (ed.). (1996). *Handbook of Chinese Psychology*. Oxford & New York: Oxford University Press.

Boswell, James. (1950). *London Journal, 1762–1763*, edited by Frederick A. Pottle. New York: McGraw-Hill.

Bourdieu, Pierre. (1998). *Die feinen Unterschiede: Kritik der gesellschaftlichen Urteilskraft*. Frankfurt: Main Publishing House.

Bowes-Smyth, Arthur. (*c.*1790). *A Journal of A Voyage from Portsmouth to New South Wales and China in the Lady Penhryn, Merchantman William Cropton Sever, Commander by Arthur Bowes-Smyth, Surgeon – 1787 – 1788 – 1789, compiled c.1790*. Manuscript, Mitchell Library, SLNSW. (ML Safe 1/ 15).

Bowring, R. (1982). *Murasaki Shikibu: Her Diary and Poetic Memoirs*. Princeton, NJ: Princeton University Press.

Braudel, Fernand. (1981). *Civilization & Capitalism, 15th–18th Century, The Structures of Everyday Life*, vol. 1, translated by Siân Reynolds. New York: Harper & Row.

Breward, Christopher. (1995). *The Culture of Fashion: A New History of Fashionable Dress Vol. 1*. London: St. Martin's Press.

——. (1999). *The Hidden Consumer: Masculinities, Fashion and City Life, 1860–1914*. Manchester: Manchester University Press.

——. (2000). Cultures, Identifies, Histories: Fashioning a Cultural Approach to Dress. In *The Fashion Business: Theory, Practice, Image*, edited by Nicola White and Ian Griffiths. 23–36. Oxford: Berg Publishers.

——. (2003). *Fashion*. Oxford: Oxford University Press.

Brown, Judith. (1986). A Woman's Place was in the Home: Women's Work in Renaissance Tuscany. In *Rewriting Renaissance*, edited by M. Ferguson, M. Quilligan and N. Vickers, 206–25. Chicago: University of Chicago.

Bruner, Edward. (1986a). Experience and its Expressions. In *The Anthropology of Experience*, edited by Victor Turner and Edward Bruner, 3–30. Urbana: University of Illinois Press.

——. (1986b). Ethnography as Narrative. In *The Anthropology of Experience*, edited by Victor Turner and Edward Bruner, 139–56. Urbana: University of Illinois Press.

Bruner, Jerome. (1986). *Actual Minds, Possible Worlds*. Cambridge, MA: Harvard University Press.

——. (1987). Life as Narrative. *Social Research* 54: 11–32.

Cabreza, Vincent and Dona Pazzibugan. (2002). Say Goodbye to 'Ukay-Ukay'. *Manila Standard*. 7 February: A1.

Capelaci, Sylvia. (2003). Haute Stuff. *ELLE* (Canada), May: 39.

Carbonell, Montserrat. (1998). 'Pledges', Transmissions and Credit Networks: Eighteenth-Century Barcelona. Unpublished papers presented at Session C59, Women and credit in European Societies: 16th to 19th Centuries, *12th International Economic History Congress*, Madrid.

Carocci, Guido. (1884). *Il Mercato vecchio di Firenze*. Florence: Tipografia della Pia Casa di Patronato.

Causey, Andrew. (2003). *Hard Bargaining in Sumatra: Western Tourists and Toba Bataks in the Marketplace of Souvenirs*. Honolulu: University of Hawaii Press.

Chant, Sylvia. (1996). Women's Roles in Recession and Economic Restructuring in Mexico and the Philippines. *Geoforum* 27 (3): 297–327.

Cheap Date. (2001). Shop Dropping. New York, 4 (Spring): 33.

Chetty, Derick. (2003). Past Perfect. *Flare* (Canada), March: 40.

Childs, Peter and Mike Storry. (1999). *Encyclopedia of Contemporary British Culture*. London: Routledge.

Chim, Jim. (1998). 30 Years Review on Fashion Trend in Hong Kong, 1950–80. *Xpress* (English translation) [Journal of the Hong Kong Designers Association], Hong Kong: 9–12.

Chong, Susan. (2000). Haute Couture Hand-Me-Downs. *National Post,* 5 August: W13–14.

Christie, Michael. (1988). *The Sydney Markets 1788–1988.* Flemington, NSW: Sydney Market Authority.

Cicolini, Alice. (2001). *Vieille Couture: Authentic Display.* MAFS thesis, London College of Fashion.

Clark, Hazel. (1997). Fashioning Diana. In *Planet Diana: Cultural Studies and Global Mourning,* edited by Re: PubLic, 133–6. Sydney: Research Centre in Intercommunnal Studies, University of Western Sydney.

Clarke, Alison and David Miller. (2002). Fashion and Anxiety. *Fashion Theory* 6 (2): 191–214.

Clarke, Patricia and Dale Spender. (1992). *Life Lines: Australian Women's Letters and Diaries, 1788–1840.* Sydney: Allen & Unwin.

Clarke, Ralph. (*c.*1790). *Journal kept on the Friendship during a Voyage to Botany Bay and Norfolk Island; and on the Gorgon returning to England, 9 March 1787– 10 March 1788, 15 February 1790–17 June 1792.* Manuscript, Mitchell Library, SLNSW. (ML Safe 1/ 27a)

Colavita, Courtney. (2003). Dolce & Gabbana's Time Machine. *WWD,* 7 April: 13.

Collins, David. (1798). *An Account of the English Colony in NSW* 1. London: T. Caddell Jun and W. Davies.

Colloredo-Mansfeld, Rudi. (1999). *The Native Leisure Class: Consumption and Cultural Creativity in the Andes.* Chicago: University of Chicago Press.

Comita, Jenny. (2002). Vogue View: Revamp, Rethink, Recycle. *Vogue,* October: 197, 198, 200, 202, 204.

Conant, E. P. (1991). Refractions of the Rising Sun: Japan's Participation in International Exhibitions 1862–1910. In *Japan and Britain: An Aesthetic Dialogue 1850–1930,* edited by Tomoko Sato and Toshio Watanabe, 79–92. London: Lund Humphries.

Cooper, Cynthia. (1997). *Magnificent Entertainments: Fancy Dress Balls of Canada's Governor General, 1876–1898.* Hull, Quebec: Canadian Museum of Civilization & Goose Lane.

Craik, Jennifer. (1994). *The Face of Fashion.* London: Routledge.

Cuenca, Minotte R. (2002). One-Woman Ukay-Ukay. *Philippine Star – Starweek Sunday Magazine,* 3 February: 4–5.

Cunningham, Peter. (1827). *Two Years in New South Wales.* London: H. Colburn.

Dalby, Liza Crihfield. (1993). *Kimono: Fashioning Culture.* New Haven and London: Yale University Press.

Daswani, Kavita. (2000). Old Look, New Trend. *South China Morning Post,* Hong Kong, 5 May: 19, 22.

Daunton, M. J. (1995). *Progress and Poverty: An Economic and Social History of Britain 1700–1850.* Oxford: Oxford University Press.

Daunton, Martin and Matthew Hilton. (2001). Material Politics: An Introduction. In *The Politics of Consumption: Material Culture and Citizenship in Europe and*

America, edited by Martin Daunton and Matthew Hilton, 1–32. Oxford and New York: Berg Publishers.

Davidsohn, Robert. (1956). *Storia di Firenze*, edited by Giovanni Miccoli. 4 vols. Florence: Sansoni.

Davis, Fred. (1979). *Yearning for Yesterday: A Sociology of Nostalgia*. New York: Free Press.

Davis, William G. (1973). *Social Relations in a Philippine Market: Self-Interest and Subjectivity*. Berkeley and Los Angeles: University of California Press.

Dei, Benedetto. (1984). *La Cronica dall'anno 1400 all'anno 1500*, edited by Roberto Barducci. Florence: Francesco Papfava editore.

De la Haye, Amy and Cathie Dingwall. (1996). *Surfers, Soulies, Skinheads & Skaters: Subcultural Style From the Forties to the Nineties*. London: Victoria & Albert Museum.

DeMello, Margo. (2000). *Bodies of Inscription: A Cultural History of the Modern Tattoo Community*. Durham, NC: Duke University Press.

DeMeulenaere, Stephen. (2000). Reinventing the Market: Alternative Currencies and Community Development in Argentina. *International Journal of Community Currency Research* 4. Available: http: //www. geog. le. ac. uk/ijccr/ (Accessed: February 2002).

de Roover, Raymond. (1948). *Money, Banking and Credit in Mediaeval Bruges: Italian Merchant-Bankers Lombards and Money-Changers, A Study in the Origins of Banking*. Cambridge, MA. : Medieval Academy of America.

de Vries, Jan. (1984). *European Urbanization, 1500–1800*. London: Methuen.

Diawara, Manthia. (1998). Moving Company: The Second Johannesburg Biennale. *Art Forum*, March: 86–89.

Dickens, Charles. (1836, reprinted 1881). *Sketches by Boz: Illustrative of Every-Day Life and Every-Day People*. London: Chapman & Hall.

Doren, Alfred. (1940–48). *Le arti fiorentine*. Florence: Felice le Monnier.

Douglas, Mary and Baron Isherwood. (1979). *The World of Goods*. New York: Basic Books.

——. (1996). *Thought Styles: Critical Essays on Good Taste*. London: Thousand Oaks.

Dubin, Tiffany and Ann E. Berman. (2001). *Vintage Style: Buying and Wearing Classic Vintage Clothes*. New York, Harper Collins.

Düllo, Thomas. (2000) Ikeaisierung der Wohnwelt. *In ZimmerWelten: Wie junge Menschen heute leben*, edited by Jan Carstensen and Thomas Düllo, 92–9. Essen: Klartext Verlag.

Durham, Deborah. (1995). The Lady in the Logo: Tribal Dress and Western Culture in a Southern African Community. In *Dress and Ethnicity*, edited by Joanne B. Eicher, 183–94. Oxford: Berg Publishers.

Durry, Aurore. (2003). Interview with Victoria Rovine. January.

Earle, Peter. (1989a). *The Making of the English Middle Class: Business, Society and Family Life in London, 1660–1730*. London: Methuen.

——. (1989b). The Female Labour Market in London in the Late Seventeenth and Early Eighteenth Centuries. *Economic History Review* 42: 328–53.

Eicher, Joanne B. (ed.). (1995). *Dress and Ethnicity*. Oxford: Berg Publishers.

Entwistle, Joanne and Elizabeth Wilson (eds). (2001). *Body Dressing*. Oxford and New York: Berg Publishers.

Erdem, Suna. (2002). Creativity: R.I.P. *Fashion Magazine* (Toronto), April: 46–8.

Errington, Shelly. (1994). Unravelling Narratives. In *Fragile Traditions. Indonesian Art in Jeopardy*, edited by Paul Taylor, 139–64. Honolulu: University of Hawaii Press.

Evans, Caroline. (1998). The Golden Dustman. *Fashion Theory* 2 (1): 73–94.

Fashion Scoops. (2003). *WWD*. 26 March: 3.

Farmar, Tony. (1991). *Ordinary Lives, The Private Lives of Three Generations of Irelands Professional Classes*. Dublin: A & A Farmar.

Feitelberg, Rosemary. (2002). Digging Up Some Old Favourites. *WWD*, 2 May: 8.

Field, Simone, Hazell Barrett, Angela Browns and Roy May. (1996). The Second-Hand Clothes Trade in the Gambia. *Geography* 81 (4): 371–4.

Finkelstein, Joanne. (1998). *Fashion: An Introduction*. New York: New York University Press.

Fischer, Volker. (1981). *Nostalgie: Geschichte und Kultur als Trödelmarkt*. Frankfurt: Main Publishing House.

Fischer-Lichte, Erika. (1998). Inszenierung und Theatralität. In *Die Inszenierun gsgesellschaft*, edited by Herbert Willems and Martin Jurga, 81–92. Opladen, Wiesbaden: Westdeutscher Verlag GmbH.

Fiske, John. (1997). Die kulturelle Ökonomie des Fantums. In *Kursbuch Jugendkultur*, edited by SpoKK. 54–69. Mannheim: Bollmann Verlag.

Fitzgerald, Shirley. (1987). *Rising Damp: Sydney 1870–1890*. Melbourne: Oxford University Press.

Flusser, Vilem. (1983). *Für eine Philosophie der Fotografie*. Göttingen: European Photography.

Fontaine, Laurence. (2002). Women's Economic Spheres and Credit in Pre-industrial Europe. In *Women and Credit: Researching the Past, Refiguring the Future*, edited by B. Lemire, R. Pearson and G. Campbell, 15–32. Oxford: Berg Publishers.

Franceschi, Franco. (1993). *Oltre il 'Tumulto': I lavoratori fiorentini dell' Arte della Lana fra Tre e Quattrocento*. Florence: Leo S. Olschki Editore.

Frick, Carole Collier. (1995). *Dressing a Renaissance City: Society, Economics and Gender in the Clothing of Fifteenth-Century Florence*. PhD dissertation, UCLA.

——. (2002). *Dressing Renaissance Florence: Families, fortunes and fine clothing*. Baltimore: The Johns Hopkins University Press.

Frost, Bill. (1997). Why Second-Hand is Chic. *The Times* (London), 24 July: 19.

Fukai, A. (1994). *Jyaponizumu in fuasshon: umi a watatta kimono*. Tokyo: Heibonsha.

Garber, Jenny and Angela McRobbie. (1979). Mädchen in Subkulturen. In. *Jugendkultur als Widerstand: Mileus, Rituale, Provokationen*, edited by Axel Honneth, 217–37. Frankfurt: Main Publishing House.

Gaugele, Elke. (2003). Ich misch das so: Jugendmode, ein Sampling von Gender, Individualität und Differenz. In *Jugend, Mode und Geschlecht: Die Inszenierung des Körpers in der Konsumkultur*, edited by Elke Gaugele, Christina Reiss, 34–49. Frankfurt: Main Publishing House.

Gell, Alfred. (1992). Barter and Gift-exchange in old Melanesia. In *Barter, Exchange and Value: An Anthropological Approach*, edited by Caroline Humphrey and Stephen Hugh-Jones, 142–168. Cambridge: Cambridge University Press.

Gill, Alison. (1998). Deconstruction Fashion: The Making of Unfinished, Decomposing and Re-assembled Clothes. *Fashion Theory* 2 (1): 25–50.

Gillen, Mollie. (1989). *The Founders of Australia: A Biographical Dictionary of the First Fleet*. Sydney: Library of Australian History.

Ginsburg, Madeleine. (1980). Rags to Riches: The Second-Hand Clothes Trade 1700–1978. *Costume* 14: 121–35.

Greci, Roberto. (1996). Donne e corporazioni: La fluidita di un rapporto. In *Il lavoro delle donne*, edited by Angela Groppi, 71–91. Rome: Laterza.

Gregson, Nicky and Louise Crewe. (2003). *Second-Hand Cultures*. New York: Berg Publishers.

——, Kate Brooks and Louise Crewe. (2000). Narratives of Consumption and the Body in the Space of the Charity/Shop. In *Commercial Cultures: Economies, Practices, Spaces*, edited by Peter Jackson, Michelle Lowe, Daniel Miller and Frank Mort, 101–23. New York: Berg Publishers.

——. (2001). Bjorn again? Rethinking 70s Revivalism Through the Reappropriation of 70s clothing. *Fashion Theory* 5 (1): 3–27.

Green, Dorothy. (1991). Louis Stone's 'Jonah': A Cinematic Novel. Introduction to Louis Stone's *Jonah*. Pymble, NSW: Collins Angus & Robertson.

Grimm, Stephanie. (1998). *Die Repräsentation von Männlichkeit im Punk und Rap*. Tübingen: Stauffenberg.

Guccerelli, Demetrio. (1985). *Stradario storico biografico della città di Firenze*. 1929. Florence: Ristampa Anastatica, Soc. Multigrafice Editrice.

Gulgong Guardian. (1872). 9 November: np.

Gunn, Molly. (2000). The Old Curiosity Shop. *The Guardian*, 19 May: (G2) 8–9.

Guy, Ali, Eileen Green and Maura Banim, (eds). (2001). *Through the Wardrobe: Women's Relationships with Their Clothes*. Oxford and New York: Berg Publishers.

Guy, John. (1998). *Woven Cargoes: Indian Textiles in the East*. London: Thames & Hudson.

Haggblade, Steven. (1990). The Flip Side of Fashion: Used Clothing Exports to the Third World. *The Journal of Development Studies* 26 (3): 505–21.

Hall, John W. (1974). Rule by Status in Tokugawa Japan. *The Journal of Japanese Studies* 1 (1): 39–49.

Hanchard, Michael. (2001). Afro-Modernity: Temporality, Politics, and the African Diaspora. In *Alternative Modernities*, edited by Dilip Parameshwar Gaonkar, 272–98. London: Duke University Press.

Hansen, Karen Tranberg. (1997). *Keeping House in Lusaka*. New York: Columbia University Press.

——. (1999). Second-Hand Clothing Encounters in Zambia: Global Discourses, Western Commodities, and Local Histories. *Africa* 69 (3): 343–65.

——. (2000a). Other People's Clothes? The International Second-hand Clothing Trade and Dress Practices in Zambia. *Fashion Theory* 4 (3): 245–274.

——. (2000b). *Salaula. The World of Secondhand Clothing and Zambia.* Chicago: University of Chicago Press.

Hardaker, A. (1892). *A Brief History of Pawnbroking.* London: Jackson Ruston and Keeson.

Harris, Phill. (1908). Paddy's Market, Sydney. A Sketch. *The Red Funnel* 7 (4), 1 November: 350.

Harte, Negley. (1991). The Economics of Clothing in the Late Seventeenth Century. In *Fabrics and Fashions: Studies in the Economic and Social History of Dress, Textile History* (special issue) 22: 277–96.

Harvey, David. (1995). Die Verdichtung von Raum und Zeit. In *Philosophische Ansichten zur Kultur der Moderne,* edited by Andreas Kuhlmann, 48–78. Frankfurt: Main Publishing House.

Haughey, Anthony. (1996). *Imeall na hEorpa: The Edge of Europe,* with an essay by Fintan O'Toole. Dublin: Roinn Ealaíon, Cultúir agus Gaeltachta in association with the Gallery of Photography.

Hawes, Edward. (1986). Artifacts, Myth and Identity in American History Museums. In *Museology and Identity. ICOFOM Study Series* 10, edited by V. Sofka: 135–39.

Healy, John. (1978). *Nineteen Acres.* Galway: Kenny's Bookshop.

Hebdige, Dick. (1974). *The Style of the Mods.* Birmingham: Stenciled Occasional Papers, Centre for Contemporary Cultural Studies.

——. (1979). *Subculture: The Meaning of Style.* London: Methuen & Co.

Heller, Agnes. (1999). *A Theory of Modernity.* Oxford: Blackwell.

Helmes-Conzett, Cornelius. (1995). *Mode – Geschichte – Politik: Die 50er Jahre und die Politischen Generationen der Bundesrepublik.* Hamburg: Kovak.

Herlihy, David. (1990). *Opera Muliebria: Women and Work in Medieval Europe.* Philadelphia: Temple University Press.

—— and Christiane Klapisch-Zuber. (1981). *Machine-readable file, Catasto of 1427.* Madison: University of Wisconsin.

—— and Christiane Klapisch-Zuber. (1985). *Tuscans and Their Families.* New Haven and London: Yale University Press.

Hewitt, Paolo. (2000). *The Soul Stylists: Forty Years of Modernism.* London: Mainstream Publishing.

Hitzler, Ronald. (1999). *Jugendszenen in NRW: Über juvenile Kultur (en) unter den Bedingungen der Spätmoderne.* Düsseldorf: Ministerium für Frauen, Jugend, Familie und Gesundheit des Landes Nordrhein-Westfalen.

Ho, Oscar. (1999). *My Poor Dear Hong Kong – Poor but Cool* (exhibition flyer). Pao Galleries, Hong Kong Arts Centre, October 7–24.

Hogendorn, Jan. (1999). Slaves as Money in the Sokoto Caliphate. In *Credit, Currencies and Culture: African Financial Institutions in Historical Perspective,* edited by Endre Stiansen and Jane I. Guyer, 56–71. Uppsala, Sweden: Nordiska Afrikainstitutet.

Horx, Matthias. (1995). *Trendbuch 2: Megatrends für die späten neunziger Jahre.* Düsseldorf: Econ Verlag.

Horyn, Cathy. (2002). Is Copying Really a Part of the Creative Process? *New York Times*, 9 April: B10.

Hoskins, Janet. (1998). *Biographical Objects: How Things Tell the Stories of People's Lives.* London and New York: Routledge.

Hosley, W. (1990). *The Japan Idea: Art and Life in Victorian America.* Hartford, CT: Wadsworth Atheneum.

Howes, David (ed.). (1996). *Cross-Cultural Consumption: Global Markets, Local Realities.* London and New York: Routledge.

Hows, W. A. II. (1847). *A History of Pawnbroking, Past and Present.* London.

Hucker, Wendy. (c.1995). Wagga Rugs, *NSW Quilt Register*, Available: www. amol. org. au/nqr/wendy. htm. (Accessed: 2001).

Hughes, Robert. (1988). *The Fatal Shore: A History of the Transportation of Convicts to Australia 1787–1868.* London: Pan Books.

Humphrey, Caroline and Stephen Hugh-Jones (eds). (1992). *Barter, Exchange and Value: An Anthropological Approach.* Cambridge: Cambridge University Press.

Hunt, Margaret. (1999). *Women, Credit and the Seafaring Community in London, 1700–1740.* Unpublished paper presented at the *Women & Credit Conference*, Fredericton, NB, Canada.

Ikegami E. (1997). Protest from the Floating World: Fashion, State, and Category Formation in Early Modern Japan. In *Political Power and Social Theory* 2: 135–80.

Illustrated Australian News (Melbourne). (1867). 28 March: 6.

Irish Folklore Collection (1940). Main Manuscript Questionnaire on Emigration. Vols. 745–57.

—— (1955). Main Manuscript Questionnaire on Emigration. Vols. 1407–11.

Jackson, J. (2001). What Does Your Style Reveal About You? *Harper's Bazaar*, November: 130–2, 134.

Jacobs, Patricia. (1994). Xuly Bet: A Brother from the 'Mother' Turns Fashion Inside Out. *Essence* 15 (1), May: 26–7, 144.

James, Deborah. (1996). 'I Dress in This Fashion': Transformations in Sotho Dress and Women's Lives in a Sekhukhuneland Village, South Africa. In *Clothing and Difference: Embodied Identities in Colonial and Post-Colonial Africa*, edited by Hildi Hendrikson, 34–65. Durham: Duke University Press.

Jameson, Fredric. (1984). Postmodernism, or the Cultural Logic of Late Capitalism. *New Left Review* (147): 53–92.

——. (1989). Nostalgia for the Present. *South Atlantic Quarterly* 88 (2, Spring): 517–37.

Jarvis, Anthea. (2003). Book review of 'The Study of Dress History' by Lou Taylor. *Costume* 37: 139–40.

Jeffs, Angela. (1998). Silk Road Trading Post for Kimono Goods, Clothes. *The Japan Times*, 6 September: 12.

Jenß, Heike. (2001). Retro-Looks in Modedesign und Jugendkultur: Tom Ford (Gucci), Anna Sui und die Mods. In *Textil – Körper – Mode: Dortmunder Reihe zu kulturanthroplogischen Studien des Textilen*, edited by Gabriele Mentges, Heide Nixdorff, 225–301. No. 1, zeit. schnitte. Berlin: Ebersbach Verlag.

——. (2002). Anziehende Vergangenheit: Über den Konsum und die Inszenierung vergangener Zeit in Jugendszenen. In *Selfaktor: Zeitformen des Textilen. Schnittformen der Zeit*, edited by Ellen Harlizius-Klück, Annette Hülsenbeck, 215–36. Berlin: Ebersbach Verlag.

——. (2004). Frisur-Kopien. Haare im Retroschnitt. *Haar tragen. Frisuren in und auf den Köpfen*, edited by Christian Janecke (ed.), 271–90. Köln: Böhlau.

Jimenez-David, Rina. (2002). 'Ukay-Ukay' Memories. *Philippine Daily Inquirer*, 8 February: A9.

Johnson, J. (2003). Secondhand Roses. *Globe and Mail*, 26 April: L5.

Johnson, Paul. (1983). Credit and Thrift and the British Working-Class, 1870–1939. In *The Working Class in Modern British History: Essays in Honour of Henry Pelling*, edited by J. Winter, 147–70. Cambridge: Cambridge University Press.

Jones, Ann Rosalind and Peter Stallybrass. (2000). *Renaissance Clothing and the Materials of Memory*. Cambridge: Cambridge University Press.

Jones, Carla and Ann Marie Leshkowich. (2003). Introduction: The Globalization of Asian Dress: Re-Orienting Fashion or Re-Orientalizing Asia? In *Re-Orienting Fashion: The Globalization of Asian Dress*, edited by Sandra Niessen, Ann Marie Leshkowich and Carla Jones, 1–48. Oxford and New York: Berg Publishers.

Jones, Rose Apodaca. (2002). Decades' Designer Revival. *WWD*, 8 April: 16.

Kaiser, Susan. (1990). *The Psychology of Clothing: Symbolic Appearance in Context*. New York: Macmillan Publishing Co.

Karino, Ayako. (2002). Weaving Old Kimonos into the Fabric of Modern Taste. *Asahi Japan*, June, 5.

Kastner, J. (2002). Art of the Sell. *The Globe and Mail*, 10 August: L1, L6.

Kelly, William. (1860). *Life in Victoria, or Victoria in 1853 and Victoria in 1858, Showing the March of Improvement Made by the Colony Within Those Periods, in Town and Country, Cities and Diggings*, vol. 1. London: Chapman and Hall.

Kennedy, Alan. (1990). *Japanese Costume: History and Tradition*. Paris: Adam Biro.

Kitagawa Morisada, annotated by Usami Hideki. (1996). *Kinsei Fûzokushi (Morisada mankō)* 1. Tokyo: Iwanami shoten.

Klapisch-Zuber, Christiane. (1992). Un salario o l'onore: come valutare le donne fiorentine del XIV–XV secolo. *Quaderni storici* 79 (1), April: 41–9.

Kondo, D. (1997). *About Face: Performing Race in Fashion and Theatre*. New York and London: Routledge.

Kopytoff, Igor. (1986). The Cultural Biography of Things: Commoditization as Process. In *The Social Life of Things: Commodities in Cultural Perspective*, edited by Arjun Appadurai, 64–91. Cambridge: Cambridge University Press.

Korda, Natasha. (1996). Household Property/Stage Property: Henslowe as Pawnbroker. *Theatre Journal* 48: 185–95.

Kouyaté, Lamine. (2003) Interview with Victoria Rovine, January.

Kuipers, Joel C. (1990). Talking About Troubles: Gender Differences in Weyéwa Ritual Speech Usage. In *Power and Difference: Gender in Island Southeast Asia*, edited by Jane M. Atkinson and Shelly Errington, 153–75. Stanford, CA: Stanford University Press.

Kwiatkowski, Lynn M. (1998). *Struggling with Development: The Politics of Hunger and Gender in the Philippines.* Boulder, CO: Westview.

Lacuarta, Gerald G. (2002). Gloria Draws Flak for Crackdown on 'Ukay-Ukay'. *Philippine Daily Inquirer,* 8 February: A7.

Laing, John. (*c.*1875). Paddy's Market. In *Something to his Advantage: an Australian Christmas Serial,* edited by R. Thatcher, 120–3. Sydney: Turner and Henderson.

Landucci, Luca. (1883, reprinted 1969). *Diario fiorentino dal 1450 al 1516.* Florence: Studio Biblos.

Langer, Erick D. (1997). Foreign Cloth in the Lowland Frontier: Commerce and Consumption of Textiles in Bolivia, 1830–1930. In *The Allure of the Foreign: Imported Goods in Postcolonial Latin America,* edited by Benjamin Orlove, 93–112. Ann Arbor: University of Michigan Press.

Larocca, Amy. (2002). Fashion Police. *New York Magazine,* 29 April: 13

Latner, Lynda. (2003). Interview with Alexandra Palmer, 17 March.

Lee, Michelle. (2003). *Fashion Victim: Our Love-Hate Relationship with Dressing, Shopping, and the Cost of Style.* New York: Broadway Books

Lees-Maffei, Grace. (2003). Introduction. Studying Advice: Historiography, Methodology, Commentary, Bibliography. *Journal of Design History* 16 (1): 1–14.

Le Guilledoux, Dominique. (1997). Xuly Bët, styliste, entre Afrique, République et acrylique. *Le Monde,* 22 November: 14–15.

Lehnert, Gertrud. (1997). Modische Inszenierungen: Mode, Puppen, Models. In *Metis: Zeitschrift für historische Frauenforschung* 12: 44–54.

——. (2000). *Geschichte der Mode im 20. Jahrhundert.* Köln: Konemann.

Lemire, Beverly. (1988). Consumerism in Preindustrial and Early Industrial England: the Trade in Secondhand Clothes. *Journal of British Studies* 27 (1): 1–24.

——. (1990a). The Theft of Clothing and Popular Consumerism in Eighteenth Century England. *Journal of Social History* 24: 255–76.

——. (1990b). The Nature of the Second-Hand Clothes Trade, the Role of Fashion and Popular Demand in England, 1680–1880. *Quederno dell' Archivio,* 29–39. Torino: Gruppo GFT.

——. (1991). Peddling Fashion: Salesmen, Pawnbrokers, Taylors, Thieves and the Second-hand Clothes Trade in England, *c.*1700–1800. *Textile History* 22: 67–82.

——. (1997). *Dress, Culture and Commerce: The English Clothing Trade before the Factory, 1660–1800.* London: Macmillan Press Ltd.

——. (1998). Petty Pawns and Informal Lending: Gender, Households and Small-scale Credit in English Communities. In *From Family Firms to Corporate Capitalism: Essays in Business and Industrial History in Honour of Peter Mathias,* edited by Kristine Bruland and Patrick O'Brien. Oxford: Oxford University Press.

——. (2000). Second-hand Beaux and 'red-armed Belles': Conflict and the Creation of Fashions in England, *c.*1600–1800. *Continuity and Change* 15: 391–417.

Lentz, Graham. (2002). *The Influential Factor.* London: GEL Publishing.

Leung, Cynthia. (2001). Digging Up Dirt on Vintage Nuggets. *South China Morning Post*, Hong Kong, May 25: Style 4.

Lewis, Virginia. (1996). La jungle fever de Xuly Bet. *Le Figaro*. 12 October: np.

Li, Tania Murray. (1999). Compromising Power: Development, Culture and Rule in Indonesia. *Cultural Anthropology* 14 (3): 295–322.

Liddell, Jill. (1989). *The Story of the Kimono*. New York: E. P. Dutton.

Liesch P. and D. Birch. (2000). Community-based LETSystems in Australia: Localised Barter in a Sophisticated Western Economy. *International Journal of Community Currency Research* 4, Available: http://www. geog. le. ac. uk/ijccr/. (Accessed: February 2002)

Lindroth, L. and D. N. Tornello. (2002). *Virtual Vintage: The Insider's Guide to Buying and Selling Online*. New York, Random House.

Linebaugh, Peter. (1991). *The London Hanged: Crime and Civil Society in the Eighteenth Century*. Harmondsworth, Middlesex: Penguin Books.

Lipovetsky, Gilles. (1994). *The Empire of Fashion: Dressing Modern Democracy*. Princeton: Princeton University Press.

Loebenthal, Joel. (1990). *Radical Rags: Fashions of the Sixties*. New York, Abbeville Press.

Lyman, M. (1984). Distant Mountains: The Influence of *Funzō-e* on the Tradition of Buddhist Clerical Robes in Japan. *Textile Museum Journal* 23: 25–41.

MacFarlane, Alan. (1970). *The Family Life of Ralph Josselin, a Seventeenth-Century Clergyman*. Cambridge: Cambridge University Press.

Macquarie, Lachlan. (1822). Journal, entry for 11 February. Mitchell Library, SLNSW. Manuscript. (ML C774)

Manila Standard (staff). (2002). DSWD [Department of Social Welfare and Development] Retracts: No Ban on 'Ukay-Ukay'. *Manila Standard*. 18 February: 2.

Manual of the Society of St Vincent de Paul. (1954 [1888]). Dublin: Society of St Vincent de Paul.

Manuel, Gren. (1995). Parents Pay Price for Lack of Affection. *South China Morning Post,* Hong Kong. November 28: 3

Marabottini, Alessandro (ed.). (1979). *Le Arti di Bologna di Annibale Carracci*. Rome: Edizioni dell'Elefante.

Marcelli, Valérie and Céline Wallut. (2003). La Restauration du suaire de Saint Lazare D'Autun: les avatars d'une broderie Hispano-Mauresque du Xie siècle. *Bulletin du CIETA* 80: 114–24.

Marin, Louis. (1984). *Utopics: Spatial play*, translated by R. A. Vollrath. New York: Macmillan Humanities.

Martin, Richard and Harold Koda. (1991). *The Historical Mode. Fashion and Art in the 1980s*. New York: Rizzoli.

——. (1994). *Orientalism: Visions of the East in Western Dress*. New York: The Metropolitan Museum of Art & Harry N. Abrams, Inc.

Martines, Lauro. (2003). *April Blood: Florence and the Plot Against the Medici*. Oxford: Oxford University Press.

Maruyama, Nobuhiko. (1994). *Clothes of the Samurai Warrior*. Kyoto: Kyoto Shoin.

Mason, Elizabeth. (2002). *Valuable Vintage: The Insiders Guide to Pricing and Collecting Important Vintage Fashions*. New York: Three Rivers Press.

Mayhew, Henry. (1861–2, reprinted 1967). *London Labour and the London Poor*, vol II. London: Cass.

Maynard, Margaret. (1994). *Fashioned from Penury: Dress and Cultural Practice in Colonial Australia*. Melbourne: Cambridge University Press.

McBryde, Isabel. (1989). '... To establish a commerce of this sort' – Cross-cultural exchange at the Port Jackson Settlement. In *Studies from Terra Australis to Australia*, edited by John Hardy and Alan Frost, 169–82. Canberra: Australian Academy of the Humanities.

McCullough, H. C. (1968). *Tales of Ise: Lyrical Episodes from Tenth-Century Japan*. Stanford, CA: Stanford University Press.

——. (1988). *The Tale of the Heike*. Stanford, CA: Stanford University Press.

McRobbie, Angela. (1989). Second-Hand Dresses and the Role of the Ragmarket. In *Zoot Suits and Second-Hand Dresses: An Anthology of Fashion and Music*, edited by Angela McRobbie, 23–49. Boston: Unwin Hyman.

——. (2002). *Postfeminist Popular Culture: Bridget Jones and the New Gender Regime*. Unpublished paper presented at: *Ringvorlesung: Gender Studien in den Kulturwissenschaften*, Dortmund University, 6 December.

Mead, Rebecca. (2002). Letter from Tokyo. Shopping Rebellion: What the Kids Want. *The New Yorker*, 18 March: 104–11.

Medicoff, Zack. (1999). Salvation Army Salutes Bargain Boutiques. *Toronto Star*, 9 December: H6.

Mentges, Gabriele. (1998). Die Besonderheit textiler Kultur. Thesen und Überlegungen für eine museale Präsentation. In *Anzeiger des Germanischen Nationalmuseums, Nürnberg*, 216–18. Nürnberg: Verlag des Germanischen Nationalmuseum.

——. (2000). Zwischen Casual Wear und Szenelook: Zum Verhältnis von Jugend und Mode. In *ZimmerWelten: Wie junge Menschen heute wohnen*, edited by Jan Carstensen, Thomas Düllo and Claudia Richartz-Sasse. 70–81. Essen: Klartext Verlag

——. (2001). Eine Einführung. In *zeit. schnitte. Kulturelle Konstruktionen von Kleidung und Mode. Textil – Körper – Mode: Dortmunder Reihe zu kulturanthropologischen Studien des Textilen*, edited by Gabriele Mentges, Heide Nixdorff, 9–14. Berlin: Ebersbach.

Miles, Steven. (1998). 'Fitting In and Sticking Out': Consumption, Consumer Meanings and Construction of Young People's Identities. *Journal of Youth Studies* 1 (1): 81–6.

Milgram, B. Lynne. (1999a). Locating 'Tradition' in the Striped Textiles of Banaue, Ifugao. *Museum Anthropology* 23 (1): 3–20.

——. (1999b). Crafts, Cultivation and Household Economies: Women's Work and Positions in Ifugao Northern Philippines. In *Research in Economic Anthropology* 20, edited by Barry Isaac, 221–61. Stamford, CT: JAI Press.

——. (2001). Situating Handicraft Market Women in Ifugao, Upland Philippines: A Case for Multiplicity. In *Women Traders in Cross-Cultural Perspective: Mediating Identities, Marketing Wares*, edited by Linda J. Seligmann, 129–59. Stanford, CA: Stanford University Press.

Milhaupt, Terry Satsuki. (2003). Tsujigahana Textiles and Their Fabrication. In *Turning Point: Oribe and the Arts of Sixteenth-Century Japan*, edited by M. Murase, 318–23. New York: The Metropolitan Museum of Art and New Haven and London: Yale University Press.

Miller, Daniel (ed.). (1997). *Material Cultures: Why Some Things Matter*. Chicago: Chicago University Press.

Miller, J. Hillis. (1990). Narrative. In *Critical Terms for Literary Study,* edited by F. Lentricchia and T. McLaughlin, 12–21. Chicago: University of Chicago Press.

Morra, Bernadette. (2003). I'm a Collector of Vintage-To-Be. *Toronto Star,* 17 April: H5.

Mower, Sarah. (2000). Yves of Reconstruction. *Vogue*, November: 302, 304.

Muensterberger, W. (1994). *Collecting. An Unruly Passion*. Princeton, New Jersey: Princeton University Press.

Muggleton, David. (2000). *Inside Subculture: The Postmodern Meaning of Style*. Oxford: Berg Publishers.

Mukerji, Chandra. (1983). *From Graven Images: Patterns of Modern Materialism*. New York: Columbia University Press.

Myers, Fred R. (ed.). (2001). *The Empire of Things: Regimes of Value and Material Culture*. Santa Fe: School of American Research.

Nagasaki, Iwao. (1993). *Kosode* 4. Kyoto: Kyoto shoin.

——. (1998). *Some to ori o tazuneru*. Tokyo: Shinchôsha.

——. (1999). *Kimono to mon'yô: Nihon no katachi to iro*. Tokyo: Kôdansha.

Neale, Walter C. (1976). *Monies in Societies*. San Francisco: Chandler & Sharp.

Neville, Richard. (1991). The Many Faces of Bungaree. *Australian Antique Collector*, July/December: 37–40.

New Brunswick Courier. 26 May 1832, 2 June 1832, 23 August 1834.

Ng Chun Bong (ed.). (1992). *Hong Kong Fashion History*. Hong Kong: Committee on Exhibition of Hong Kong Fashion History.

Niessen, Sandra, Ann Marie Leshkowich and Carla Jones (eds). (2003). *Re-Orienting Fashion: The Globalization of Asian Dress*. Oxford and New York: Berg Publishers.

Norris, Lucy. (2004). Shedding Skins: The Materiality of Divestment in India. *Journal of Material Culture*, 9 (1): 59–71.

Nunome Junro (1992). *Me de miru sen'i no kōkogaku: sen'i ibutsu shiryō shūsei – The Archaeology of Fiber before your Eyes*. Kyoto: Senshoku to seikatsusha.

O'Carroll, Ide. (1990). *Models for Movers; Irish Women's Emigration to America*. Dublin: Attic Press.

O'Hagan, Anne. (2003). High-End Hoarding: From Madonna's Shoes to Vintage Lingerie, Fashion is the Latest Collectible. *Fashion Magazine* (Toronto), March: 136–9.

O'Hara, Georgina. (1986). *The Encyclopedia of Fashion*. New York: Thames and Hudson.

Ontrup, Rüdiger and Christian Schicha. (1999). Die Transformation des Theatralischen. In *Medieninszenierungen im Wandel: Interdiszplinäre Zugänge*, edited by Rüdiger Ontrup and Christian Schicha, 7–18. Münster: LIT Verlag.

Orlove, Benjamin and Arnold J. Bauer. (1997). Giving Importance to Imports. In *The Allure of the Foreign: Imported Goods in Postcolonial Latin America*, edited by Benjamin Orlove, 1–29. Ann Arbor: University of Michigan Press.

Packer, George. (2002). How Susie Bayer's T-Shirt Ended Up on Yusuf Mama's Back. *New York Times*, 31 March (7) 54–9.

Pagnini, Giovanni F. (1765–6). *Della decima e di varie altre gravezze imposte Dal comune di Firenze. Della moneta e della mercatura de'Fiorentini dino al secolo XVI. Lisbona e Lucca* 2. Florence: G. Bouchard.

Palmer, Alexandra. (2001). *Couture & Commerce: The Transatlantic Fashion Trade in the 1950s*. Vancouver: University of British Columbia Press.

Paul, Margot. (1984). A Creative Connoisseur: Nomura Shōjirō. In *Kosode: 16th–19th Century Textiles from the Nomura Collection*, Amanda Mayer Stinchecum, 12–21. New York: Japan Society and Kodansha International.

Philippine Star (staff). (2002). 'Ukay-Ukay' Imports. *Philippine Star*, 7 February: 1, 7.

Phillips, Ruth B. and Christopher B. Steiner (eds). (1999). *Unpacking Culture: Art and Commodity in Colonial and Postcolonial Worlds*. Berkeley, CA: University of California Press.

Pike, Laurie. (2002). Fashion Detective. *Jalouse*, January: 24–5.

Polhemus, Ted. (1994). *Streetstyle: From Sidewalk to Catwalk*. London: Thames and Hudson London.

——. (1996). *Stylesurfing: What to Wear in the Third Millenium*. London: Thames and Hudson London.

Polkinghorne, Donald. (1988). *Narrative Knowing and the Human Sciences*. Buffalo, NY: State University of New York Press.

Rainey, Ronald. (1985). *Sumptuary Legislation in Renaissance Florence*. PhD dissertation, Columbia University.

Reddy, William. (1987). *Money & Liberty in Modern Europe: A Critique of Historical Understanding*. Cambridge: Cambridge University Press.

Reiss, Christina. (2003). Heute bin ich so morgen bin ich anders: Postmoderne Lebensstile als Medium jugendlicher Identitätsbildungen. In *Jugend, Mode und Geschlecht: Die Inszenierung des Körpers in der Konsumkultur*, edited by Elke Gaugele and Christina Reiss, 16–33. Frankfurt: Main Publishing House.

Renaux, Pascale. (1994). Pari Dakar de Xuly Bët. *Glamour* (63), April: 112–17.

Revue Noire. (1997–98). Special Issue: *Fashion* 27 (December–January): 71.

Ribeiro, Aileen. (2002). *Dress in Eighteenth Century Europe 1715–1789*. New Haven and London: Yale University Press.

Richard, Birgit. (1998). Die oberflächlichen Hüllen des Selbst: Mode als ästhetisch-medialer Komplex. *Kunstforum* 141, July–September: 49–93.

Roberts, Allen F. and Mary Nooter Roberts. (2003). *A Saint in the City: Sufi Arts of Urban Senegal*. Los Angeles: UCLA Fowler Museum of Cultural History.

Roche, Daniel. (1994). *The Culture of Clothing: Dress and Fashion in the 'Ancien Regime'*, translated by Jean Birrell. Cambridge: Cambridge University Press.

——. (2000). *A History of Everyday Things: The Birth of Consumption in France, 1600–1800*. Cambridge: Cambridge University Press.

Rodgers, Susan. (1995). *Telling Lives, Telling History: Autobiography and Historical Imagination in Modern Indonesia*. Berkeley, CA: University of California Press.

Rolfe, Margaret. (1998). *Australian Quilt Heritage*. Rushcutters Bay, NSW: Fairfax Press.

Rokushō. (1998), 'Kogire no miryoku,' Kyoto: Maria shobō, 26: 74–7.

Rosaldo, Renato. (1986). Ilongot Hunting as Story and Experience. In *The Anthropology of Experience*, edited by Victor Turner and Edward Bruner, 97–138. Urbana: University of Illinois Press.

——. (1993). *Culture & Truth: The Remaking of Social Analysis*. Boston, MA: Beacon Press.

Rosati, V. (ed.). (1976). Le lettere di Margherita Datini. *Archivio Storico Pratese* 522: 25–152.

Rovine, Victoria L. (2001). *Bogolan: Shaping Culture through Cloth in Contemporary Mali*. Washington DC: Smithsonian Institution Press.

Roy, Tirthankar (ed.). (1996). *Cloth and Commerce: Textiles in Colonial India*. New Delhi: Sage Publications India Pvt. Ltd.

Said, Edward. (1978). *Orientalism*. New York: Pantheon Books.

Sanderson, Elizabeth. (1997). Nearly New: The Second-Hand Clothing Trade in Eighteenth-Century Edinburgh. *Costume* 31: 38–48.

——. (1996). *Women and Work in Eighteenth-Century Edinburgh*. Basingstoke: Macmillan.

Sartini, Ferdinando (ed.). (1940–8). *Statuti dell' Arte dei Rigattieri e Linaioli di Firenze (1296–1340)*. Florence: Felice Le Monnier Editore.

Schraven, Jorim. (2000). The Economics of Local Exchange and Trading Systems: a Theoretical Perspective. *International Journal of Community Currency Research* 4. Available: http://www. geog. le. ac. uk/ijccr/. (Accessed: February 2002)

Schrift, Melissa. (2001). *Biography of a Chairman Mao Badge: The Creation and Mass Consumption of a Personality Cult*. New Brunswick, NJ: Rutgers University Press.

Schwartz, Hillel. (2000). *Déjà vu: Die Welt im Zeitalter ihrer tatsächlichen Reproduzierbarkeit*. Berlin: Aufbau-Verlag.

Screech, T. (2002). Dressing Samuel Pepys: Japanese Garments and International Diplomacy in the Edo Period. *Orientations* 33 (2): 52–5.

Seeling, Charlotte. (1999). *Fashion: The Century of the Designer (1900–1999)*. Cologne: Könemann.

Shapiro, S. (1996). Modern Internet Boosts the Vintage Clothing Market. *Toronto Star*, 24 October: K3.

Shea, Christina. (2001). Who Wants to be a Designer? *Vogue*, November: 311–12, 316.

Shively, Donald H. (1964–65). Sumptuary Regulation and Status in Early Tokugawa Japan. *Harvard Journal of Asiatic Studies* 25: 123–64.

Silver, Cameron. (2002) Interview with Alexandra Palmer, 3 February.

——. (2003) Correspondence with Alexandra Palmer, 5 July.

Silverman, Kaja. (1994). Fragments of a Fashionable Discourse. In *On Fashion,* edited by Shari Benstock and Suzanne Ferriss, 183–95. New Brunswick, NJ: Rutgers University Press.

Silverstein, Cory. (2001). *Clothed Encounters: The Power of Dress in Relations between Anishnaabe and British Peoples in the Great Lakes Region 1760–2000.* Ph.D. Dissertation, McMaster University.

Simmel, Georg. (1971). The Stranger. In *On Individuality and Social Forms,* edited by Donald Levine, 143–9. Chicago: University Of Chicago Press.

Skov, L. (1996). Fashion Trends, Japonisme and Postmodernism, or 'What is so Japanese About Comme Des Garçons?' In *Contemporary Japan and Popular Culture,* edited by J. W. Treat, 137–68. Honolulu: University of Hawaii Press.

Smith, Adam. (1776, reprinted 1976). *An Inquiry into the Nature and causes of the Wealth of Nations,* vols. 1 & II. Indianapolis: Liberty Classics.

Sōsaku ichiba 6. (1997). 'Konuno ni asobu.' Kyoto: Maria shobō.

Spindler, Amy M. (1993). Prince of Pieces. *The New York Times,* 2 May: (9) 1,13.

Spooner, Brian. (1986). Weavers and Dealers: the Authenticity of an Oriental Carpet. In *The Social Life of Things: Commodities in Cultural Perspective,* edited by Arjun Appadurai, 195–235. Cambridge: Cambridge University Press.

Spufford, Margaret. (1984). *The Great Reclothing of Rural England: Petty Chapmen and their Wares in the Seventeenth Century.* London: Hambledon.

——. (2000). The Cost of Apparel in Seventeenth-Century England. *Economic History Review* 53: 677–705.

Staley, Edgcumbe. (1906). *The Guilds of Florence* (2nd ed). London: Methuen and Co.

Stallybrass, Peter. (1998). Marx's Coat. In *Border Fetishisms: Material Objects in Unstable Places,* edited by Patricia Spyer, 183–207. New York: Routledge.

Stannage, Tom (ed.). (2001). *Gold and Civilisation.* Canberra: Art Exhibitions Australia & National Museum of Australia.

Steele, Valerie. (1997a). Anti-Fashion: The 1970s. *Fashion Theory* 1 (3): 279–95.

——. (1997b). *Fifty Years of Fashion: New Look to Now.* New Haven: Yale University Press.

Steiner, Christopher B. (1994). *African Art in Transit.* Cambridge: Cambridge University Press.

——. (1995). The Art of the Trade: On the Creation of Value and Authenticity in the African Art Market. In *The Traffic in Culture. Refiguring Art and Anthropology,* edited by G. E. Marcus and F. R. Myers, 151–65. Berkeley, Los Angeles, London: University of California Press.

Stella, Alessandro. (1993). *La Révolte des Ciompi: Les hommes, les lieux, le travail.* Paris: Editions de l'Ecole des Hautes Etudes en Sciences Sociales.

Sterckx, P. (2001). Landscape of Events Seen at Speed. In *Virilio Live: Selected interviews,* edited by J. Armitage, 144–53. London, Thousand Oaks, New Delhi: Sage Publications.

Stevens, Kimberly. (1998). Where Designers Seek the Future in the Past. *The New York Times,* 8 February: (S9) 5.

Stewart, Kathleen. (1996). *A Space on the Side of the Road: Cultural Poetics in an 'Other' America.* Princeton, NJ: Princeton University Press.

Stone, Louis. (1907). *Jonah: a tale of Larrikin Life.* London: Methuen.

Stow, John. (1987). *The Survey of London,* edited by H. B. Wheatley. London: Dent.

Strathern, M. (1988). *The Gender of the Gift.* Berkeley, CA: University of California Press.

Strutt, William. (*c.*1890). *Autobiography, 1825–1856.* Manuscript, Strutt Papers, Mitchell Library, SLNSW. (ML MSS 867)

Subido, Paulo. (2003). A Guide to the Ukay-Ukay Safari. *The Philippine Star,* 11 April: H2

Sullivan, Robert. (2000). Let's Make A Deal. *Vogue,* November: 278, 301.

Sydney City and Suburban Sewerage and Health Board: Eleventh Progress Report 1875–76. (1876). Sydney: NSW Legislative Assembly, Thomas Richards Government Printer.

Sydney Gazette and New South Wales Advertiser. (1820). G. Howe. 20 May: 4.

Takeda, Sharon S. (2002). Fashionable Dress or Theatrical Costume: Textiles and the Evolution of Noh Robes. In *Miracles & Mischief: Noh and Kyōgen Theater in Japan,* 70–90. Los Angeles: Los Angeles County Museum of Art.

Talking Fashion. (2002). *Vogue,* October: 189.

Talley, André Leon. (2002). Stylefax: Jump. *Vogue,* October: 112.

Tarlo, Emma. (1996a). *Clothing Matters: Dress and Identity in India.* Chicago: University of Chicago Press.

——. (1996b). Fabricating Regional Value: Embroidery Traders from Gujarat. Unpublished paper presented at the 4th *European Modern South Asia Conference,* Copenhagen.

Taylor, Lou. (2000). The Hilfiger Factor and the Flexible Commercial World of Couture. In *The Fashion Business: Theory, Practice, Image,* edited by Nicola White and Ian Griffiths, 121–42. Oxford: Berg Publishers.

Tebbutt, Melanie. (1983). *Making Ends Meet: Pawnbroking and Working-Class Credit.* London: Methuen.

Thirsk, Joan. (1973). The Fantastical Folly of Fashion: the English Stocking Knitting Industry, 1500–1700. In *Textile History and Economic History: Essays in Honour of Miss Julia de Lacy Mann,* edited by N. B. Harte and K. G. Ponting, 50–73. Manchester: Manchester University Press.

——. (1978). *Economic Policy and Projects: The Development of a Consumer Society in Early Modern England.* Oxford: Clarendon Press.

Thomas, Nicholas. (1991). *Entangled Objects: Exchange, Material Culture, and Colonialism in the Pacific.* Cambridge, MA and London: Harvard University Press.

Thompson, Michael. (1979). *Rubbish Theory: The Creation and Destruction of Value.* Oxford: Oxford University Press.

Thornton, Sarah. (1995). *Club Cultures: Music, Media and Subcultural Capital.* Cambridge: Polity.

Thrift Shops Make the Most of Their Time in the Fashion Spotlight. (1996). *Wall Street Journal*, 14 November : A1.

Thurman, Judith. (2003). Used Goodies: A Holiday Guide for Thrifters. *The New Yorker.* 8 December: 84, 86, 88–9.

Ti Similla [UP faculty, Newsletter for the University of the Philippines]. (2002). An 'Ukay' Dictionary. *Ti Similla*, (Office of Public Affairs). March: 12.

Tolkien, Tracy. (2000). *Vintage: The Art of Dressing Up.* Great Britain: Pavillion Books Limited.

Trautman, Pat. (1991). Witches' Weeds. In *Dress and Popular Culture*, edited by Patricia Cunningham and Susan Voso Lab, 146–53. Bowling Green, OH: Bowling Green University Press.

Trebay, Guy. (2002). Fashion Replay. Imitation is the Mother of Invention. *New York Times*, 7 July: (4)10.

Trexler, Richard A. (1972). Le Célibat à la fin du Moyen Age: les religieuses de Florence. *Annales, E.S.C.* 27: 1329–50.

Trosse, Sabine. (1999). *Geschichte/n im Anzug: Über den Retro-Trend im Bekleidungsdesign.* Münster: Waxmann Verlag.

Tse, Donald K. (1996). Understanding Chinese People as Consumers: Past Findings and Future Propositions. In *The Handbook of Chinese Psychology*, edited by Michael Harris Bond, 352–63. Hong Kong: Oxford University Press.

Tsing, Anna. (2000). The Global Situation. *Cultural Anthropology* 15 (3): 327–60.

Turudich, Daniela et al. (2002). *The Vintage Fashion Directory. The National Sourcebook for Vintage Fashion Retailers.* Long Beach, California: Streamline Press.

Ulrich, Laurel Thatcher. (2001) *The Age of Homespun: Objects and Stories in the Creation of an American Myth.* New York: Alfred A. Knopf.

United Nations. (1996). *International Trade Statistics Yearbook 1995.* Vol. 2, Trade by Commodity. New York: United Nations.

——. (1999). *International Trade Statistics Yearbook 1998.* Vol. 2, Trade by Commodity. New York: United Nations.

Unseen C. Z. (2003). *Harper's Bazaar*, February: 80–83.

van der Plas, Els and Marlous Willemsen (eds). (1998). *The Art of African Fashion.* The Netherlands and New Jersey: Prince Claus Fund and Africa World Press.

van Wijngaarden, Hilde (1998). Credit as a Way to Make Ends Meet. The Use of Credit by Poor Women in Zwolle, 1650–1700. Unpublished papers presented at Session C59, *Women and credit in European Societies: 16th to 19th Centuries'*, *12th International Economic History Congress*, Madrid.

Veblen, Thorstein. (1899, reprinted 1979). *The Theory of the Leisure Class.* New York: Penguin Books.

Vieilles Robes de Chine. (1921). *Femina*, (10) np.

Vellard, Veronique. (2000). Xuly Bet: An African on the Paris Fashion Show. *The International Telegraph,* 10 October: np.

Vintage Diva. (2001). *Harper's Bazaar*, September: 170.

von Hahn, Karen. (2001). This Old Thing? *Fashion Magazine* (Toronto), October: 98.

Weill, Christina. (1999). *Secondhand Chic: Finding Fabulous Fashion at Consignment, Vintage and Thrift Stores*. New York, Pocket Books.

Weiner, Annette. (1992). *Inalienable Possessions*. Berkeley, CA: University of California Press.

—— and Jane Schneider (eds). (1989). *Cloth and Human Experience*, Washington and London: Smithsonian Institution Press.

Wentworth, Michael Justin. (1980). Tissot and Japonisme. In *Japonisme in Art: An International Symposium*, edited by The Society for the Study of Japonisme, 127–46. Japan: Kodansha International.

Whitley, Nigel. (1987). *Pop Design: From Modernism to Mod*. London: The Design Council.

Wiesner, Merry E. (1993). *Women and Gender in Early Modern Europe*. Cambridge: Cambridge University Press.

Wilk, Richard. (1990). Consumer Goods as Dialogue about Development. *Culture and History* 7: 79–100.

Wilson, Elizabeth. (1985). *Adorned in Dreams: fashion and modernity*. London: Virago Press.

——. (1992). Fashion and the Postmodern Body. In *Chic Thrills: A Fashion Reader*, edited by Juliet Ash and Elizabeth Wilson, 6–16. London: Pandora.

——. (1998). Bohemian Dress and the Heroism of Everyday Life. *Fashion Theory* 2 (3): 225–44.

Wilson, Elizabeth. (2002). Interview of Asiatica owner/designer with Terry Milhaupt.

Wilson, Verity. (1999). Studio and Soiree: Chinese Textiles in Europe and America, 1850 to the Present. In *Unpacking Culture. Art and Commodity in Colonial and Postcolonial Worlds*, edited by R. B. Philips and C. B. Steiner, 229–42. Berkeley, Los Angeles: University of California Press.

——. (2002). Western Modes and Asian Clothes: Reflections on Borrowing Others People's Dress. *Costume* 36: 139–57.

Winter, Rainer. (1997). Medien und Fans: Zur Konstitution von Fankulturen. In *Kursbuch Jugendkultur*, edited by SpoKK, 40–53. Mannheim: Bollmann Verlag.

Witchel, Alex. (1999). I'll Try the One Like Nicole Wore. *New York Times*, 21 February: (9) 1, 7.

Wolff, Zoe. (2002). Good as old. *Time Out, New York*, 31 January–7 February: 21–3.

Worgan, George. (1788). *Journal kept on a voyage to New South Wales with the First Fleet, with a letter written to his brother Richard, 12–18 June 1788*. Manuscript, Mitchell Library, SLNSW (ML Safe 1/ 114)

Wrightson, Keith. (2000). *Earthly Necessities: Economic Lives in Early Modern Britain*. New Haven, CT: Yale University Press.

Wrigley, E. A. (1988). *Continuity, Chance and Change: The Character of the Industrial Revolution*. Cambridge: Cambridge University Press.

Yūhō Y. (1976). The Merit of Kasaya (Kesa Kudoku). In *Zen Master Dōgen: An Introduction with Selected Writings*, 88–106. New York/Tokyo: Weatherhill.

Zimbalist, Kristina. (2002a). When can you wear 'It' again? *Harper's Bazaar,* April: 124–127.

——. (2002b). Is Twice as Nice? *Vogue,* December: 129–30.

Websites

www.dadadress.com

www.decadesinc.com

www.didierludot.com

www.geocities.com/SoHo/4473

www.geocities.com/SunsetStrip/Lounge/3773/PaulWeller_en.html

www.Hintmag.com

www.preloved.ca

www.thescene.de

www.vintagecouture.com

www.uni-frankfurt.de/uniform.com

Archives

Archivio de Stato, Firenze (ASF)

Florence, Italy / Frick

    Archivio di Stato

    Carte Strozziane

    Catasto

    Matricole del' Arte di Por Santa Maria

    Mercanzia

Biblioteca Laurenziana, Acquisiti & Doni

London, England, Metropolitan Archives. MJ/SP/MSP1701 AP/45/108

Index

Note: page numbers in italics refer to illustrations